POLICE SELECTION
AND EVALUATION

POLICE SELECTION AND EVALUATION
Issues and Techniques

EDITED BY **Charles D. Spielberger**
University of South Florida

● **HEMISPHERE PUBLISHING CORPORATION**

Washington • New York • London

PRAEGER PUBLISHERS
Praeger Special Studies

New York • London • Sydney • Toronto

The quotes on pages 157, 158, and 160 were reprinted from *Manual for the Strong-Campbell Interest Inventory,* Form 325 (Merged Form) of the STRONG VOCATIONAL INTEREST BLANK, SECOND EDITION, by David P. Campbell, with the permission of the publishers, Stanford University Press, Copyright © 1974, 1977, by the Board of Trustees of the Leland Stanford Junior University.

Copyright © 1979 by Hemisphere Publishing Corporation. All rights reserved. No part of this book may be reproduced in any form, by photostat, microform, retrieval system, or any other means, without the prior written permission of the publisher.

Hemisphere Publishing Corporation
1025 Vermont Ave., N.W., Washington, D.C. 20005

Distributed exclusively by Praeger Publishers, A Division of Holt, Rinehart and Winston, CBS Inc., 383 Madison Ave., New York, N.Y. 10017.

1 2 3 4 5 6 7 8 9 0   D O D O   7 8 3 2 1 0 9

Library of Congress Cataloging in Publication Data

Main entry under title:

Police selection and evaluation.

 Bibliography: p.
 Includes indexes.
 1. Police—Recruiting—Addresses, essays, lectures.
2. Police—Labor productivity—Addresses, essays,
lectures. I. Spielberger, Charles Donald, 1927–
HV7936.R5P63 363.2 78-9958
ISBN 0-03-050976-9 (Praeger)

Printed in the United States of America

812069

LIBRARY
ALMA COLLEGE
ALMA, MICHIGAN

CONTENTS

Preface   xi

I SELECTION OF LAW ENFORCEMENT OFFICERS

1 An Overview of Police Selection: Some Issues, Questions, and Challenges
John Furcon   3

The "Jet Streams" of Change   4
Some Critical Roles and Their Challenges   5
Some Major Issues in Police Selection—Progress and Problems   8
Positive Signs and Future Perspectives   9
References   10

2 **A Model for the Selection of Law Enforcement Officers**
Charles D. Spielberger, John C. Ward, and Harry C. Spaulding   11

Predictor Variables in Police Selection   13
Performance Criteria in Police Selection Research   18
A Model for the Selection of Law Enforcement Officers   21
Summary   23
References   24

II JOB ANALYSIS AND PERFORMANCE EVALUATION OF POLICE OFFICERS

3 Job Analysis in Police Selection Research
Melany E. Baehr and Arnold B. Oppenheim   33

Development of Job Analysis Procedures   33
A Comparison of Two Different Types of Quantitative Job
Description   46

Implications for the Use of Different Job Description Instruments   54
Summary   59
References   59

4 The Development and Use of Supervisory and Peer Scales for Police Performance Appraisal
James L. Farr and Frank J. Landy   61

Development of BAS for the Police Patrol Officer Position   62
Results of Field Testing the BAS   67
Implementation of the BAS Evaluation System   69
Adapting the BAS to a Particular Police Department   74
Feasibility of Cooperative Research Efforts   74
References   75
Reference Notes   75

5 Preentry Assessment and Training: Performance Evaluation of Police Officers
Joseph M. Fabricatore   77

Preemployment Evaluation   77
Training Evaluation   80
Summary   84
References   85
Reference Notes   85

6 Objective and Subjective Measures of Police Officer Performance
Ernest C. Froemel   87

Research Procedures   90
Results   93
Discussion   103
Continuing Research   109
Summary   110
References   110
Reference Notes   111

III BIOGRAPHICAL FACTORS, APTITUDES, INTERESTS, AND VALUES IN POLICE SELECTION

7 The Civil Service Exam Has Been Passed: Now What?
Wayne F. Cascio and Leslie J. Real   115

Educational Standards for Police Officers   117
The Selection Interview   120

The Background Investigation   130
Biographical Predictors of Police Performance   134
Summary   140
References   140

8 The Development of a Written Test for Police Applicant Selection
   Andrew Crosby, Michael Rosenfeld, and Richard F. Thornton   143

   The Project Context   143
   Approaches to Police Selection   145
   Project Design Decisions and the Resulting Product   146
   Test Development Procedure   147
   Validation of the Test   150
   Application of the Test   152
   References   153

9 Using the Strong–Campbell Interest Inventory in Police Selection
   Robert T. Flint   155

   Technical Information about the SCII   157
   Interests of Police Officers   158
   The SCII Police Officer Occupational Scale   159
   Race and Sex Differences on the SCII   160
   Using the SCII in Police Selection   161
   Summary and Conclusions   164
   References   165

10 Changing Police Values
    Samuel D. Sherrid   167

    Methodology   169
    Procedure   170
    Results   172
    Discussion and Conclusion   172
    Summary   174
    References   174

IV THE USE OF PSYCHOLOGICAL TESTS IN POLICE SELECTION

11 Criterion-related Validity of Personality and Aptitude Scales: A Comparison
    of Validation Results under Voluntary and Actual Test Conditions
    Norman D. Henderson   179

    Some Previous Research on Personality and Aptitude Measures   180
    Internal and External Validity of Police Validation Studies   182

The Cleveland Project   183
An Examination of External Validity of Validation Procedures   185
Internal Validity of Validation Procedures, with Special Reference
to Differential Validation   189
Summary   194
References   194
Reference Notes   195

12 Police Corruption: Screening Out High-Risk Applicants
    Allen E. Shealy   197

Moral Development   199
Measurement of Moral Judgment   200
An Empirical Study of Police Corruption   201
Future Directions   204
The Screening Process   205
Summary   207
References   208
Reference Notes   209

13 The Assessment Center Method in the Selection of Law Enforcement
    Officers
    Robert J. Filer   211

What Is an Assessment Center?   212
The History of Assessment Centers   213
Determination of Performance Dimensions   215
The Selection of Appropriate Exercises   216
Training of Assessors   217
Use of Assessment Centers by Law Enforcement Agencies for Promotion
(City of Richmond)   218
The Assessment Center for Entry-level Selection (Ft. Collins, Colorado,
Police Department)   222
Concluding Remarks   224
Summary   226
References   228

14 Selection of Effective Law Enforcement Officers: The Florida Police
    Standards Research Project
    *Charles D. Spielberger, Harry C. Spaulding, Margie T. Jolley,
    and John C. Ward*   231

Development of the FPSRP   232
Predictor Variables and Criterion Measures   234

Preliminary Findings in the FPSRP   242
Summary and Conclusions   249
References   251

V FAIR EMPLOYMENT PRACTICES AND CIVIL RIGHTS COMPLIANCE IN POLICE SELECTION

15 Impact of Civil Rights Legislation and Court Actions on Personnel Procedures and Practices
Melany E. Baehr   **255**

Introduction   **255**
Major Trends in Legislation over the Past Decade   **256**
Results and Implications of Selection Test Validations Conducted under EEOC Guidelines   **261**
Requirements of the FEA and EEOC Guidelines, with Suggestions for Future Accepted Test Usage   **269**
Summary   **274**
References   **275**

16 Some Implications of Equal Employment Opportunity Procedures: A Practitioner's Point of View
Gene Fox   **277**

The Time Bind   **280**
The Minimum Qualification Standard   **282**
Economic Constraints   **284**
The Vagarious System   **286**
Conclusion   **288**
References   **289**

Appendix: Proceedings of the National Working Conference on the Selection of Law Enforcement Officers   **291**

Agenda for the National Working Conference   **293**
Roster of Speakers and Participants   **294**

Author Index   **299**

Subject Index   **305**

PREFACE

A major responsibility of every police administrator is the selection of recruits who have the potential to become effective law enforcement officers. This is a difficult job because of the multifaceted nature of police work. In order to deal with problems ranging from minor traffic accidents to crimes of violence, an effective officer must not only possess a variety of professional skills, but also be emotionally stable, compassionate, and sensitive to the needs of people.

The selection of qualified police officers has always been a demanding responsibility for the law enforcement administrator, but there are now additional pressures that require police administrators to expend even more time and energy on selection. In 1973 the National Advisory Commission on Criminal Justice Standards and Goals recommended that every police agency "employ a formal process for the selection of qualified police applicants. This process should include a written test on mental ability or aptitude, an oral interview, a physical examination, a psychological examination, and an in-depth background investigation."

Although the use of psychological tests in police selection has been strongly recommended by the advisory commission, recent decisions in state and federal courts have criticized standardized tests because of evidence that they discriminate against women and minority groups. Consequently, the assessment and testing procedures that are used to identify applicants with the requisite qualifications to become successful law enforcement officers must also conform to Equal Employment Opportunity Commission (EEOC) guidelines with regard to the employment of minorities and women.

Many different psychological assessment techniques are currently used in the screening and selection of law enforcement officers, but relatively little objective evidence is available with respect to the validity of these procedures as predictors of effective on-the-job performance in carrying out the diverse duties of a police officer. Over the past decade, however, the Law Enforcement

Assistance Administration, the International Association of Chiefs of Police, the Police Foundation, and other agencies concerned with law enforcement have funded a number of research projects in which procedures for selecting police officers and criteria for evaluating officer performance have been investigated. Consequently, there is now emerging a great deal of information with regard to the predictive validity of specific assessment procedures in police selection.

The diverse and changing duties of police officers, increasing demands for the employment of minority group members and women, and the range of complex methodological problems encountered in police selection research have all contributed to the police administrators' need for carefully validated selection procedures. Consistent with this need, the three major goals of this volume are (1) to review and evaluate the present state of knowledge about police selection, (2) to facilitate communication of research findings among behavioral scientists and police administrators currently involved in the selection of law enforcement officers, and (3) to identify methodological and practical problems encountered in the development of valid procedures for the selection of minority group members and women for positions in law enforcement.

The contributors to this volume are behavioral scientists and leading researchers in the field of police selection. A common denominator among the contributors is that they are vitally concerned with the selection of effective law enforcement officers and are currently engaged in research in this field. Individual chapters provide authoritative presentations of conceptual and methodological issues in research on police selection as well as on-the-job analysis and performance appraisal of law enforcement officers. Other chapters describe recent research on the use of biodata and psychological assessment procedures in police selection. The final two chapters are concerned with the impact of civil rights legislation and EEOC guidelines on personnel procedures and employment practices in police selection.

This volume should be of considerable interest to behavioral scientists, police administrators, and personnel officers who are involved in the selection and promotion of law enforcement officers. This book will also be of interest to industrial and clinical psychologists and should prove useful as a supplementary textbook in courses in criminal justice administration, personnel psychology, and psychological assessment.

The present volume grows out of the National Working Conference on the Selection of Law Enforcement Officers held in October 1976 at the FBI National Academy, Quantico, Virginia, under the sponsorship of the Law Enforcement Assistance Administration (LEAA) and the FBI. The general purpose of the conference was to provide a forum for the exchange of information among law enforcement officials and researchers concerned with police selection. Information about the working conference and a roster of the participants are provided in the Appendix.

For their contributions to planning and organizing the conference, I am deeply indebted to Ronald D. Branch, LEAA Office of Civil Rights Compliance; Sid Epstein, National Institute of Law Enforcement and Criminal Justice; Donald Fish and Joel Pate, Florida Police Standards and Training Commission; John W. Pfaff and Lawrence Monroe, FBI National Academy; J. Price Foster, LEAA Office of Criminal Justice Education and Training; and Charles F. Rinkevich and Carol Blair, LEAA Atlanta Regional Office. I would also like to acknowledge with appreciation the encouragement and assistance of Dr. William M. Mooney, assistant director of the FBI when the working conference was held, and Dr. Kenneth Joseph, academic chief at the FBI National Academy, in the planning and implementation of the working conference.

Special thanks are due to Harry C. Spaulding and John C. Ward of the University of South Florida for their invaluable help in working out the administrative arrangements for the conference and for their significant contributions in reviewing the manuscripts for this book and writing chapters 2 and 14. Finally, I would like to express my gratitude to Linda Fry, Florence Frain, Jean Goltermann, Diane Ludington, and Peggy McPherson for their expert technical and clerical assistance in the processing and preparation of the manuscript for publication.

Charles D. Spielberger

I

SELECTION OF LAW ENFORCEMENT OFFICERS

AN OVERVIEW
OF POLICE SELECTION
Some Issues, Questions,
and Challenges

John Furcon
*Industrial Relations Center, The University of Chicago,
Chicago, Illinois*

From the point of view of the citizens of our communities, the uniformed police officer is the most visible, the most prevalent, and the most frequently called on representative of the nation's criminal-justice system. Experiences in the turbulent 1960s and the even more complex 1970s support the conclusions that the challenges faced by the individual police officer are becoming increasingly more difficult and that the rate of change and the level of complexity of these challenges are rapidly increasing. For these reasons the question of standards—and in particular the question of *personnel selection procedures,* as these are related to standards—has come under greater and greater scrutiny in the law enforcement profession.

Several recent publications and reports (most notably Gottesman, 1969; Heckman, Groner, Dunnette, & Johnson, 1972; Kent & Eisenberg, 1972; Lefkowitz, 1977) have provided excellent and detailed reviews of the technical progress in research on police officer selection. Rather than reviewing this work, which quite satisfactorily describes the "state of the art" at a technical and empirical level, this chapter will examine important concepts, frameworks, questions, and issues at a more general level.

The issues that will be considered pertain to factors that influence police selection. They also provide worthwhile challenges and goals that should be considered in future efforts in the police selection and employment area. The major areas that are addressed include (1) "jet streams" of change, (2) critical roles in police selection and their challenges, (3) some major issues in police selection—problems and progress, and (4) positive signs and future perspectives.

THE "JET STREAMS" OF CHANGE

This analogy, based on environmental sciences, has proved useful in understanding present and anticipated developments in the field of police selection. Jet streams at the upper altitudes have a controlling force on specific future weather conditions at a given geographical location. There are five important jet streams to watch in the area of police selection, since their current status and future promise hold controlling influence over progress in this field. These major jet streams include:

1. *Legislation.* In recent years the human resources area has been greatly affected by major legislation, including the 1964 Civil Rights Act and acts related to age discrimination, rights of the handicapped, and privacy. The trend in all of this is to clearly recognize the dignity, the worth, and the rights of the individual. This trend may make our work somewhat more cumbersome and complicated, but any such inconveniences are judged to be a small price to pay for the major benefits that we all receive in the form of individual freedom.

2. *Judicial decisions.* The last several years have seen a number of major court decisions in the employment area, including *Griggs* v. *Duke Power Company, Albermarle* v. *Moody*, and most recently, *Davis* v. *Washington.* The trend is to support the basic thrust of the 1964 Civil Rights Act, although further clarification is needed on the full implications of the recent Davis decision for the employment process.

3. *Administrative actions.* A number of administrative agencies in the executive branch at the state and federal level of government have prepared guidelines related to the human resources area and to the employment process in particular. At the federal level for several years the Equal Employment Opportunity Coordinating Council (EEOCC) has been working toward the development of uniform federal guidelines in the employment area. In this area we find much conflict and ambiguity. However, the trend seems to be movement toward more uniform and realistic guidelines and more supportable and understandable standards.

4. *Professional psychology.* We see burgeoning interest in occupational analysis (e.g., Baehr, 1976) and the emergence of new interdisciplinary approaches and interests (e.g., the Psychology-Law Society), although there have been no major technical "breakthroughs." In fact, there is more evidence for revival and renewal of interest surrounding techniques that have been available for some time, such as the J-coefficient in job analysis, the moderator variable in prediction, and the situational testing of the assessment center. New techniques have arisen in the area of job performance

measurement, with the advent of the job behavior description scales, behaviorally anchored paired-comparison ratings, and other methods. There are also new procedures for multivariate analysis. There is growing awareness of the need to focus on the effectiveness of the total assessment or employment system rather than merely dealing with isolated specific elements of the employment process.

5. *Professional law enforcement.* The trend here is a growing recognition of a need for a more sophisticated approach in the employment area and declining satisfaction with traditional employment procedures. For example, the literature in police selection has a long past but a short history, since prior to 1950 very little sound work was published in this area. A review of the literature in the last 5 years would evidence a strong growth curve in this regard. Perhaps one of the most promising signs at this time in this area is the proliferation of local, state, and national project efforts aimed at improving the selection process of police agencies.

SOME CRITICAL ROLES
AND THEIR CHALLENGES

There are at least five occupational roles that can and do have a critical influence on the direction, content, and conduct of the police selection process. With respect to psychologists working in this field, three types or specialties are apparent: (1) clinical psychologists, (2) psychometric psychologists, and (3) industrial-organizational (I-O) psychologists. In addition, educators and administrators play an important part in this process. Each of these critical roles has one or more challenges or needs that I would like to point out. These comments are intended to identify opportunities for growth or increased effectiveness, but I realize that, in addition to being a source of encouragement, these comments run the risk of angering some people.

The Clinical Psychologist

Many psychologists who work with police agencies have a clinical background. The clinical orientation seems to be insulated from the "big picture" in the employment area or at least specifically from the need to demonstrate the linkage of clinical predictions to job performance. Clinical psychologists need to understand the technical issues surrounding job-criterion-related forms of validity and also need to gain an understanding of the legal and administrative issues surrounding the employment process in police agencies. For example, in a recent civil service hearing in a major city a psychiatrist who testified in support of his recommendation to reject a number of minority candidates indicated under cross-examination that he did not keep notes on his clinical analysis leading to the recommendations and that he had never been involved in the analysis of a police officer's job or utilized the results of any occupational analysis work as a basis for his clinical judgment. He lost, that is, his recommendations were overturned. No matter how expert his clinical assessment may have been, it seems that it would have been much improved by preparatory job analysis work and that ignorance of legal and administrative requirements only put him at a further disadvantage.

The Psychometric Psychologist

The major challenge here is to develop more effective instrumentation in the selection area—for example, to develop a selection test for police officers that is simultaneously job related, equitable, and professionally acceptable to the psychologist and to those in law enforcement. One national scope project (Furcon, 1976) aimed at developing a selection test for use in screening police applicants for the 61 major municipal agencies and for the 49 state police and highway patrol agencies is a case in point.

Specialists in psychometrics need to develop and implement research on program methodologies that support and enhance the employment process but that are comprehensible to operational and personnel managers in law enforcement agencies and to appointing authorities. At times a communications gap exists between specialists working in psychometrics and the practical people who operate our police and civil service agencies.

The I-O Psychologist

For the I-O psychologist there is a need to provide models and procedures for dealing with the change process within police and civil service organizations. Change takes a long time. In my experience, it takes 3-5 years for these organizations to move from the discussion of an idea to actually getting a project effort funded and started. Then the project must be completed. Another time lag occurs before the implementation of results. Better ways must be found to manage the innovation, development, and change process in law enforcement organizations. Another challenge I would propose to I-O psychologists would be that they develop models and procedures for the total assessment of people and for career-long planning and utilization of human talent in police agencies. There is also a need for better integration of psychometric and clinical assessment models; perhaps this can best be accomplished by I-O psychologists.

The Educator

The one challenge I would like to present to professionals working in the police education field is based on my experience as a board member for the implementing organization of the statewide police selection system set up by our police chiefs and police commissioners in the state of Illinois (Furcon &

Froemel, 1973). Several complaints have been brought to the board concerning police applicants who are college graduates and even graduates of police science programs but have failed the examination process. This circumstance may actually be more directly a problem of expectations than of the exam process. It seems to me that in the area of entry into police service there are some tall expectations being generated in some police science programs. These expectations include the belief that anyone who gets a police science degree can get a job as a police officer and that with such a degree rapid promotion is likely. As a matter of fact, many police science graduates will be unable to get jobs anywhere in the criminal-justice system, since there are many graduates and since the qualifications for entering a specific job have not been among the qualifications for entering the education program.

This problem is not unique to police science programs, but it does represent a key problem in the area of police selection. The challenge is to effectively prescreen people interested in entering police science programs so that the probability of a graduate's selection as a police officer is enhanced or at least the potential student will be advised in advance of his or her chances of eventual employment.

The Administrator

Of all the roles discussed in this section, the role of the administrator or agency head is the most difficult. While each of the above-mentioned roles has its own problems, my observation is that the job of keeping agencies operating, keeping the government moving, and providing the services that people need in the community and on the street is really a challenge. My charge to administrators is that they establish priorities in the human resources area and allocate resources wisely.

Two observations support this recommendation. First, personnel research and development of the type that we are discussing are the most perishable delicacies in the organization fruitbasket. How often do you find a fruitbasket on sale that contains fresh strawberries? Personnel research is among the first items to be cut in the finalization of agency budgets. Training would be the next most vulnerable item. I wonder if in the long run it is wise to limit or eliminate allocations in the personnel research area? The second observation is also related to budgets. The percentage of the annual police budget allocated to personnel salaries and benefits usually ranges from 75 to 90% of the total. This allocation simply illustrates the importance of the human services provided by the police agency. The percentage of the budget related to vehicle fleet purchase is ordinarily far less. Ironically, however, we find that the amount spent on vehicle operation and maintenance is many times the amount expended for personnel selection and development and training activities.

SOME MAJOR ISSUES IN POLICE SELECTION—
PROGRESS AND PROBLEMS

The progress that has been made in police selection, as assessed by the literature in this field, is considerable, and has already been addressed in part in the preceding sections of this chapter. Some major problems in the police selection area include the following:

1. Current employment practices in police agencies have not changed significantly for many years. In fact, entry testing procedures in many departments resemble the written tests first developed around the time of World War I, as exemplified by the Army Alpha and the Army General Classification tests.

2. Police personnel professionals do not at this time implement contemporary personnel procedures in their agencies.

3. There is not yet a good model for disseminating information and for initiating and managing innovations in operational practices. In market research, for example, the "key communicator" model has been identified as a means of understanding the process by which physicians in a geographical area adopt drugs for use in treating patients.

4. There are serious limitations on the significance of our concurrent test validation strategy, but often it is our best available approach. New ground must be broken in order to provide more effective validation methodologies.

5. The question of transferability or "portability" of validation results is a relatively new question in search of good answers. While experts may disagree on the appropriateness or value of different validation methodologies, they will probably agree that it is neither cost effective nor realistic to expect each and every police agency to individually validate the various elements of its selection process.

6. The handling of racial differences and sex differences in employment practices remains a widespread and controversial problem. These differences exist; the challenge is to address them in a fair and effective manner.

7. Another problem exists in the measurement of police officer job performance. The police officer's job is complex. The criterion measure that is used in assessing job success is the limiting factor; predictions of job success made on the basis of test performance can be no better than the horizon set by the reliability and meaningfulness of the chosen form of measure.

8. In general, the technical validity of traditional applicant screening procedures has not been established. The best examples of this problem situation are found in the areas of height, weight, and physical agility requirements. Because of the "adverse impact" of such requirements on women and members of certain minority groups and because of the absence of suitable evidence of validity or "job relatedness," courts have been setting aside these requirements in specific cases. The potential for similar problems

exists in the area of personal background investigation procedures, another important traditional part of police applicant screening.

9. Police organizations are changing. There is a gradual, almost imperceptible shift to newer forms of organization. This shift is evidenced by structural changes, such as the advent of team policing and by the suspension of the traditional structure, as when a temporary task force group sets aside rank and works to develop a solution to a specific need or problem. The demographic composition of agencies is also changing. Entering officers are better educated and represent a much more heterogeneous group with respect to sex and race. The problem facing the selection specialist is the need to take these changing circumstances into account in developing and updating selection procedures for the police agency.

POSITIVE SIGNS AND FUTURE PERSPECTIVES

One important positive sign is the increasing number of psychologists who are on the permanent staff of either police departments or agencies having the responsibility for appointing police officers. Staff professionals who are permanent employees are in a different (and possibly more advantageous) position in terms of initiating and managing improvement in police selection, since their presence is long term rather than related to a specific grant or short-term project.

Good technical alternatives for police selection testing are becoming available. For example, at the nationwide level, two test development and validation projects have been completed. The project conducted by Heckman, Groner, Dunnette, and Johnson (1972) was the earliest project at this level. The recently completed project conducted by the International Association of Chiefs of Police, the International Personnel Management Association, and the Educational Testing Service is another example (Rosenfeld & Thorton, 1976). Another project (Furcon, 1976) is nearing completion. These project efforts represent somewhat different approaches to police selection testing, both in terms of the validation strategy and methodology and in terms of the construct areas represented in the test material.

While there is no riskier business than attempting to predict the future, a conservative extrapolation of current trends suggests the following prospects for the future in the police employment area:

1. More rather than less legal and administrative attention directed at an agency's personnel practices.
2. Increased complexity of personnel practices, to meet changing conditions and job requirements, as well as to meet legal, administrative, and professional guidelines for fairness and effectiveness.
3. A reorganization and renewal in civil service and appointing-authority agencies. In part, this renewal will be structural, as evidenced by the shift

to "departments of human resources." This renewal will also be characterized by the increased number of professionals with advanced education in psychology, the behavioral sciences, and personnel administration who will be moving into these agencies.

4. A higher priority being placed on the need to have police managers and appointing-authority officials educated, trained, and updated in the technical and professional developments in this area.

5. More appreciation of the difficulty and complexity of managing the personnel-staffing and decision-making process in police organizations.

6. Increased attention to the issue of the effective identification, utilization, and retention of leaders, that is, supervisors, managers, and executives, in the police agency. At present, nearly all leaders in police organizations come from within, working their way up from the bottom. Although there is much activity in the area of promotion, this activity is mainly along traditional lines. Much work needs to be done to upgrade the technical quality of promotional assessment work carried out in police agencies.

REFERENCES

Baehr, M. E. A practitioner's view of EEOC requirements with special ret 'rence to job analysis. Occasional paper 37. Chicago: University of Chicago, Industrial Relations Center, 1976.

Furcon, J. E. Municipal and state police officer selection test development project: progress and implications. In J. Lefkowitz (Chair), *Police selection: Impact of administrative, professional, social and legal considerations.* Symposium presented at the meeting of the American Psychological Association, Washington, D.C., 1976.

Furcon, J. E., & Froemel, E. C. *The relationship of selected psychological tests to measures of police officer job performance in the State of Illinois.* Chicago: University of Chicago, Industrial Relations Center, 1973.

Gottesman, J. *Personality patterns of urban police applicants as measured by the MMPI.* Hoboken, N.J.: Stevens Institute of Technology, 1969.

Heckman, R. W., Groner, D. M., Dunnette, M. D., & Johnson, P. D. *Development of psychiatric standards for police selection.* Report submitted to the National Institute of Law Enforcement and Criminal Justice, U.S. Department of Justice, Law Enforcement Assistance Administration, 1972.

Kent, D. A., & Eisenberg, T. The selection and promotion of police officers: A selected review of the literature. *The Police Chief,* 1972, *39,* 20–29.

Lefkowitz, J. Industrial-organizational psychology and the police. *American Psychologist,* 1977, *32,* 346–364.

Rosenfeld, M., & Thorton, R. F. *The development and validation of a multijurisdictional police examination.* Princeton, N.J.: Educational Testing Service, 1976.

2

A MODEL FOR THE SELECTION OF LAW ENFORCEMENT OFFICERS

Charles D. Spielberger, John C. Ward, and Harry C. Spaulding
Department of Psychology, University of South Florida,
Tampa, Florida

The importance to U.S. society of selecting effective law enforcement officers has been increasingly recognized. A major goal in police selection is to screen out "misfits" from positions in law enforcement. Examples of police misconduct cited by the U.S. President's Commission on Law Enforcement (1967) include instances in which police officers were involved in criminal activities ranging from "rolling drunks" and accepting bribes to participating in large-scale burglary rings. Unfortunately, the findings of the commission may come as no surprise to the average citizen, who is likely to encounter similar stories in any newspaper.

In recent years personnel selection procedures have come under critical review because of alleged unfair or discriminatory employment practices. The Equal Employment Opportunity Commission (EEOC) report of 1970 delineated specific cautions and guidelines for validating selection procedures for particular employment positions or fields (Boyer & Griggs, 1974). On the basis of these guidelines, court decisions during the past 5 years have mandated equal employment opportunities for minority group members and women and have given added importance to job-related validation.[1]

---

[1] For a detailed analysis of the impact of civil rights legislation and court actions on personnel practices, see Baehr, chapter 15 of this volume. Also, in chapter 16 of this volume Fox examines some of the practical implications of the EEOC guidelines for the police administrator.

Many different assessment techniques and screening procedures are currently used in the selection of police officers. Yet relatively little objective evidence is available with respect to the validity of these procedures. The prediction of effective performance is difficult because of the diverse and complex duties of a police officer. Furthermore, selection methods must be adaptable to changing conditions but not so involved or costly that their use becomes prohibitive when applied to increasing numbers of candidates.

The usefulness of any selection procedure must be determined through empirical investigations that evaluate the relationship between initial selection standards (predictors) and the actual job performance of police officers. The report of the Police Task Force of the U.S. President's Commission on Law Enforcement (1967) states:

> Standards set for selection must not only be realistic, but should correlate positively with on-the-job performance. In other words, if a characteristic makes absolutely no difference as to whether or not a man would make a good patrolman, it should not be used as a criterion for selection. (p. 7)

The process of establishing the relationship between initial selection standards and job performance is termed *validation*. In one approach to validation, which is called *concurrent validity*, the skills and personal characteristics of police officers who are already employed are assessed. A more rigorous validation procedure, referred to as *predictive validity*, requires determining how well initial standards predict a candidate's success (or failure) as a police officer.

During the past 5 years, the Law Enforcement Assistance Administration, the International Association of Chiefs of Police (IACP), the Police Foundation, and other agencies concerned with law enforcement have supported a number of validation research projects investigating procedures for selecting police officers and criteria for assessing officer performance (Cruse & Rubin, 1973; Dunnette & Motowidlo, 1976; Eisenberg, Kent, & Wall, 1973; Landy & Farr, 1975). Consequently, there is now emerging a great deal of knowledge with regard to specific selection procedures, but it is difficult for decision makers in law enforcement agencies to evaluate and utilize these research findings in selecting new police officers.

The major goal of this chapter is to present a model to guide the validation efforts of researchers and administrators involved in the selection of law enforcement officers. Prior to the description of this model, three general categories of predictor variables will be defined and examples of research using specific predictor measures within each of these categories will be described. In addition, the criteria for successful performance that are most often employed in police selection research will be examined and specific research examples of how these criteria have been assessed will be reported.

PREDICTOR VARIABLES IN POLICE SELECTION

In research on the selection of law enforcement officers, a variety of predictor measures have been employed, both singly and in combination. These selection devices may be grouped into the following three general categories: (1) physical, biographical, and demographic characteristics of applicants; (2) psychological tests, including civil service examinations, measures of intelligence and aptitude, measure of values, attitudes, and interests, and tests of personality and motivation; and (3) situational tests, in which selected job functions are simulated or candidates' behavior is observed in "test" situations, such as oral interviews and polygraph examinations. Each of these categories is examined below, and the findings of representative studies of specific predictor measures are described.

Physical, Biographical, and Demographic Predictor Variables

Traditionally, height requirements have been used in police selection, but researchers who have examined the validity of height as a predictor of successful performance have reported inconsistent and/or equivocal results (Archuleta, 1974; Dempsey, 1974; Goldstein, 1974; Halling, 1974; Hoobler & McQueeney, 1973; Kollender & McQueeney, 1977; Marsh, 1962; Nolting, 1929; O'Conner, 1962; Prelutsky, 1974; Spencer & Jewell, 1963). While height requirements have not been found to be an occupational necessity, Eisenberg and Reinke (1973) recommend that these requirements be maintained until more definitive research results are available. However, some agencies, such as the FBI (Yates, 1977), have abolished height as a selection standard.[2]

Since police selection standards based on height and weight potentially discriminate against female applicants, it has been suggested that measures of physical agility can be better justified as standards for selecting police officers (Byrd, 1976; McGhee, 1976; Osborne, 1976; Stamford, Kley, Thomas, & Nevin, 1977; Tolbert, 1976). Since the results in studies of physical agility have not been replicated, the generalizability of these findings is questionable. Thus there is little empirical support for the use of physical agility tests in police selection at this time.

The biographical characteristics of applicants for positions in law enforcement have traditionally been considered important factors in determining fitness for police work (Goldstein, 1972; Kates, 1950; Matarazzo, Allen, Saslow, & Wiens, 1964; Terman, 1917; Thurstone, 1922). The biodata used in police selection has included education, previous military and

---

[2] This information was reported by Robert Yates at the National Working Conference on the Selection of Law Enforcement Officers (Spielberger & Spaulding, 1977).

employment experience, financial status, and criminal and accident history. In general, the background of applicants accepted for employment as police officers differs from the background of those who have been rejected (Goldstein, 1972), but the results of descriptive studies have not established the validity of biodata in predicting successful performance in police work.

Empirical studies have investigated the predictive validity of a number of biographical variables, such as marital status, number of dependents, highest salary previously attained, education, hobbies, previous employment, length and type of military experience, records of traffic violations, and birthplace (Azen, Montgomery, Snibbe, Fabricatore, & Earle, 1974; Cross & Hammond, 1951; Levy, 1967, 1971; McAllister, 1970). Of these, only previous military experience appears to predict the performance of police officers in a reasonably consistent manner. Unfortunately, most researchers have used large numbers of biographical predictors with too few subjects, which has resulted in significant correlations occurring by chance (Monte Carlo effects). The criterion of success has also varied considerably from study to study. Thus, more research is needed to determine whether the biographical characteristics of applicants can contribute to the prediction of police officer performance (see Cascio & Real, chapter 7 of this volume).

A subcategory of biodata predictor variables, generally referred to as demographic characteristics, includes the age, race, and sex of applicants. While minimum and maximum age limits have been traditional considerations in the selection of law enforcement officers, there are inconsistencies in the research findings on the validity of age requirements (Cross & Hammond, 1951; Levy, 1967, 1971). Until more definitive research is available, the usefulness of age as a predictor of on-the-job performance cannot be determined.

EEOC guidelines make it illegal to use race or sex as standards for the selection of police officers, and compliance with these guidelines requires researchers to examine their procedures in order to prevent potential discrimination against females or minority group members. Accordingly, in recent studies, the data have been separately analyzed as a function of race (Baehr, Saunders, Froemel, & Furcon, 1971; Cohen & Chaiken, 1972; Snibbe, Fabricatore, Azen, & Snibbe, 1975; Spencer & Nichols, 1971). On the basis of their findings, Baehr et al. (1971) concluded that race must be separately examined in the validation of police selection techniques, but Snibbe et al. (1975) contend that this may not be necessary for all sections of the country.

The sex of police applicants has also received a great deal of attention and recent research findings have indicated that physical agility requirements may discriminate unfairly against female applicants (Osborne, 1976). It should be noted that most previous studies of police selection were conducted at a time when there were relatively few female officers. As the number of women employed in law enforcement positions increases, research will be needed in which relationships between predictor measures and criterion variables are analyzed separately for male and female police officers. Only then can compliance with federal guidelines and court rulings be ensured.

Psychological Assessment in Police Selection

In one of the earliest studies of police selection, Terman (1917) considered intelligence to be an important factor in fitness for police work and recommended a minimum IQ of 80 for employment as a police officer. Intellectual ability is even more important in police selection today, and studies indicate that at least average intelligence is required of police officers (Gordon, 1969; Kole, 1962; Matarazzo et al., 1964; Merrill, 1927; Thurston, 1922). In general, intelligence and ability tests have proved useful as predictors of police academy performance (Dubois & Watson, 1950; Mullineaux, 1955; Pounian, 1959) but are less reliable for predicting job performance as measured by supervisor ratings. Furthermore, measures of intelligence do not appear to differentiate between police officers who perform poorly and average or superior officers (Dubois & Watson, 1950; Hess, 1973; Martin, 1923; Pounian, 1959).

In many police departments, to be eligible for employment, a candidate must pass a civil service screening examination, and scores on civil service tests are highly correlated with measures of aptitude and intelligence (Abbatiello, 1969; Blum, 1961; Blum, Goggin, & Whitmore, 1961; Spencer & Nichols, 1971). Since adverse racial impact may result from civil service testing (Cohen & Chaiken, 1972), compliance with EEOC guidelines may require examination of the civil service preselection process, as well as the tests that are actually used in screening law enforcement applicants.

Psychological tests are often used in police selection to assess values, attitudes, and interests. Police applicants' values and attitudes have been measured with the Allport-Vernon-Lindzey Study of Values (Colarelli & Siegel, 1964; Hooke & Krauss, 1971; Rush, 1963), the Niederhoffer (1967) Cynicism Scale, and the Rokeach Terminal Value Survey (Rokeach, Miller, & Snyder, 1971). The Kuder Preference Record (Azen, Snibbe, & Montgomery, 1973; Marsh, 1962; Spaulding, 1948; Sterne, 1960), and the Strong Vocational Interest Blank (Barnabas, 1976; Blum, 1961, 1964; Dubois & Watson, 1950; Kates, 1950) have been widely used to assess the interest patterns of candidates for law enforcement positions.

The value, attitude, and interest profiles of police officers differ from those of the general population (Bennett & Greenstein, 1975; McNamara, 1967; Niederhoffer, 1967; Rokeach et al., 1971; Tift, 1974), and this so-called value gap has been investigated in various ways. Some researchers have examined police officers' values and attitudes as these are related to education and training (Bennett & Greenstein, 1975; Guller, 1972; Sherrid & Beech, 1976; Smith, Locke, & Walker, 1967; Sparling, 1975; Weiner, 1976; Zacker, 1971), while others have investigated the influence of the "organizational climate" of a department on the values and attitudes of police recruits (Balch, 1972; Meyer, 1973; Miller & Fry, 1975).

Most studies of the values, attitudes, and interests of police officers have been largely descriptive, and the few criterion-related validity studies have not been cross-validated or replicated. Thus it is difficult to evaluate the usefulness of value, attitude, and interest measures in the prediction of the success of law enforcement officers, and much more research on the predictive validity of these measures is needed. The use of the Strong-Campbell Interest Inventory (SCII) to assess attitudes and interest patterns of law enforcement officers is described by Flint in chapter 9 of this volume, and Sherrid discusses changes in the values of police officers in chapter 10.

The personality characteristics of recruits and tenured officers have been the subject of extensive research (e.g., Gallati, 1960a, 1960b), and the use of psychiatrists and psychologists in screening police applicants is on the increase (Eisenberg et al., 1973; Murphy, 1972; Oglesby, 1957; Wolfe, 1970). The personality assessment devices most often employed in police selection research are the Rorschach inkblots (Blum, 1964; Kates, 1950; Matarazzo et al., 1964; Rankin, 1957), the Minnesota Multiphasic Personality Inventory (MMPI) (Barnabas, 1976; Blum, 1964; Colarelli & Seigel, 1964; Gottesman, 1975; Hooke & Krauss, 1971; Marsh, 1962; Matarazzo et al., 1964; Nowicki, 1966; Rankin, 1957; Rush, 1963; Shealy, 1977), the California Psychological Inventory (CPI) (Hogan, 1971; Parker & Roth, 1973), and the Eysenck Personality Inventory (EPI) (Fenster & Locke, 1973). In most concurrent validity studies in which the MMPI, the CPI, and the EPI were employed, the profiles of successful police officers were not different from those of the general population. In police selection research with the MMPI and the Rorschach, a higher incidence of pathology was observed in the profiles of terminated or poorly performing officers (see Shealy, chapter 12, this volume).

Gottesman (1975) contends that the use of the MMPI in police selection is questionable. Since this test was standardized on relatives of hospitalized medical patients, Gottesman concludes that the MMPI norms are not appropriate for applicants for law enforcement positions. The CPI (often referred to as the sane man's MMPI may provide a more useful personality assessment device for use in research on police selection. Data on the predictive validity of the CPI in police selection research is reported in chapter 14 of this volume.

The importance of considering the effects of stress and anxiety on police officer performance has been suggested by a number of investigators (Cruse & Rubin, 1973; Kroes, Margolis, & Hurrell, 1974; Reiser, 1976; Symonds, 1970). In a concurrent validity study of successful police applicants, Matarazzo et al. (1964) reported that candidates for positions in law enforcement scored in the "healthy" range for anxiety. However, the predictive validity of anxiety measures in police selection remains to be investigated.

Saunders (1977) has recently suggested that the relationship between an applicant's anxiety and his or her performance as a police officer may be very complex. Saunders observes that anxiety may enhance the relationship between some predictor and criterion measures, but the direction of this relationship may actually be reversed when other predictors and criteria are examined. In essence, Saunders posits that anxiety acts as a "moderator variable" in police selection research in improving the predictive validity of other variables, but anxiety measures cannot stand alone as predictors of successful police performance. In order to examine the contribution of anxiety measures to police selection, it may be necessary to employ highly sophisticated statistical procedures.

The Use of Situational Tests in Police Selection

Situational tests are being increasingly used to supplement other procedures in selecting applicants for law enforcement positions (Shavelson, Beckum, & Brown, 1974). Chenoweth (1961), who was among the first to advocate these procedures in assessing police applicants, describes situational testing as a technique for evaluating the reactions of candidates to structured stimuli in order to predict job-related behavior. While research on the validity of situational testing in police selection shows promising results (e.g., Dillman, 1963; Mills, 1976; Mills, McDevitt, & Tonkin, 1966), the cost and complexity of constructing and administering situational tests limit the feasibility of including such procedures in the initial screening of recruits (Chenoweth, 1961).

The use of polygraphs in examining police applicants may be considered a special type of situational test. In polygraph testing, a trained examiner evaluates applicants' responses to specific questions designed to assess personal qualities that are critical in the performance of a police officer's duties. Since polygraph examinations are expensive and since the predictive validity studies have produced equivocal results (Arther, 1967; Blum, 1967; Stephens, 1969; Swank & Haley, 1972; Territo, 1974), the use of the polygraph screening by individual police agencies would seem difficult to justify at this time.

During the past decade, situational testing procedures have been incorporated in "assessment centers" for the selection and promotion of law enforcement officers. Research on the contributions of the assessment center approach has been encouraging (D'Arcy, 1974; Dunnette & Motowidlo, 1976; Gavin & Hamilton, 1975; Kent, Wall, & Bailey, 1974). Typically, assessment centers use inexpensive screening methods to reduce the number of applicants who are evaluated by more expensive and time-consuming situational tests. Several police agencies may also combine resources in the operation of assessment centers to further reduce costs. An application of the assessment center approach in the evaluation of law enforcement officers is described by Filer in chapter 13 of this volume.

With few exceptions, research on the selection of law enforcement officers has focused on the concurrent and predictive validity of the variables employed in the selection process. In this research, successful performance as a police officer has been defined in many different ways, and there is little consistency from one study to another. On the basis of their review of ten years of research in police selection, Kent and Eisenberg (1972) conclude that "a usefully valid and unbiased procedure for selecting police officers has not been demonstrated as yet. . . . The criterion problem stands out as one of the major stumbling blocks to improved police selection and promotion procedures" (p. 28).

Further progress in the development of valid and cost-effective procedures for the selection of law enforcement officers will require clarification of the criteria for successful performance. The performance criteria traditionally used in police selection research are reviewed in the next section of this chapter.

PERFORMANCE CRITERIA IN POLICE SELECTION RESEARCH

In research on the selection of law enforcement officers, performance criteria have been assessed in a number of ways. While the specific criteria have varied from study to study, most investigators have obtained measures of (1) performance at the police academy or (2) performance on the job during the probationary period and/or as tenured patrol officers. Police academy criteria have included academic achievement (grades, class rank, etc.) and instructor and peer (classmate) ratings. Measures of the performance of probationary and tenured patrol officers have included supervisor and peer ratings, objective indexes (commendations, reprimands, etc.), and employment status (employed vs. terminated or resigned). For tenured patrol officers promotion in rank has been examined as an important criterion of success.

In order to be certified as law enforcement officers, recruits are generally required to successfully complete a police academy training program. Measures of ability and intelligence are generally good predictors of academic achievement at police academies (Abbatiello, 1969; Dubois & Watson, 1950; Morman, Hankey, Kennedy, & Jones, 1966; Mullineaux, 1955; Shealy, 1972). In contrast, the interests and personality characteristics of applicants have generally not been found to be related to academy grades (Morman, Hankey, Heywood, & Liddle, 1966; Morman, Hankey, Kennedy, & Jones, 1966). On the other hand, interest and personality measures are positively correlated with instructor and peer evaluations of general suitability for police work (Azen et al., 1974; Chiaramonte, 1974). Since peers at the police academy may observe behaviors that are often hidden from instructors, Azen et al. (1974) suggest that peer ratings may also be useful as predictors of later job performance. While the training program at the police academy is designed to prepare recruits to carry out the complex duties and responsibilities of a police officer, there is little opportunity for the recruits to demonstrate that they can apply the principles that they learn at the academy. Nevertheless, as has been noted by McCreedy (1974), "There is almost an implied bias in law enforcement agencies that those who have completed the academy training have received the 'stamp of approval'" (p. 42). During the probationary period, however, officers are continuously observed as they actually perform on the job, and a decision must be made on whether or not each officer will be retained or terminated. Thus measures of performance during the probationary period would seem to provide better criteria for validating selection procedures than would performance at the police training academy.

During the probationary period, supervisor ratings provide the major basis for evaluating performance, and personality measures appear to be better than measures of intellectual ability in predicting these ratings (Blum et al., 1961). Since it is not always possible for working supervisors to observe closely the performance of each probationary officer, many departments have established field training officer (FTO) positions (Fabricatore, 1977; Roberts, 1977). Typically, the FTOs are experienced, well-trained officers who are assigned full time to ride with probationary officers and to observe and evaluate their day-to-day performance. Although the cost of obtaining FTO ratings may be relatively high, such ratings provide especially valuable criteria for validating initial selection standards.

Evaluations of actual performance on the job are generally considered to be the most meaningful criteria for validating police selection procedures. In evaluating probationary officers and tenured patrol officers, the same types of supervisor and peer ratings have been employed (Azen et al., 1973; Baehr et al., 1971; Hooke & Krauss, 1971). These ratings have been criticized because they are often based on subjective, arbitrary judgments and are low in reliability (Dudycha, 1956). In response to such criticisms, sophisticated behaviorally anchored rating scales have been developed, and these appear to provide more objective and reliable scaling procedures for assessing police performance (Dunnette & Motowidlo, 1976; Landy & Farr, 1975). Dunnette's scales consist of behavioral statements that describe specific police duties related to crime prevention, traffic maintenance and control, detecting and investigating criminal activities, and so forth. Landy and Farr have developed similar rating scales, which are described in detail in chapter 4 of this volume.

Commendations, reprimands, and citizens' complaints recorded in a police officer's personnel file may also provide objective information that is useful in evaluating performance. Specific indexes that have been used as performance criterion measures for probationary and tenured police officers include (1) absenteeism or time lost from sickness or injury, (2) formal recognition of outstanding performance, (3) disciplinary charges, (4) arrests, (5) services rendered, and (6) allegations of criminal misconduct (e.g., Cohen & Chaiken, 1972; Colarelli & Siegel, 1964; McAllister, 1970). Since most of these measures generally occur with low frequency, their usefulness as performance criteria is limited. In addition, such measures have been criticized because they may not be "relevant 'yardsticks' as far as community/human relations and social interactions are concerned" (Badalamente, George, Halterlein, Jackson, Moore, & Rio, 1973, p. 452).

A potentially important performance criterion in the evaluation of probationary police officers is whether the officer is retained or was terminated on or before completion of the probationary period (Blum, 1964). For those who were terminated, it is essential to determine if the officer was involuntarily dismissed, was performing satisfactorily but resigned for personal reasons, or was disqualified because of medical problems.

Employment status has also been used as one of the criteria for evaluating the performance of tenured patrol officers (Blum, 1964). A major contributor to this area, Levy (1971), has defined and labeled three categories of employment status: "currents," "failures," and "nonfailures." Currents are employed police officers who are performing satisfactorily. Failures are officers who have been terminated because of unsatisfactory performance. Nonfailures are terminated officers who are considered rehirable by their departments. These criteria appear to be useful in police selection research and are further discussed in chapter 14 of this volume.

Supervisor ratings, objective indexes of performance, and employment status have been used to evaluate both probationary and tenured officers. Advancement in rank provides a unique measure of success in the evaluation of the performance of tenured law enforcement officers. While advancement has been used as a criterion for validating initial selection procedures (Blum, 1964; Cohen & Chaiken, 1972), it should be noted that some people who function adequately as patrol officers do not possess the leadership qualities generally required for promotion. Therefore the use of advancement as a criterion for validating initial selection procedures may screen out officers who perform patrol duties in a highly satisfactory manner.

On the basis of the preceding review of the police selection literature, we have come to the unhappy conclusion that Kent and Eisenberg (1972) are essentially correct; the methodology in many police selection studies is faulty, the statistical analyses are often inappropriate, cross-validation of research findings is rare, and with a few exceptions, programmatic research is lacking. To provide a conceptual framework for evaluating police selection studies and planning future research in this field, a predictive model for the selection of law enforcement officers has been formulated. This model is discussed in the final section of this chapter.

A MODEL FOR THE SELECTION OF LAW ENFORCEMENT OFFICERS

In research on the selection of law enforcement officers a variety of predictor and criterion measures have been employed. Since the predictor and criterion measures have varied from one study to another, a meaningful comparison of the research findings on police selection is extremely difficult to achieve. A tentative model for evaluating and classifying previous research on the selection of law enforcement officers is proposed in Figure 1.

The model groups the predictor variables used in police selection research into three major categories or classes, each with several subclasses. These categories, which are listed in the lefthand column of the model, are physical, biographical and demographic characteristics; psychological assessment procedures; and situational tests. Specific variables relating to physical, biographical, or demographic characteristics are height, weight, age, educational level, marital status, and type and amount of previous employment experience (see Cascio and Real, chapter 7 of this volume).

The second general category of predictor variables consists of psychological tests for assessing intellectual ability and aptitude; values, attitudes, and interests; and personality and motivational factors. The third major category is composed of situational tests, including observations of performance in situations analogous to those in which police officers must function (criterion samples) and instruments used to evaluate physiological changes, such as the polygraph and the psychological stress evaluator (PSE). Some departments have developed assessment centers, in which combinations of situational tests and other assessment procedures are employed in a "multiple hurdles" technique (Blum, 1964).

Critical employment decisions are generally made by law enforcement agencies based on performance evaluations at the police academy or during a specified probationary period. These practices are recognized in the proposed police selection model by dividing the criteria for successful performance into the three major groupings listed in Figure 1 as column headings: performance at police academy; performance during probationary period; and performance in patrol status. The police selection literature suggests that different predictor variables may be required to predict performance during each of these periods.

Most agencies require candidates for law enforcement positions to pass physical examinations and background investigations as part of their employment screening procedures, but the validity of physical, biographical and demographic predictors of police performance has yet to be established. Furthermore, court decisions and EEOC guidelines make it illegal for police selection procedures to discriminate against minority groups and women. Therefore, in investigating the potential contribution of physical, biographical,

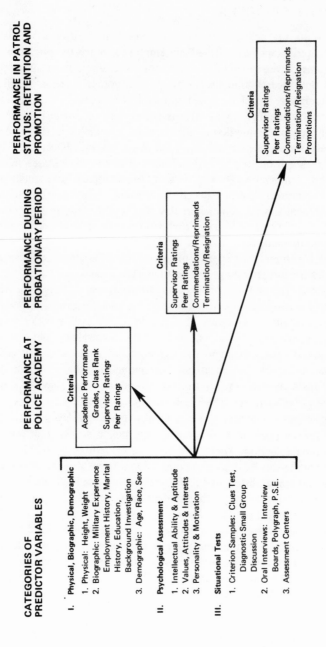

FIGURE 1 A model for the selection of law enforcement officers.

and demographic variables in predicting performance during each of the employment periods specified by the model, police selection researchers should develop separate prediction equations for women and minorities.

In the psychological assessment of applicants for positions in law enforcement, intellectual ability and aptitude have proved useful in predicting success or failure at police academies, but these measures are not good predictors of performance on the job. Recently, the IACP developed a police aptitude test on the basis of an in-depth analysis of the job of a police patrol officer. The IACP test shows great promise and is described in detail by Crosby, Rosenfeld, and Thornton in chapter 8 of this volume.

As previously noted, the usefulness of measures of values, attitudes, and interests in police selection is difficult to evaluate, and more research on the predictive validity of these measures is needed. As was mentioned above, the use of the SCII in police selection is discussed by Flint in chapter 9 of this volume, and a study in which the SCII was used in the prediction of performance at police academies and during the probationary period is described in chapter 14.

In research on the personality and motivational characteristics of candidates for positions in law enforcement, the Rorschach Inkblots Test and the MMPI have been most widely used. The Rorschach lacks objectivity, and it is expensive to administer and score. The MMPI has demonstrated predictive validity in identifying the characteristics of police officers who perform poorly on the job (see Shealy, chapter 12 of this volume), but this test has been criticized as inappropriate for evaluating police applicants (Gottesman, 1975). The use of the CPI in police selection research is discussed in chapter 14 of this volume.

Research on the validity of situational tests has shown encouraging results, and these tests are becoming more popular in police selection and promotion programs (see Filer, chapter 13 of this volume). However, situational tests are expensive to construct and administer, and cost-effectiveness considerations must be taken into account in decisions about including situational tests in research on the initial selection of candidates.

The model for the selection of law enforcement officers described in Figure 1 provides a general framework for evaluating research on police selection that may also prove useful in planning future investigations. It is recommended that one or more variables from the first two general predictor categories specified by the model be included in future investigations of the selection of law enforcement officers. A predictive validity research design that examines specific performance criteria for each of the three employment periods is also recommended. Of course, cross-validation of results is an essential requirement in law enforcement selection research.

SUMMARY

In this chapter a predictive model was proposed to guide the validation efforts of researchers and administrators involved in the selection of law enforcement officers. Three general categories of predictor variables were defined, and examples of research using specific predictor measures within each of these categories were described. The criteria for successful performance that are most often employed in police selection research were also examined, and specific research examples of how these criteria have been assessed were reported.

REFERENCES

Abbatiello, A. *A study of police candidate selection.* Paper presented at the 77th annual convention of the American Psychological Association, Washington, D.C., 1969.

Archuleta, A. O. Comment on "A question of height" (by R. I. Hoobler & J. A. McQueeney in *The Police Chief,* 1973). *The Police Chief,* 1974, *41,* 12.

Arther, R. O. Polygraph picks potential policemen. *The Journal of Polygraph Studies,* 1967, *2.*

Azen, S. P., Montgomery, H. R., Snibbe, H. M., Fabricatore, J. M., Earle, H. H. Predictors of resignation and performance in law enforcement officers. *American Journal of Community Psychology,* 1974, *2,* 79–86.

Azen, S. P., Snibbe, H. M., & Montgomery, H. R. A longitudinal predictive study of success and performance of law enforcement officers. *Journal of Applied Psychology,* 1973, *57,* 190–192.

Badalamente, R. V., George, C. E., Halterlein, P. J., Jackson, T. T., Moore, S. A., & Rio, R. Training police for their social role. *Journal of Police Science and Administration,* 1973, *1,* 440–453.

Baehr, M. E., Saunders, D. R., Froemel, E. C., & Furcon, J. E. The prediction of performance for black and for white police patrolmen. *Professional Psychology,* 1971, *2,* 46–57.

Balch, R. W. The police personality: Fact or fiction. *Journal of Criminal Law, Criminology, and Police Science,* 1972, *63,* 106–119.

Barnabas, B. Profile of a good police officer. *Law and Order,* 1976, *24,* 32–44.

Bennett, R. R., & Greenstein, T. The police personality: A test of the predispositional model. *Journal of Police Science and Administration,* 1975, *3,* 334–339.

Blum, R. H. *A further study of deputy sheriff selection procedures.* Unpublished manuscript, 1961.

Blum, R. H., *Police selection.* Springfield, Ill.: Thomas, 1964.

Blum, R. H. The polygraph examination in law enforcement personnel selection. *Police,* 1967, *12,* 60–75.

Blum, R. H., Goggin, W. L., & Whitmore, E. A study of deputy sheriff selection procedures. *Police,* 1961, *6,* 59–63.

Boyer, J. K., & Griggs, E. *Equal employment opportunity program development manual.* Washington, D.C.: U.S. Department of Justice, Law Enforcement Assistance Administration, Office of Civil Rights Compliance, 1974.

Byrd, D. A. Impact of physical fitness on police performance. *The Police Chief,* 1976, *43,* 30–32.

Chenoweth, J. H. Situational tests–A new attempt at assessing police candidates. *Journal of Criminal Law, Criminology, and Police Science,* 1961, *52,* 232–238.

Chiaramonte, R. M. Applicant screening. *The Police Chief,* 1974, *41,* 49–50.

Cohen, B., & Chaiken, J. *Police background characteristics and performance: Summary report,* (No. R-999-DOJ). New York: Rand Institute, 1972.

Colarelli, N. J., & Siegel, M. A method of police personnel selection. *Journal of Criminal Law, Criminology, and Police Science,* 1964, *55,* 287–289.

Cross, A. C., & Hammond, K. R. Social differences between "successful" and "unsuccessful" state highway patrolmen. *Public Personnel Review,* 1951, *12,* 159–161.

Cruse, D., & Rubin, J. Determinants of police behavior: A summary. (Criminal Justice Monograph, U.S. Department of Justice, Stock: #2700-00215). Washington, D.C.: U.S. Government Printing Office, 1973.

D'Arcy, P. F. In New York City assessment center program helps test managerial competence. *The Police Chief,* 1974, *41,* 52.

Dempsey, C. A. A study of police height requirements. *The Police Chief,* 1974, *41,* 34–35.

Dillman, E. G. Role-playing as a technique in police selection. *Public Personnel Review,* 1963, *24,* 116–118.

Dubois, P. H., & Watson, R. K. The selection of patrolmen. *Journal of Applied Psychology,* 1950, *34,* 90–95.

Dudycha, G. J. Rating and testing policemen. *Police,* 1956, *1,* 37–49.

Dunnette, M. D., & Motowidlo, S. J. Police selection and career assessment (Grant No. 73-N1-99-0018-G and 74-N1-99-0001-G). Washington, D.C.: National Institute of Law Enforcement and Criminal Justice, Law Enforcement Assistance Administration, U.S. Department of Justice, November 1976.

Eisenberg, T., Kent, D. A., & Wall, C. R. *Police personnel practices in state and local governments.* Gaithersburg, Md.: International Association of Chiefs of Police and Police Foundation, in cooperation with Educational Testing Service, December 1973.

Eisenberg, T., & Reinke, R. W. The use of written examinations in selecting police officers: Coping with the dilemma. *The Police Chief,* 1973, *40,* 24–26.

Fabricatore, J. M. Performance evaluation at the police academy. In C. D. Spielberger & H. C. Spaulding (Eds.), *Proceedings of the National Working Conference on the Selection of Law Enforcement Officers,* 1977, 51–57.

Fenster, C. A., & Locke, B. Neuroticism among policemen: An examination of police personality. *Journal of Applied Psychology,* 1973, *57,* 358–359.

Gallati, R. R. J. Police personnel testing experience of the New York City Police Department. *Police,* 1960, *5,* 76–77. (a)

Gallati, R. R. J. Police personnel testing experience of the New York City Police Department. *Police,* 1960, *5,* 23–25. (b)

Gavin, J. F., & Hamilton, J. W. Selecting police using assessment center methodology. *Journal of Police Science and Administration*, 1975, *3*, 166–176.

Goldstein, L. S. Characteristics of police applicants. *The Police Chief*, 1972, *39*, 58–60.

Goldstein, L. S. Comment on "A question of height" (by R. I. Hoobler, & J. A. McQueeney in *The Police Chief*, 1973). *The Police Chief*, 1974, *41*, 11.

Gordon, G. C. *Perspectives on law enforcement: I. Characteristics of police applicants.* Princeton, N.J.: Educational Testing Service, 1969.

Gottesman, J. *The utility of the MMPI in assessing the personality patterns of urban police applicants.* Hoboken, N.J.: Stevens Institute of Technology, 1975.

Guller, I. B. Higher education and policemen: Attitudinal differences between freshmen and senior police college students. *Journal of Criminal Law, Criminology, and Police Science*, 1972, *63*, 396–401.

Halling, B. E. Comment on "A question of height" (by R. I. Hoobler & J. A. McQueeney in *The Police Chief*, 1973). *The Police Chief*, 1974, *41*, 10–11.

Hess, L. R. Police entry tests and their predictability of score in police academy and subsequent job performance. *Dissertation Abstracts International*, 1973, *33-B*, 5552.

Hogan, R. Personality characteristics of highly rated policemen. *Personnel Psychology*, 1971, *24*, 679–686.

Hoobler, R. I., & McQueeney, J. A. A question of height. *The Police Chief*, 1973, *40*, 43–48.

Hooke, J. F., & Krauss, H. H. Personality characteristics of successful police sergeant candidates. *Journal of Criminal Law, Criminology, and Police Science*, 1971, *62*, 104–106.

Kates, S. L. Rorschach responses, Strong blank scales, and job satisfaction among policemen. *Journal of Applied Psychology*, 1950, *34*, 249–254.

Kent, D. A., & Eisenberg, T. The selection and promotion of police officers: A selected review of recent literature. *The Police Chief*, 1972, *39*, 20–29.

Kent, D. A., Wall, C. R., & Bailey, R. L. A new approach to police personnel decisions. *The Police Chief*, 1974, *41*, 72–77.

Kole, D. M. A study of intellectual and personality characteristics of medical students. Unpublished master's thesis, University of Oregon, 1962.

Kollender, W. B., & McQueeney, J. A. A Question of height–Additional thoughts. *The Police Chief*, 1977, *44*, 56–58.

Kroes, W. H., Margolis, B. L., & Hurrell, J. J. Job stress in policemen. *Journal of Police Science and Administration*, 1974, *2*, 145–155.

Landy, F. J., & Farr, J. L. *Police performance appraisal.* University Park, Pa.: Pennsylvania State University, Department of Psychology, 1975.

Learned, K. E. Police selection procedures. *Law and Order*, 1976, *24*, 68–72.

Levy, R. J. Predicting police failures. *Journal of Criminal Law, Criminology, and Police Science*, 1967, *58*, 265–276.

Levy, R. J. *Investigation of a method for identification of the high risk police applicant.* Berkeley, Calif.: Institute for Local Self-Government, 1971.

Marsh, S. H. Validating the selection of deputy sheriffs. *Public Personnel Review*, 1962, *23*, 41–44.

Martin, E. M. An aptitude test for policemen. *Journal of Criminal Law*, 1923, *14*, 376–404.

Matarazzo, J. D., Allen, B. V., Saslow, G., & Wiens, A. N. Characteristics of successful policemen and firemen applicants. *Journal of Applied Psychology*, 1964, *48*, 123–133.

McAllister, J. A. A study of the prediction and measurement of police performance. *Police*, 1970, *15*, 58–64.

McCreedy, K. R. Selection practices and the police role. *The Police Chief*, 1974, *41*, 41–43.

McGhee, G. L. Job-related pre-employment physical agility tests. *The Police Chief*, 1976, *43*, 42–43.

McNamara, R. Uncertainties in police work: The relevance of police recruits' backgrounds and training. In D. Bordua (Ed.), *The police: Six sociological essays*, New York: Wiley, 1967.

Merrill, M. A. Intelligence of policemen. *Journal of Personnel Research*, 1927, *5*, 511–515.

Meyer, J. C. Police attitudes and performance appraisal: The forest and some trees. *Journal of Police Science and Administration*, 1973, *1*, 201–208.

Miller, J., & Fry, L. Re-examining assumptions about education and professionalism in law enforcement. *Journal of Police Science and Administration*, 1975, *3*, 189–196.

Mills, R. B. Use of diagnostic small groups in police recruit selection and training. *Journal of Criminal Law, Criminology, and Police Science*, 1969, *60*, 238–241.

Mills, R. B. Simulated stress in police recruit selection. *Journal of Police Science and Administration*, 1976, *4*, 179–186.

Mills, R. B., McDevitt, R. J., & Tonkin, S. Situational tests in metropolitan police recruit selection. *Journal of Criminal Law, Criminology, and Police Science*, 1966, *57*, 99–104.

Morman, R. R., Hankey, R. O., Heywood, H. L., & Liddle, L. R. Predicting state traffic officer cadet academic performance from theoretical TAV selection system scores. *Police*, 1966, *11*, 54–58.

Morman, R. R., Hankey, R. O., Kennedy, P. K., & Jones, E. M. Academy achievement of state traffic officer cadets related to TAV selection system plus other variables. *Police*, 1966, *11*, 30–34.

Mullineaux, J. E. An evaluation of the predictors used to select patrolmen. *Public Personnel Review*, 1955, *16*, 84–86.

Murphy, J. J. Current practices in the use of psychological testing by police agencies. *Journal of Criminal Law, Criminology, and Police Science*, 1972, *63*, 570–576.

Niederhoffer, A. *Behind the shield: The police in urban society*. Garden City, N.Y.: Doubleday & Co., Inc., 1967.

Nolting, O. F. Important considerations in the selection of patrolmen. *The American City*, 1929, *40*, 124–125.

Nowicki, S. A study of the personality characteristics of successful policemen. *Police*, 1966, *11*, 39–41.

O'Connor, G. W. Survey of selection methods. *The Police Chief*, 1962, *31*, 8.

Oglesby, T. W. Use of emotional screening in the selection of police applicants. *Public Personnel Review*, 1957, *18*, 228–231, 235.

Osborne, G. D. Validating physical agility tests. *The Police Chief*, 1976, *9*, 43–46.

Parker, L. C., & Roth, M. C. The relationship between self-disclosure, personality, and a dimension of job performance of policemen. *Journal of Police Science and Administration*, 1973, *1*, 282–287.

Pounian, C. A. Selection, assessment, and performance of Chicago police officers. *Proceedings of the 67th Annual Convention of the American Psychological Association*, 1959, 956–957.

Prelutsky, B. Second thoughts. *Human Behavior*, 1974, *3*, 9–10.

Rankin, J. H. Psychiatric screening of police selection recruits. *Public Personnel Review*, 1957, *18*, 191–196.

Reiser, M. Stress, distress, and adaptation in police work. *The Police Chief*, 1976, *43*, 24–27.

Roberts, M. D. Post-employment probationary selection: The San Jose model of field training and evaluation. In C. D. Spielberger & H. C. Spaulding (Eds.), *Proceedings of the National Working Conference on the Selection of Law Enforcement Officers*, 1977, 58–60.

Rokeach, M., Miller, M., & Synder, J. The value gap between police and policed. *Journal of Social Issues*, 1971, *27*, 155–171

Rush, A. C. Better police personnel selection. *The Police Chief*, 1963, *30*, 18–26.

Saunders, D. R. Moderator variables and police selection. In C. D. Spielberger & H. C. Spaulding (Eds.), *Proceedings of the National Working Conference on the Selection of Law Enforcement Officers*, 1977, 111–116.

Shavelson, R. J., Beckum, L. C., & Brown, B. Criterion sampling approach to selecting patrolmen. *The Police Chief*, 1974, *41*, 55–61.

Shealy, A. E. Psychological screening of policemen. Paper presented at the 80th Annual Convention of the American Psychological Association, Honolulu, September 1972.

Shealy, A. E. The MMPI and the Meyer-Briggs type indicator in police selection. In C. D. Spielberger & H. C. Spaulding (Eds.), *Proceedings of the National Working Conference on the Selection of Law Enforcement Officers*, 1977, 95–102.

Sherrid, S. D., & Beech, R. P. Self-dissatisfaction as a determinant of change in police values. *Journal of Applied Psychology*, 1976, *61*, 273–278.

Smith, A. B., Locke, B., & Walker, W. F. Authoritarianism in college and non-college oriented police. *Journal of Criminal Law, Criminology, and Police Science*, 1967, *58*, 128–132.

Snibbe, H. M., Fabricatore, J., Azen, S. P., & Snibbe, J. R. Race differences in police patrolmen: A failure to replicate the Chicago study. *American Journal of Community Psychology*, 1975, *3*, 155–160.

Sparling, C. L. The use of education standards as selection criteria in police agencies: A review. *Journal of Police Science and Administration*, 1975, *3*, 332–334.

Spaulding, V. V. A study of nurse and police applicants. *Delaware State Medical Journal*, 1948, 177–178.

Spencer, G., & Jewell, K. Police leadership: A research study. *The Police Chief*, 1963, *32*, 40–45.

Spencer, G., & Nichols, R. A study of Chicago police recruits: Validation of selection procedures. *The Police Chief*, 1971, *38*, 50–55.

Spielberger, C. D., & Spaulding, H. C. (Eds.), *Proceedings of the National Working Conference on the Selection of Law Enforcement Officers*, 1977.

Stamford, B. A., Kley, J., Thomas, D., & Nevin, J. Physical fitness criteria: An avant-garde approach. *The Police Chief*, 1977, *44*, 59.

Stephens, E. C. The value of pre-employment polygraph examinations. *The Journal of Polygraph Studies*, 1969, *3*.

Sterne, D. M. Use of the Kuder Preference Record, Personal, with police officers. *Journal of Applied Psychology*, 1960, *44*, 323–324.

Swank, C. J., & Haley, K. N. The objections to polygraph screening of police applicants. *The Police Chief*, 1972, *39*, 73–76.

Symonds, M. Emotional hazards of police work. *American Journal of Psychoanalysis*, 1970, *30*, 155–160.

Terman, L. M. A trial of mental and pedagogical tests in a civil service examination for policemen and firemen. *Journal of Applied Psychology*, 1917, *1*, 17–19.

Territo, L. The use of the polygraph in the pre-employment screening process. *The Police Chief*, 1974, *41*, 51–53.

Thurstone, L. L. The intelligence of policemen. *Journal of Personnel Research*, 1922, *1*, 64–74.

Tift, L. L. The "cop" personality reconsidered. *Journal of Police Science and Administration*, 1974, *2*, 266–278.

Tolbert, C. C. Physical fitness: A number one priority. *The Police Chief*, 1976, *43*, 36–37.

U.S. President's Commission on Law Enforcement. *Task force report: The police*. Washington, D.C.: U.S. Government Printing Office, 1967.

Weiner, N. L. The educated policeman. *Journal of Police Science and Administration*, 1976, *4*, 450–457.

Wolfe, J. B. Some psychological characteristics of American policemen: A critical review of the literature. *Proceedings of the 78th Annual Convention of the American Psychological Association*, 1970, *5*, 453–454.

Yates, R. A. Job analysis of the F.B.I. special agent position. In C. D. Spielberger & H. C. Spaulding (Eds.), *Proceedings of the National Working Conference on the Selection of Law Enforcement Officers*, 1977, 29–41.

Zacker, J. W. The effects of experiential training upon empathy, interpersonal sensitivity, cynicism and alienation in police recruits. *Dissertation Abstracts International*, 1971, *31-A*, 7615–7616.

II

JOB ANALYSIS AND PERFORMANCE EVALUATION OF POLICE OFFICERS

3

JOB ANALYSIS IN POLICE SELECTION RESEARCH

Melany E. Baehr and Arnold B. Oppenheim
Industrial Relations Center, The University of Chicago, Chicago, Illinois

DEVELOPMENT OF JOB ANALYSIS PROCEDURES

In 1966 the Industrial Relations Center (IRC) of the University of Chicago initiated a large-scale study to validate a test battery for the selection of police officers for the Chicago police department (Baehr, Furcon, & Froemel, 1969). A follow-up longitudinal study was subsequently completed in the same department (Furcon, Froemel, Franczak, & Baehr, 1971). Since then, we have undertaken a number of other public-sector studies, in particular, a local police officer selection validation in the state of Illinois (Furcon & Froemel, 1973) and a national validation of selection procedures for bus operators (Baehr, 1977).

In the course of our studies, we have refined some of the traditional approaches to job analysis. We have also developed new methodologies, which are being applied in ongoing studies to validate selection procedures used by two municipal departments for various police positions, as well as in a national validation for municipal police officers and state troopers. Data from these continuing studies will be used in this chapter to illustrate two important procedural issues arising out of the process of job analysis.

One of the issues concerns the method of the job analysis. The IRC has routinely used the traditional procedures for job analysis, including literature search, review of extant job descriptions or recruiting materials, interviews with such "key" people as incumbents, and personal observations of performance on the job, which take the form of "ride-alongs" in police departments. However, in the validation study for the selection of bus operators, which was conducted for the Department of Transportation (DOT), we strove for a "numerical hold" on the problem by concentrating our attention on the development of a standardized and quantified instrument for describing the basic functions performed on a job and their relative importance for overall performance.

In constructing such an instrument, there are two clear choices for the content of the items. They could consist of the actual day-to-day activities, at various levels of specificity, that are performed on the job, or they could consist of the human skills and attributes required for the performance of these activities. Data on both these approaches will be presented here, since we have developed both types of instruments in various forms. In their final form, both instruments are pencil-and-paper inventories, with items written in nontechnical language and a forced, four-interval, rectangular distribution response format.

The Skills and Attributes Inventory (SAI) deals with basic human abilities (Baehr, 1976). It is designed for use across a number of occupational fields. Its prototype employed a forced-normal-distribution card-sort as a response format, but since its bulk made it inconvenient and expensive for national administrations, it was abandoned in favor of the pencil-and-paper booklet. The Job Functions Inventory for Police Officers (JFI), developed in the course of the national police validation study, focuses on the specific day-to-day activities performed by police officers (n.d.). Both these instruments are relatively easy to administer. Since their items are written in nontechnical language, the job descriptions can be produced by incumbents or supervisors and do not require a trained job analyst. This feature is almost unique among the few existing instruments of this type.

The second procedural issue arose when the IRC implemented its first consortium validation studies in the supermarket industry in 1968 and in DOT in 1970. We soon realized that, apart from the validation procedure itself, one of the critical issues in such studies was that of the "transportability" of the validated selection test battery. Data illustrating the following two types of transportability will be discussed.

1. The use of a validated test battery for seemingly similar occupations that did not participate in the consortium validation
2. The use of a test battery validated by one particular organization or department by another organization or department with a seemingly similar job and employee population

A discussion of these two types of transportability is presented below.

Transportability to a Nonparticipant
in a Consortium Study

In the DOT (bus operator) study, we were concerned with the first type of transportability—use of the test battery by an organization that had not participated in the study. It occurred to us, however, that the quantified job descriptions developed for the job analysis through use of the SAI could be used for a prior purpose, that of determining whether the jobs in the five participating companies were similar enough to be combined in one validation study.

The description of the bus operator's job at the five participating transit authorities was obtained in terms of the importance of the skills and attributes required for overall good performance. Profiles for the five authorities are given in Figure 1. Source scores are given in Table 1, results of a multivariate analysis of variance (MANOVA) in Table 2. Although there is

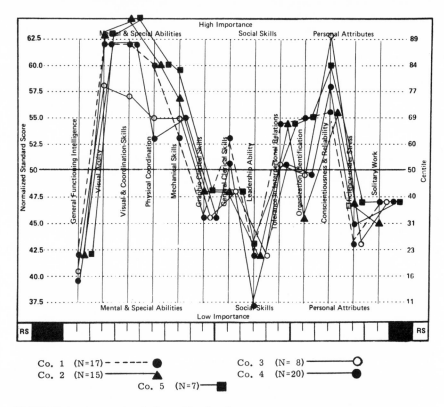

Co. 1 (N=17) - - - - - - ●
Co. 2 (N=15) ————————▲
Co. 5 (N=7) ——■
Co. 3 (N= 8) ————————○
Co. 4 (N=20) ————————●

FIGURE 1 Composite SAI profiles for five transportation authorities participating in a consortium validation study.

TABLE 1 Raw score means, equivalent normalized standard scores, and standard deviations on SAI factor scores for bus operators at five transit authorities

Skills and attributes	1 (N = 17)			2 (N = 15)			3 (N = 8)			4 (N = 20)			5 (N = 7)		
	Mean	NSS	SD	Mean	NSS	SD	Mean	NSS	SD	Mean	NSS	SD	Mean	NSS	SD
Mental abilities and specific aptitudes															
General functioning intelligence	21.94	42	5.55	22.00	42	5.04	21.25	41	8.24	18.65	39	4.40	21.57	42	3.36
Visual acuity	18.06	62	3.36	18.67	63	2.72	15.88	58	5.57	18.35	62	2.85	19.14	63	3.48
Visual and coordination skills	14.18	62	2.51	14.80	65	2.48	11.75	57	4.50	13.60	62	2.56	15.43	65	3.26
Physical coordination	10.88	60	3.18	11.53	60	3.00	9.25	55	2.55	8.25	53	3.67	11.14	60	3.80
Mechanical skills	6.24	53	4.02	7.60	57	2.50	7.00	55	2.00	6.70	55	3.31	9.00	59	2.83
Graphic clerical skills	11.65	46	6.31	12.73	48	4.43	12.12	46	5.82	11.80	46	4.73	13.29	48	2.87
General clerical skills	15.06	53	3.90	13.47	48	2.17	13.50	48	4.50	13.85	51	3.41	13.14	48	3.44
Interpersonal skills															
Leadership ability	8.12	42	5.97	7.80	42	4.68	7.62	42	4.34	3.40	36	3.03	9.29	43	2.81
Tolerance in interpersonal relations	22.29	54	3.20	22.00	54	2.90	21.12	51	3.98	20.90	51	3.19	22.43	54	2.57
Personal attributes															
Organization identification	22.65	55	3.37	20.13	46	3.40	20.62	49	4.50	21.35	49	3.15	22.71	55	3.69
Conscientiousness and reliability	23.29	56	4.73	23.00	56	4.68	25.88	63	3.80	23.65	58	2.89	25.00	60	3.96
Efficiency under stress	19.53	43	3.36	20.73	47	3.08	19.00	43	2.62	19.75	45	3.97	20.86	47	3.02
Solitary work	16.00	47	2.81	15.53	45	3.09	15.88	47	4.70	15.60	47	3.05	15.71	47	2.36

TABLE 2 Analysis of variance (F ratios) on SAI factor scores across the five authorities in the validation study

Skills and attributes	Univariate F	p
Mental abilities and specific aptitudes		
General functioning intelligence	1.248	0.300
Visual acuity	1.132	0.350
Visual and coordination skills	2.042	0.098
Physical coordination	2.822	0.032
Mechanical skills	1.103	0.363
Graphic clerical skills	0.199	0.936
General clerical skills	0.643	0.637
Interpersonal skills		
Leadership ability	4.079	0.005
Tolerance in interpersonal relations	0.656	0.627
Personal attributes		
Organization identification	1.452	0.227
Conscientiousness and reliability	0.898	0.472
Efficiency under stress	0.563	0.694
Solitary work	0.058	0.991

some variation in these profiles, only one univariate F is significant beyond the .05 level. On the basis of this finding and of other information obtained in the course of the job analysis, we decided to proceed with a single consortium study. The composite profile for the five authorities thus became the "standard" against which the similarity of the bus operator's job in nonparticipating authorities would be judged.

The standard profile and the profile for the first "test case" transit company are shown in Figure 2, the source statistics in Table 3, and the F ratios in Table 4. All the F ratios are nonsignificant. Since the completion of the study, more than 30 transit authorities have completed the SAI in card-sort form and had their resulting profiles compared with the standard. A special computer program has been developed to test profile similarity (Baehr, 1977). In the great majority of cases, reasonably similar profiles have been obtained. Sometimes the reason for apparent profile differences could be traced to the use of unsuitable raters, and this situation has been rectified. In only three cases were there unresolvable profile differences. Two of these were very small companies with fewer than 20 vehicles. The other was a large urban company, but its applicants were from an ethnic group (French Canadian) that had not been studied for the validation. This, to date, represents our experience in checking the requirements for nonparticipating companies to use a consortium validation selection test battery. It is probable that we will need

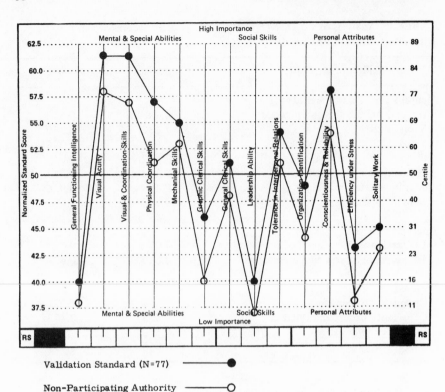

Validation Standard (N=77) ————————●

Non-Participating Authority ————————○

FIGURE 2 Composite SAI standard profile for a consortium study and for a nonparticipating authority.

to use a similar approach in applying the test battery being developed in our national police study.

Transportability from One Organization or Department to Another

A police selection validation undertaken in a municipal department (police department 1) in 1971 is of particular interest here, since we wished to use the results from this study to develop an interim procedure for the selection of police officers in another municipal department (police department 2) where urgent recruiting needs made prior local validation unfeasible. This would be the second type of transportability—from one organization or department to another.

The SAI job descriptions for patrol officers, sergeants, and lieutenants in police department 1 are given in Figure 3, and descriptions for these positions in police department 2 are given Figure 4. The source statistics for these two figures appear in Tables 5 and 6, and the F ratios across the three ranks of patrol officer, sergeant, and lieutenant appear separately for the two departments in Table 7. For the first police department there are 9 and for the second 10 out of the 13 p values that are significant beyond the .05 level of confidence, with the majority of these beyond the .001 level. It is clear that the dimensions where there are differences and the directions of these differences are "sensible" in the light of other information about these three police ranks. For example, sergeants and lieutenants score dramatically higher than patrol officers on the dimension of "leadership ability" but lower to the same extent of difference on the "visual acuity" and "physical coordination" skills.

Although the SAI profiles show marked differences between ranks, their stability for any one rank is illustrated in Figures 5, 6, and 7, which compare results for each of the three ranks across the two departments. The three sets

TABLE 3   SAI factor scores for the composite of bus operators at five transit authorities and results for bus operators in a nonparticipating authority

Skills and attributes	Bus operators ($N = 77$)			N-P ($N = 10$)		
	Mean	NSS	SD	Mean	NSS	SD
Mental abilities and specific aptitudes						
General functioning intelligence	20.46	40	5.65	17.80	38	7.00
Visual acuity	17.92	62	3.52	16.50	58	3.92
Visual and coordination skills	13.75	62	3.01	12.20	57	2.90
Physical coordination	9.74	57	3.58	7.50	51	3.66
Mechanical skills	6.88	55	3.30	5.70	53	3.92
Graphic clerical skills	11.82	46	4.98	9.50	40	4.48
General clerical skills	13.84	51	3.34	13.10	48	2.73
Interpersonal skills						
Leadership ability	6.35	40	4.92	4.00	37	4.97
Tolerance in interpersonal relations	21.60	54	3.24	21.00	51	3.94
Personal attributes						
Organization identification	21.12	49	3.54	18.80	44	3.46
Conscientiousness and reliability	23.60	58	3.90	22.10	54	2.47
Efficiency under stress	19.49	43	3.62	16.50	38	4.09
Solitary work	15.49	45	3.13	13.90	43	3.11

TABLE 4 Multivariate analysis of variance (F ratios) on SAI factor scores across one bus company and the "standard" composite of five companies

Skills and attributes	Univariate F	p
Mental abilities and specific aptitudes		
General functioning intelligence	2.5911	0.1117
Visual acuity	1.8941	0.1729
Visual and coordination skills	3.1480	0.0801
Physical coordination	4.7065	0.0333
Mechanical skills	1.4825	0.2272
Graphic clerical skills	2.5371	0.1154
General clerical skills	0.5684	0.4533
Interpersonal skills		
Leadership ability	2.6817	0.1057
Tolerance in interpersonal relations	0.3882	0.5352
Personal attributes		
Organization identification	5.1856	0.0257
Conscientiousness and reliability	1.7092	0.1951
Efficiency under stress	8.6566	0.0044
Solitary work	3.0651	0.0841

Note. Multivariate F ratio $= 1.3946$; $p < .1873$; numerator degrees of freedom $= 13$; denominator degrees of freedom $= 63$.

of F ratios given in Table 8 produce only 3 out of the total of 39 p values that are significant beyond the .05 level of confidence.

On the basis of these results, we implemented an interim procedure in the second police department. Since then, the department has started its own concurrent validation for the patrol officer position, and the ranks of sergeant and lieutenant have been included in the validation research to be undertaken in the current year (1978).

The job analysis for the second department produced some additional and very interesting job description information concerning different race and sex groups. SAI job descriptions for the position of patrol officer done by groups of whites, blacks, and Latins are given in Figure 8. The source statistics are given in Table 9, the results of a MANOVA across ranks and races in Table 10. The MANOVA indicates that there are no significant variations on any dimension and, even visually, there are remarkably few variations in the profiles considering the small sample sizes of 19 whites, 7 blacks, and 6 Latins.

SAI job descriptions for the patrol officer position done by groups of males and females are given in Figure 9. The source statistics and MANOVA results are shown in Table 11. Essentially the same conclusions are reached

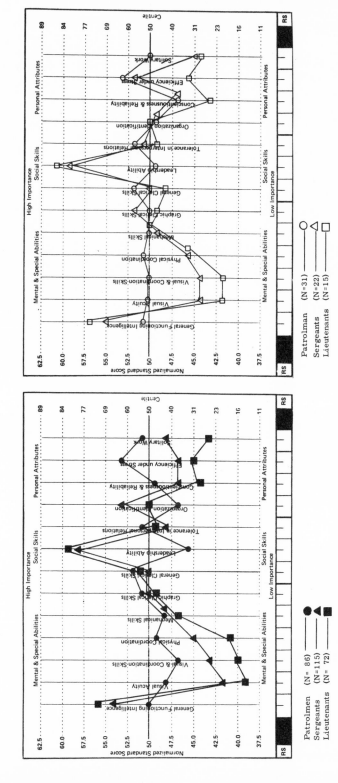

FIGURE 3 Composite SAI profiles for the positions of patrol officer, sergeant, and lieutenant in police department 1.

FIGURE 4 Composite SAI profiles for the positions of patrol officer, sergeant, and lieutenant in police department 2.

Patrolmen   (N = 86)
Sergeants   (N = 115)
Lieutenants (N = 72)

Patrolman   (N = 31)
Sergeants   (N = 22)
Lieutenants (N = 15)

41

TABLE 5 SAI factor scores for groups of patrol officers, sergeants, and lieutenants

Skills and attributes	Patrol officers (N = 86)			Sergeants (N = 115)			Lieutenants (N = 72)		
	Mean	NSS	SD	Mean	NSS	SD	Mean	NSS	SD
Mental abilities and specific aptitudes									
General functioning intelligence	26.95	50	5.09	28.44	54	3.50	29.44	56	3.74
Visual acuity	10.07	48	3.85	6.43	42	4.45	4.32	39	3.87
Visual and coordination skills	7.51	47	3.52	5.57	43	3.55	3.71	40	3.21
Physical coordination	5.67	49	3.60	3.72	45	3.10	2.17	41	2.56
Mechanical skills	4.02	48	3.07	4.02	48	3.35	3.55	47	2.48
Graphic clerical skills	14.62	51	4.65	14.16	50	4.07	13.35	49	3.76
General clerical skills	14.62	52	3.23	13.73	50	3.60	13.85	51	3.84
Interpersonal skills									
Leadership ability	11.07	46	4.75	19.40	58	3.48	19.93	59	2.83
Tolerance in interpersonal relations	21.00	51	4.03	19.81	48	3.41	18.87	49	3.54
Personal attributes									
Organization identification	20.41	47	3.23	22.31	53	3.31	21.43	50	2.60
Conscientiousness and reliability	19.53	49	4.83	18.54	47	4.66	17.10	44	4.15
Efficiency under stress	23.60	53	3.55	21.21	47	4.14	20.00	45	3.63
Solitary work	17.79	51	3.66	16.27	48	3.78	14.11	43	3.57

TABLE 6 SAI factor scores for groups of patrol officers, sergeants, and lieutenants

Skills and attributes	Patrol officers (N = 31)			Sergeants (N = 22)			Lieutenants (N = 15)		
	Mean	NSS	SD	Mean	NSS	SD	Mean	NSS	SD
Mental abilities and specific aptitudes									
General functioning intelligence	27.45	51	3.91	28.68	55	3.62	30.07	57	6.10
Visual acuity	10.74	50	4.10	7.68	44	4.56	5.60	42	4.94
Visual and coordination skills	8.68	50	3.64	6.32	44	3.66	5.13	42	4.07
Physical coordination	7.13	51	4.06	3.95	46	3.96	4.00	46	3.36
Mechanical skills	4.93	50	3.50	4.45	49	3.29	5.13	50	3.46
Graphic clerical skills	14.32	50	4.49	14.73	52	4.80	13.60	49	4.35
General clerical skills	14.41	52	4.18	13.59	50	2.30	13.13	48	4.21
Interpersonal skills									
Leadership ability	13.64	49	4.73	20.14	59	3.24	20.67	61	4.35
Tolerance in interpersonal relations	21.35	52	4.42	20.77	51	4.24	20.06	49	4.49
Personal attributes									
Organization identification	20.97	49	3.00	21.09	49	3.49	21.40	50	2.29
Conscientiousness and reliability	18.71	47	5.52	18.68	47	3.93	16.47	43	4.88
Efficiency under stress	23.35	53	4.54	22.95	52	3.21	20.47	46	3.70
Solitary work	17.55	50	4.17	15.23	45	4.27	14.60	44	4.52

TABLE 7   Analysis of variance (F ratios) on SAI factor scores across ranks for two police departments

Skills and attributes	1		2	
	Univariate F	p	Univariate F	p
Mental abilities and specific aptitudes				
General functioning intelligence	1.76	0.1738	3.1524	0.0301
Visual acuity	35.48	0.0001	8.0531	0.0002
Visual and coordination skills	24.23	0.0001	6.3563	0.0007
Physical coordination	30.00	0.0001	4.3803	0.0069
Mechanical skills	0.99	0.3719	0.6015	0.6162
Graphic clerical skills	3.07	0.0483	0.2243	0.8792
General clerical skills	2.57	0.0784	0.4844	0.6942
Interpersonal skills				
Leadership ability	117.90	0.0001	15.1204	0.0001
Tolerance in interpersonal relations	11.07	0.0001	0.3194	0.8114
Personal attributes				
Organization identification	7.44	0.0008	1.5969	0.1977
Conscientiousness and reliability	8.54	0.0003	1.3922	0.2522
Efficiency under stress	16.41	0.0001	5.6021	0.0017
Solitary work	20.78	0.0001	2.7839	0.0470

here. While the small sample of four females caused some visual fluctuations in the profile, none of the observed differences is statistically significant.

The implications of these results are that there is fair agreement in the job description profiles for three police positions in this department produced by incumbents of different rank, race, and sex. In addition, we have comparable job descriptions for the three positions produced in the first department, where a selection test battery had been validated. In the absence of other conflicting job description data, we felt justified in utilizing this validation to set up an interim selection procedure for patrol officers in police department 2.

We have now discussed two types of transportability. The national police study in progress will provide the opportunity to investigate a third. It seems that we now have the tools and techniques to develop procedures not only to determine whether a nonparticipating department's job requirements will

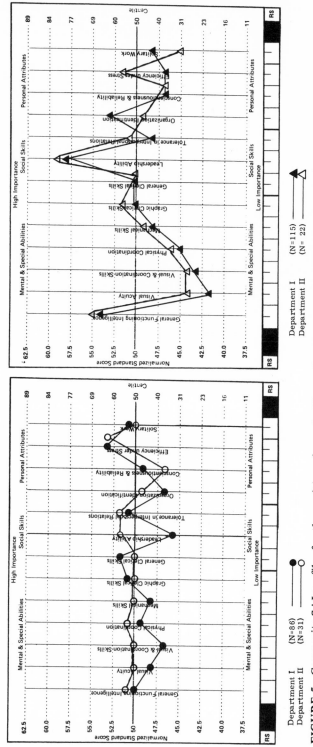

FIGURE 5 Composite SAI profiles for the position of patrol officer in two police departments.

Department I (N=86) ●——●
Department II (N=31) ○——○

FIGURE 6 Composite SAI profiles for the position of sergeant in two police departments.

Department I (N=115) ▲——▲
Department II (N=22)   △——△

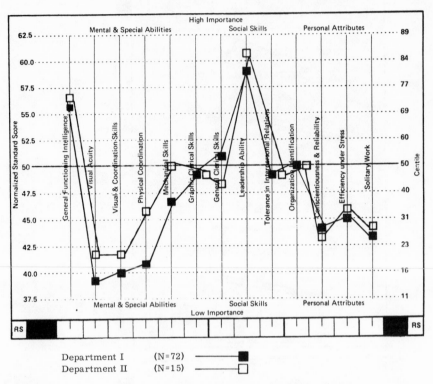

Department I   (N=72) ──────■
Department II   (N=15) ──────□

FIGURE 7   Composite SAI profiles for the position of lieutenant in two police departments.

warrant use of a validated selection test battery but to take a step forward and adjust the validated test battery for a more precise "fit" to the requirements of the job in the nonparticipating department. This brings us both to the national police study and to our second topic.

A COMPARISON OF TWO DIFFERENT TYPES OF QUANTITATIVE JOB DESCRIPTION

The national police study includes consortium validation studies for two positions—municipal patrol officer and state trooper. Five departments participated in each study, in which both forms of job description (activities and attributes) were used.

Results of SAI job descriptions implemented by the site advisory boards for the study were essentially similar to those obtained in the bus-operator study. No statistically significant differences were found in the descriptions given for a single occupation at any of the five municipal patrol officer sites or at any of the five state trooper sites. However, the results of the

TABLE 8 Analysis of variance (F ratios) on SAI factor scores separately for patrol officers, sergeants, and lieutenants across two departments

Skills and attributes	Patrol officers[a] (N = 117)		Sergeants[b] (N = 137)		Lieutenants[c] (N = 87)	
	Univariate F	p	Univariate F	p	Univariate F	p
Mental abilities and specific aptitudes						
General functioning intelligence	0.2445	0.6220	0.0847	0.7715	0.2701	0.6047
Visual acuity	0.6721	0.4141	1.4364	0.2328	1.2313	0.2703
Visual and coordination skills	2.4557	0.1199	0.8025	0.3720	2.2213	0.1399
Physical coordination	3.4732	0.0650	0.0950	0.7584	5.6836	0.0194
Mechanical skills	1.8641	0.1749	0.3165	0.5747	4.3380	0.0403
Graphic clerical skills	0.0924	0.7618	0.3419	0.5598	0.0531	0.8184
General clerical skills	0.0720	0.7890	0.0305	0.8616	0.4159	0.5208
Interpersonal skills						
Leadership ability	6.7192	0.0108	0.8458	0.3594	0.6856	0.4101
Tolerance in interpersonal relations	0.1674	0.6832	1.3616	0.2453	1.2755	0.2619
Personal attributes						
Organization identification	0.7142	0.3998	2.4716	0.1183	0.0018	0.9665
Conscientiousness and reliability	0.6149	0.4346	0.0181	0.8932	0.2689	0.6055
Efficiency under stress	0.0879	0.7675	3.5018	0.0635	0.2041	0.6526
Solitary work	0.0926	0.7615	1.3431	0.2486	0.2114	0.6469

[a]Multivariate F ratio = 1.2445; $p < 0.2596$; numerator degrees of freedom = 13; denominator degrees of freedom = 103.
[b]Multivariate F ratio = 1.2472; $p < 0.2547$; numerator degrees of freedom = 13; denominator degrees of freedom = 123.
[c]Multivariate F ratio = 1.5417; $p = 0.1233$; numerator degrees of freedom = 13; denominator degrees of freedom = 73.

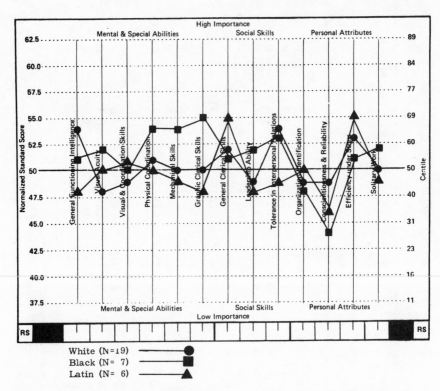

White (N=19) ——————●
Black (N= 7) ——————■
Latin (N= 6) ——————▲

FIGURE 8 Composite SAI profiles for the position of patrol officer done by groups of whites, blacks, and Latins.

comparisons between the composites of the state and the municipal departments were surprising. The three sets of F ratios for these comparisons are shown in Table 12. It can be seen from the table only 4 out of a possible 13 differences between the composite state and the composite municipal departments were significant at the .05 level, and of these, only one was significant beyond the .001 level. This dimension represented the ability to work on one's own, or to do solitary work, which was rated as being of considerably greater importance for the state trooper. This may, indeed, be the only behaviorally different requirement for these two occupations.

A check on these results was made by obtaining job descriptions through the use of the behavior attributes included in the Position Analysis Questionnaire (PAQ) by Mecham and McCormick (1969). The composite profiles for the five municipalities and for the five states are given in Figures 10 and 11, the source statistics and F ratios in Table 13. These profiles show absolutely no differences either visually or statistically between the behavioral requirements for the two positions.

TABLE 9 SAI factor scores for groups of whites, blacks, and Latins rating the position of police patrol officer

Skills and attributes	White (N = 19)			Black (N = 7)			Latin (N = 6)		
	Mean	NSS	SD	Mean	NSS	SD	Mean	NSS	SD
Mental abilities and specific aptitudes									
General functioning intelligence	28.32	54	3.11	27.43	51	2.15	25.33	47	6.77
Visual acuity	10.05	48	3.84	12.43	52	5.47	11.50	50	2.74
Visual and coordination skills	8.58	49	3.75	8.86	50	3.76	9.33	51	3.67
Physical coordination	6.84	51	3.88	8.57	54	3.95	6.50	50	4.72
Mechanical skills	4.84	50	3.24	6.71	54	3.99	4.67	49	5.35
Graphic clerical skills	14.16	50	4.59	16.43	55	3.82	13.00	48	4.69
General clerical skills	14.42	52	4.05	14.14	51	4.67	15.67	55	4.89
Interpersonal skills									
Leadership ability	13.58	49	4.17	15.43	52	5.09	12.67	48	6.38
Tolerance in interpersonal relations	21.84	54	3.67	21.71	53	4.15	20.00	49	6.90
Personal attributes									
Organization identification	21.11	49	3.30	20.57	48	2.76	21.17	50	2.32
Conscientiousness and reliability	19.53	49	6.09	17.00	44	4.69	17.83	46	4.02
Efficiency under stress	23.47	53	3.95	22.57	51	5.65	24.17	55	5.31
Solitary work	17.42	50	4.46	18.43	52	4.54	16.83	49	2.48

TABLE 10   Analysis of variance (F ratios) on SAI factor scores for police positions across groups of white, black, and Latin police officers

Skills and attributes	Univariate F	p
Mental abilities and specific aptitudes		
General functioning intelligence	2.42	0.100
Visual acuity	1.46	0.243
Visual and coordination skills	0.45	0.640
Physical coordination	0.87	0.427
Mechanical skills	1.59	0.214
Graphical clerical skills	0.92	0.407
General clerical skills	0.16	0.854
Interpersonal skills		
Leadership ability	1.57	0.219
Tolerance in interpersonal relations	0.94	0.397
Personal attributes		
Organization identification	1.44	0.248
Conscientiousness and reliability	0.20	0.823
Efficiency under stress	0.44	0.647
Solitary work	0.07	0.929

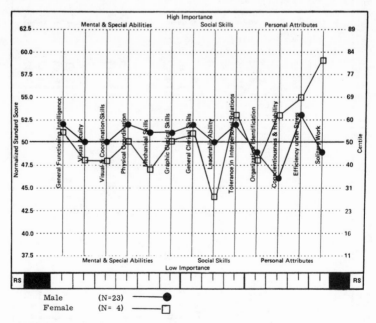

FIGURE 9   Composite SAI profiles for the position of patrol officer done by groups of males and females.

TABLE 11 SAI factor scores across groups of male and female police officers

Skills and attributes	Male (N = 28)			Female (N = 4)			Univariate F	p
	Mean	NSS	SD	Mean	NSS	SD		
Mental abilities and specific aptitudes								
General functioning intelligence	27.61	52	3.95	27.25	51	4.11	0.0284	0.8673
Visual acuity	11.00	50	4.30	9.75	48	1.71	0.3225	0.5744
Visual and coordination skills	8.89	50	3.71	8.00	48	3.37	0.2068	0.6526
Physical coordination	7.29	52	4.06	6.25	50	3.86	0.2296	0.6353
Mechanical skills	5.43	51	3.90	3.75	47	2.99	0.6761	0.4175
Graphic clerical skills	14.54	51	4.61	13.75	50	3.77	0.1053	0.7479
General clerical skills	14.68	52	4.49	14.00	51	1.63	0.0876	0.7694
Interpersonal skills								
Leadership ability	14.39	50	4.63	9.75	44	3.86	3.6306	0.0664
Tolerance in interpersonal relations	21.43	52	4.61	21.75	53	2.87	0.0181	0.8940
Personal attributes								
Organization identification	21.07	49	2.96	20.50	48	3.32	0.1275	0.7236
Conscientiousness and reliability	18.25	46	5.65	21.50	53	2.38	1.2599	0.2706
Efficiency under stress	23.29	53	4.74	24.25	55	2.06	0.1579	0.6940
Solitary work	16.96	49	4.00	21.50	59	2.38	4.8007	0.0364

Note. Multivariate F ratio = 0.8253; $p < 0.6320$; numerator degrees of freedom = 13; denominator degrees of freedom = 8.

TABLE 12 Analysis of variance (F ratios) on SAI factor scores separately across groups of municipalities and groups of states and between the composites for municipalities and states

Skills and attributes	Across municipalities[a]		Across states[b]		Across municipalities and states[c]	
	Univariate F	p	Univariate F	p	Univariate F	p
Mental abilities and specific aptitudes						
General functioning intelligence	1.041	0.395	0.845	0.503	1.301	0.313
Visual acuity	1.170	0.334	1.183	0.325	10.629	0.002
Visual and coordination skills	0.343	0.848	1.043	0.392	7.846	0.006
Physical coordination	0.747	0.567	1.008	0.410	2.744	0.096
Mechanical skills	1.268	0.293	0.216	0.927	7.034	0.009
Graphic clerical skills	0.785	0.542	1.543	0.198	0.581	0.453
General clerical skills	0.595	0.670	0.162	0.954	3.199	0.072
Interpersonal skills						
Leadership ability	1.452	0.228	1.858	0.126	0.301	0.591
Tolerance in interpersonal relations	1.166	0.335	1.063	0.382	1.608	0.204
Personal attributes						
Organization identification	1.469	0.223	0.200	0.936	1.066	0.304
Conscientiousness and reliability	1.871	0.127	1.622	0.177	0.511	0.483
Efficiency under stress	2.143	0.086	0.971	0.430	4.031	0.044
Solitary work	0.404	0.807	0.777	0.546	21.364	0.000

[a]Numerator degrees of freedom = 57; denominator degrees of freedom = 4.
[b]Numerator degrees of freedom = 73; denominator degrees of freedom = 4.
[c]Numerator degrees of freedom = 138; denominator degrees of freedom = 1.

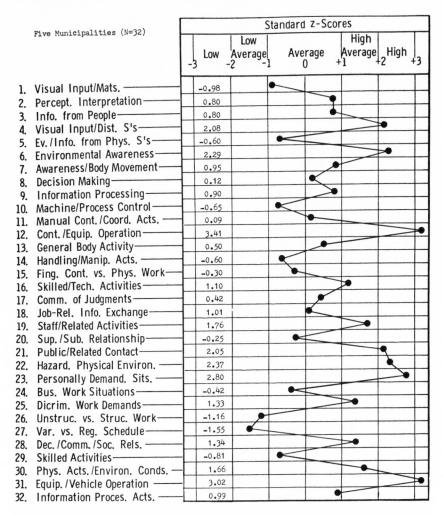

Five Municipalities (N=32)

	Standard Z-Scores					
	Low -3	Low Average -2	-1	Average 0	High Average +1	High +2 +3

1. Visual Input/Mats. — **-0.98**
2. Percept. Interpretation — **0.80**
3. Info. from People — **0.80**
4. Visual Input/Dist. S's — **2.08**
5. Ev./Info. from Phys. S's — **-0.60**
6. Environmental Awareness — **2.29**
7. Awareness/Body Movement — **0.95**
8. Decision Making — **0.12**
9. Information Processing — **0.90**
10. Machine/Process Control — **-0.65**
11. Manual Cont./Coord. Acts. — **0.09**
12. Cont./Equip. Operation — **3.41**
13. General Body Activity — **0.50**
14. Handling/Manip. Acts. — **-0.60**
15. Fing. Cont. vs. Phys. Work — **-0.30**
16. Skilled/Tech. Activities — **1.10**
17. Comm. of Judgments — **0.42**
18. Job-Rel. Info. Exchange — **1.01**
19. Staff/Related Activities — **1.76**
20. Sup./Sub. Relationship — **-0.25**
21. Public/Related Contact — **2.05**
22. Hazard. Physical Environ. — **2.37**
23. Personally Demand. Sits. — **2.80**
24. Bus. Work Situations — **-0.42**
25. Dicrim. Work Demands — **1.33**
26. Unstruc. vs. Struc. Work — **-1.16**
27. Var. vs. Reg. Schedule — **-1.55**
28. Dec./Comm./Soc. Rels. — **1.34**
29. Skilled Activities — **-0.81**
30. Phys. Acts./Environ. Conds. — **1.66**
31. Equip./Vehicle Operation — **3.02**
32. Information Proces. Acts. — **0.99**

FIGURE 10 Composite PAQ profile for the position of municipal police officer for five municipalities participating in a consortium validation study.

However, we get a strikingly different picture when we make the same series of comparisons using profiled job descriptions produced by the Job Functions Inventory for Police Officers (n.d.). These descriptions represent the rated importance of specific activities performed on the job. The three sets of F ratios—across cities, across states, and between cities and states—are given in Table 14. Only 2 out of a possible 24 comparisons are not significant beyond the .01 level. In other words, described in terms of the specific activities performed, the patrol officer's job is different in the five cities, the state trooper's job is different in the five states, and the patrol officer's job and the

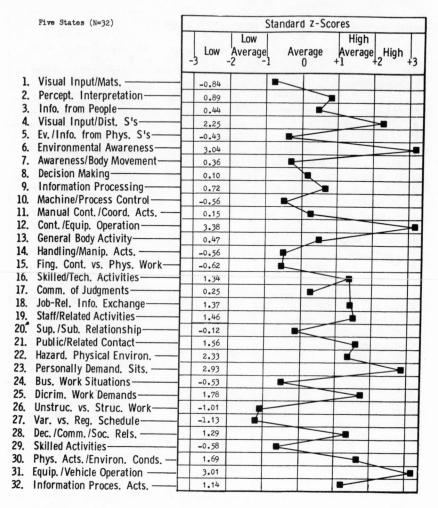

Five States (N=32)	Standard Z-Scores

	Low -3	Low Average -2	-1	Average 0	High Average +1	High +2	+3
1. Visual Input/Mats.	-0.84						
2. Percept. Interpretation	0.89						
3. Info. from People	0.44						
4. Visual Input/Dist. S's	2.25						
5. Ev./Info. from Phys. S's	-0.43						
6. Environmental Awareness	3.04						
7. Awareness/Body Movement	0.36						
8. Decision Making	0.10						
9. Information Processing	0.72						
10. Machine/Process Control	-0.56						
11. Manual Cont./Coord. Acts.	0.15						
12. Cont./Equip. Operation	3.38						
13. General Body Activity	0.47						
14. Handling/Manip. Acts.	-0.56						
15. Fing. Cont. vs. Phys. Work	-0.62						
16. Skilled/Tech. Activities	1.34						
17. Comm. of Judgments	0.25						
18. Job-Rel. Info. Exchange	1.37						
19. Staff/Related Activities	1.46						
20. Sup./Sub. Relationship	-0.12						
21. Public/Related Contact	1.56						
22. Hazard. Physical Environ.	2.33						
23. Personally Demand. Sits.	2.93						
24. Bus. Work Situations	-0.53						
25. Dicrim. Work Demands	1.78						
26. Unstruc. vs. Struc. Work	-1.01						
27. Var. vs. Reg. Schedule	-1.13						
28. Dec./Comm./Soc. Rels.	1.29						
29. Skilled Activities	-0.58						
30. Phys. Acts./Environ. Conds.	1.69						
31. Equip./Vehicle Operation	3.01						
32. Information Proces. Acts.	1.14						

FIGURE 11   Composite PAQ profile for the position of state trooper for five states participating in a consortium validation study.

state trooper's job are different except that, very oddly, the nonsignificant comparisons appear in these series. These two composite profiles are presented in Figure 12.

IMPLICATIONS FOR THE USE OF DIFFERENT JOB DESCRIPTION INSTRUMENTS

The national police study has thus produced apparently conflicting information when the patrol officer's and the state trooper's jobs are

TABLE 13 PAQ dimensions across groups of municipal patrol officers and state troopers

Dimensions	Municipal patrol officers (N = 32) Mean	SD	State troopers (N = 32) Mean	SD	Univariate F	p
Visual input/materials	−0.98	0.38	−0.84	0.70	0.982	0.327
Perception interpretation	0.80	0.57	0.88	0.54	0.370	0.551
Information from people	0.80	0.35	0.44	0.39	15.159	0.000
Visual input/distal S's	2.08	0.45	2.25	0.57	1.724	0.191
Evaluation information from physical S's	−0.60	0.81	−0.43	0.72	0.822	0.372
Environmental awareness	2.29	1.12	3.04	0.95	8.296	0.006
Awareness/body movement	0.95	1.05	0.35	1.13	4.712	0.032
Decision making	0.12	0.31	0.10	0.34	0.070	0.687
Information processing	0.90	0.69	0.72	0.63	1.209	0.275
Machine process control	−0.65	0.51	−0.56	0.48	0.449	0.512
Manual control/coordination actions	−0.09	0.57	0.15	0.72	0.119	0.682
Control equipment operation	3.41	0.94	3.38	1.34	0.008	0.551
General body activity	0.50	0.61	0.47	0.92	0.031	0.652
Handling/manipulating activities	−0.60	0.56	−0.56	0.58	0.085	0.689
Finger control vs. physical work	−0.30	0.76	−0.62	0.77	2.696	0.102
Skilled/technical activities	1.09	0.56	1.34	0.67	2.564	0.111
Communication of judgments	0.42	0.47	0.25	0.46	2.161	0.143
Job related information exchange	1.01	1.42	1.37	1.57	0.897	0.350
Staff/related activities	1.76	1.06	1.46	1.12	1.191	0.279
Supplemental/substituted relationship	−0.25	0.62	−0.12	0.34	1.094	0.300
Public/related contact	2.05	0.84	1.56	1.13	3.874	0.051
Hazardous physical environment	2.37	1.07	2.33	1.11	0.018	0.614
Personally demanding situations	2.80	0.56	2.93	0.63	0.744	0.396

TABLE 13 PAQ dimensions across groups of municipal patrol officers and state troopers (*continued*)

Dimensions	Municipal patrol officers (N = 32)		State troopers (N = 32)		Univariate F	p
	Mean	SD	Mean	SD		
Businesslike work situations	−0.42	0.29	−0.53	0.48	1.338	0.250
Discriminatory work demands	1.33	0.52	1.78	0.65	9.570	0.003
Unstructured vs. structured work	−1.16	0.45	−1.01	0.47	1.855	0.175
Variety vs. regular schedule	−1.55	0.74	−1.13	1.00	3.744	0.054
Decisions/community/social relations	1.34	0.23	1.29	0.31	0.505	0.487
Skilled activities	−0.81	0.23	−0.58	0.41	7.862	0.007
Physical acts/environmental conditions	1.66	0.68	1.69	0.90	0.028	0.646
Equipment/vehicle operation	3.02	0.78	3.01	0.88	0.004	0.508
Information processing actions	0.99	0.40	1.14	0.49	1.675	0.198

TABLE 14 Analysis of variance (F ratios) on JFI factor scores separately across groups of municipalities and groups of states and between the composites for municipalities and states

JFI	Across municipalities[a] Univariate F	p	Across states[b] Univariate F	p	Across municipalities and states[c] Univariate F	p
Patrol activities	11.780	0.000	31.841	0.000	0.681	0.414
Interpersonal relations	20.974	0.000	6.906	0.000	393.875	0.000
Traffic patrol	8.811	0.000	6.714	0.000	313.977	0.000
Police procedures	13.602	0.000	23.373	0.000	11.260	0.001
Security and surveillance	3.778	0.005	16.083	0.000	262.702	0.000
Emergency services	3.098	0.015	29.164	0.000	0.065	0.686
Special assignments	29.059	0.000	37.090	0.000	24.533	0.000
Self-development and specialized knowledge	11.568	0.000	10.195	0.000	108.149	0.000

[a]Numerator degrees of freedom = 4; denominator degrees of freedom = 696.
[b]Numerator degrees of freedom = 4; denominator degrees of freedom = 646.
[c]Numerator degrees of freedom = 1; denominator degrees of freedom = 1350.

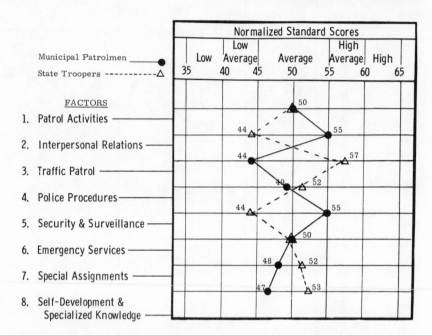

FIGURE 12 Composite JFI job dimension profiles for the position of municipal police officer and state trooper for participants in a consortium validation study.

described in terms of the importance of the activities performed rather than in terms of the importance of the skills and attributes required to perform these. We have had similar results for other occupational groups, such as two types of mechanics in the transit industry, and on the basis of both studies, we are reasonably convinced that these are not irreconcilable differences. The specific activities performed in the two police positions are observably different, but the underlying behaviors, and thus the skills and attributes required to perform the activities, are largely similar. The two forms of job descriptions yield different information, which can be used for different purposes.

Description in terms of the activities performed lends itself to

the development of standard job descriptions and of programs for job clarification
the development of training curricula
procedures for performance appraisal
the construction of behavior-anchored rating scales

The implication for this last, however, is that it may have to be adjusted for each site. In other words, its transportability must be investigated.

Description in terms of required skills and attributes, on the other hand, leads naturally to

identification or construction of tests to be validated for selection or promotion
programs of self-directed self-development

In the future the IRC will probably continue to use both forms of job description in its studies. It is to be hoped that some of this valuable data obtained at the time of selection and some of the techniques used to obtain it will be incorporated into the standard personnel procedures for placement, training, and promotion used by organizations participating in such studies.

SUMMARY

In the course of local and national studies for the validation of selection procedures in the public sector, the IRC has used and refined many of the traditional approaches to job analysis. It has also developed some new methodologies for this process, particularly in the area of quantified job description by incumbents and supervisors. Two of these methodological or procedural issues are discussed in this chapter.

One issue concerns the particular method of quantified job analysis to be employed. Results are compared for descriptions of the patrol officer's job based on the day-to-day activities of that job and for descriptions based on the human skills and attributes required for successful performance of the activities. Implications for the use of both types of description are outlined.

The other issue concerns the increasingly important question of the transportability of validated test batteries. Two types of transportability are illustrated—results from a consortium validation used in a similar but nonparticipating organization and results from a municipal police department to a police department in another city.

REFERENCES

Baehr, M. E. *Skills and attributes inventory (importance rating).* Chicago, Ill.: University of Chicago, Industrial Relations Center, 1976.

Baehr, M. E. *National validation of a selection test battery for male transit bus operators: Final report.* To be published by National Technical Information Service, Springfield, Virginia (printed in limited run by IRC, 1977).

Baehr, M. E., Furcon, J. E., & Froemel, E. C. *Psychological assessment of patrolman qualifications in relation to field performance.* Washington, D.C.: U.S. Government Printing Office, 1969.

Furcon, J. E., & Froemel, E. C. *The relationship of selected psychological tests to measures of police officer job performance in the state of Illinois.* Chicago, Ill.: University of Chicago, Industrial Relations Center, 1973.

Furcon, J. E., Froemel, E. C., Franczak, R. G., & Baehr, M. E. *A longitudinal study of psychological test predictors and assessments of patrolman field performance.* Chicago, Ill.: University of Chicago, Industrial Relations Center, 1971.

Job functions inventory for police officers. Chicago, Ill.: University of Chicago, Industrial Relations Center, n.d.

Mecham, R. C., & McCormick, E. J. *The rated attribute requirements of job elements in the Position Analysis Questionnaire.* Lafayette, Ind.: Purdue University, Occupational Research Center, January 1969.

4

THE DEVELOPMENT AND USE OF SUPERVISORY AND PEER SCALES FOR POLICE PERFORMANCE APPRAISAL

James L. Farr and Frank J. Landy
Department of Psychology, Pennsylvania State University,
University Park, Pennsylvania

The evaluation of police officer performance has not kept pace with the changing demands of the job of police officer. Both technological and societal factors have contributed to an increase in the complexity and challenge that today exist in such a position. Yet in most police agencies the ways in which officers' job performance is evaluated have not changed substantively for many years. The typical police department evaluates the job performance of its patrol officers by means of a supervisory rating, and many of the larger municipal departments use such a rating as the predominant, if not only, method of evaluation (Landy & Farr, Note 1).

The reliance on supervisory ratings as an important measure of job performance is not unique to police agencies. In many jobs, including that of police patrol officer, objective or countable measures of job performance (e.g., number of arrests, number of absences, etc.) are either incomplete indexes of overall performance or are not comparable from individual to individual (e.g., consider the difficulties in comparing directly the arrest records of one officer assigned to an affluent residential district and another officer assigned to an inner-city area). Since objective measures may not provide sufficient information about all aspects of the job performance of police officers, police department administrators usually find it necessary to employ some kind of

The research described in this chapter was supported by grants NI-71-063-G and NI-73-99-0036-G from the LEAA of the U.S. Department of Justice.

rating scale. Unfortunately, while the task of rating the job performance of a subordinate appears reasonably simple, the process is likely to be beset with a number of problems. These potential difficulties with rating scales as criteria of job performance have been described by Guion (1965, chap. 4), Landy and Trumbo (1976, chap. 4), and Smith (1976), among others, and space will not be devoted here to a detailed account of such difficulties. Suffice it to say that the problems can be considerable and can seriously undermine the usefulness of ratings for administrative and counseling purposes.

Smith and Kendall (1963) developed a procedure for constructing rating scales that attempts to overcome the difficulties found in traditional scales. The important characteristics of the Smith-Kendall scales are (a) the involvement of individuals representative of future raters in the development of the dimensions of job performance to be rated and (b) the use of scaling procedures to select rating scale anchors that are behaviorally based and relatively unambiguous in terms of the behavior each anchor is describing. We will refer to these types of scales as Behaviorally Anchored Scales (BAS) in subsequent sections of this chapter.

In the next section we will describe a multiyear, multidepartment effort to develop BAS for the job of police patrol officer. Then we will discuss the use of such scales in a performance evaluation system. Finally we will examine the implications for future work in police departments.

DEVELOPMENT OF BAS FOR THE POLICE PATROL OFFICER POSITION

The rationale for the research project to be described here was based on several considerations related to scientific rigor and to practicality. The Smith and Kendall approach to the development of rating scales was chosen because of the possible improvements that this method offers for measuring job performance. It was also considered desirable to involve a large number of police departments in the development of the BAS, because this would increase the transportability of the final evaluation system. At a more practical level, the involvement of many departments would result in less need for the time and manpower of any single department. Thus departments would be able to participate in the project without having to commit large amounts of resources.

In addition, it was decided that two sets of rating scales should be developed, one for use by supervisory officers to rate their subordinates and one for use by patrol officers to rate the job performance of their fellow patrol officers. As a result of the nature of patrol officers' duties, much of their work is done under conditions of little or no direct supervision. Thus, fellow officers or peers may be able to provide information that would not be available from a supervisory officer.

Sample

A total of 58 police departments in 28 states and the District of Columbia participated in at least one phase of the project. All geographical regions of the continental United States were represented in the sample. All the cities whose police departments were included in the study had populations of 40,000 or more.

Procedure

Only an overview of the project procedure will be presented here. Further details are available in Landy and Farr (1976) and Landy, Farr, Saal, and Freytag (1976). Further descriptions of the BAS methodology may be found in Campbell, Dunnette, Arvey, and Hellervik (1973); Landy and Farr; and Smith and Kendall (1963).

Performance dimension identification and definition for the job of municipal police patrol officer occurred in a series of working conferences conducted with project personnel and representatives from a total of 15 police departments. In two conferences attended by supervisory officers, eight performance dimensions were identified and labeled as (1) job knowledge, (2) judgment, (3) initiative, (4) dependability, (5) demeanor, (6) attitude, (7) relations with others, and (8) communication. In two conferences attended by patrol officers (peers) the following nine performance dimensions were named: (1) job knowledge, (2) judgment, (3) use of equipment, (4) dealing with the public, (5) reliability, (6) demeanor, (7) compatibility, (8) communication, and (9) work attitude. The definitions for each of the supervisory and peer rating scale dimensions are shown in Table 1.

Specific instances of job behaviors that exemplify the performance dimensions were generated at the supervisory and peer conferences and by mail from conference participants. Several hundred behavioral examples were obtained by this process and were empirically evaluated for usefulness as performance dimension anchors according to the usual BAS methodology. The behavioral examples were randomly ordered and administered to approximately 50 patrol officers and 50 supervisory police officers in several cities for allocation to performance dimensions. Those behavioral examples that were categorized to a single dimension by two-thirds or more of the officers were retained for further development. This step in the scale development process ensured that various officers agreed that each behavioral description was an example of a single dimension of job performance. Furthermore, this agreement was also found across police departments, a fact that added to the generalizability of the allocation step.

The behavioral examples that satisfied the allocation step were next evaluated by approximately 100 supervisory officers and 175 patrol officers in

TABLE 1 Performance dimensions and definitions

Peers	Supervisors
Job knowledge. Use of knowledge of law, procedures, policies and techniques related to the patrol function including the application of prior training. *Judgment.* Analytic assessment of the situation and taking of necessary and appropriate action after consideration of alternative approaches. *Use of equipment.* Knowledge of and skill in the use of firearms and other special equipment (radio, first aid, vehicles, etc.). *Dealing with the public.* Ability to deal with public in a respectful, tactful style, while attempting to to meet their expectation if possible. *Reliability.* Dependability in job attendance, effort expenditure, acceptance of responsibility, reaction to stress and accuracy in all details of work. *Demeanor.* Personal and professional pride as shown by personal neatness and grooming and physical appearance. *Compatibility.* Ability to work with fellow officers, including accepting and giving constructive criticism, mutual decision making, and taking an equal share of the work load. *Communication.* Ability to make oneself understood in face-to-face situations and to transmit information in written form. *Work attitude.* Interested in serving the public by the performance of the job; gains satisfaction from doing the job well, which include the fair and objective enforcement and administration of the law.	*Job knowledge.* Awareness of procedures, laws, and court rulings and of changes in them. *Judgment.* Observation and assessment of the situation and taking of appropriate action. *Initiative.* Conduct of individual personal performance without either direct supervision or commands, including suggestions for improved departmental procedures. *Dependability.* Predictable job behavior, including attendance, promptness, and reaction to boredom, stress, and criticism. *Demeanor.* Professional bearing as determined by overall neatness of uniform, personal grooming, and general physical condition. *Attitude.* General orientation toward the law enforcement profession and the department. *Relations with others.* Ability to deal with the public, fellow officers, supervisory personnel, and other people one comes into contact with during the performance of the job. *Communication.* Ability to make oneself understood and to gather and transmit information, both in oral and written fashion.

several cities. Evaluations were made in terms of a 9-point continuum of performance favorability, and the decision to retain or to drop a behavioral example for further work was based principally on the size of the standard deviation of the ratings given to the item by the officers. Items with relatively small standard deviations were retained, since a small standard deviation would indicate general agreement by the raters with regard to the level of job performance described in a particular example. Large standard deviations, of course, indicate disagreement. The mean ratings given to particular behavioral examples were also examined. It was desirable to have examples that represented as much as possible of the 9-point continuum of performance favorability.

Final Performance Evaluation Scales

The scale development process resulted in two sets of evaluation instruments, one set to be used by supervisory officers to rate their subordinates and the other to be used by patrol officers to evaluate their peers. The final format of the scales consisted of a vertical, 9-point scale for each performance dimension, which was located beneath the definition of the dimension. The eight supervisory scales were placed in a 4-page booklet (one $8\frac{1}{2}'' \times 22''$ sheet, folded once) and the 9 peer scales appear in a separate 4-page booklet. Each booklet provides for the evaluation of one officer by one rater. An example of a rating scale appears in Figure 1.

Two characteristics distinguished our project's final performance evaluation scales from the traditional BAS format. First, the behavioral anchors did not appear on our scales themselves. Rather, the examples of job performance previously categorized and scaled for favorability level were presented in a separate booklet. One booklet was developed for the eight supervisory scales and one for the nine peer scales. The booklets also contained instructions for using the scales and cautions regarding various rating errors. This procedure permitted a less bulky rating booklet for each officer being rated. A reduction in paper and space needs is a practical advantage, as any personnel manager knows.

Early in the development of the scales, the anchors, or behavioral descriptions, did appear on the actual rating scales themselves, connected to the scales by a series of arrows that indicated the mean value of each of the anchors. Raters would occasionally question the position of a particular anchor, thinking that it should be higher or lower than was suggested by the rating scale. While this was not surprising, due to the large number of cities and individuals involved in the research, one result was that the credibility of the scales suffered when such objections were raised. When the anchors were placed in the separate booklet form, the arrows connecting the anchors to the scales were eliminated. The use of the separate booklet format and the

Judgment - Observation and assessment of the situation

and taking appropriate action.

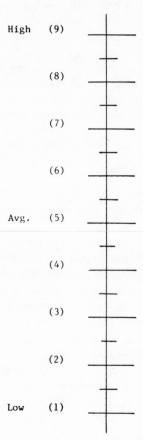

FIGURE 1   Example of Behavior Anchored Scale (BAS),
performance dimension of judgment (supervisory scales).

elimination of the arrows seemed to minimize problems related to anchor
placement by scale users.

Our scales also departed from the traditional BAS format by eliminating
the "could be expected to" stem from the behavioral examples. Several
representatives from cooperating departments pointed out that the use of such
a stem suggested that the rating given to an officer was an anticipation
regarding *future* performance, not a description of *past* performance. It was
felt that this impression was counter to the principal purpose of the scales and

could also have implications if an officer sought legal action regarding a protested rating.

An example of a section of the instructional booklet indicating the behavioral anchors for one performance dimension is shown in Table 2.

RESULTS OF FIELD TESTING THE BAS

Psychometric Properties of the Scales

A total of 2,545 patrol officers in 48 departments were rated on the supervisory scales, and 2,030 officers in 37 departments were rated on the peer scales. The scale ratings were examined for the existence of rating errors such as halo, central tendency, and leniency. The reliabilities of the scales were also estimated. Because of the large number of departments participating in this research, the data were not pooled across departments; rather, psychometric analyses were conducted for each department. The resulting departmental statistics were then used to form sampling distributions of the various indexes of the psychometric properties of the scales. Because of the voluminous data, only the highlights will be presented here. For more details, the interested reader is referred to Landy and Farr (1976) and Landy, Farr, Saal, and Freytag (1976).

The average rating (across all performance dimensions and all departments) was about 6.60 for the peer scales and 6.45 for the supervisory scales. The standard deviation averaged about 1.80 for the peer scales and 1.72 for

TABLE 2 Behavioral examples for the performance dimension of judgment, supervisory scales

	Judgment: Observation and assessment of the situation and taking appropriate action
High	Calls for assistance and clears the area of bystanders before confronting a barricaded, heavily-armed suspect.
	Radios in his position and discontinues a high-speed chase before entering areas of high vehicle and pedestrian traffic, such as school areas.
Average	Issues warnings instead of tickets for traffic violations that occur at particularly confusing intersections.
	Does not leave a mother and daughter in the middle of a fight just because no law is being violated.
Low	Enters a building with a broken door window instead of guarding the exits and calling for a backup unit.
	Continues to write a traffic violation when hearing a report of a nearby robbery in progress.

the supervisory scales. Both peer and supervisory scales tended to have negatively skewed—but in other respects normal—rating distributions.

In general, the data suggested little evidence for central tendency in the ratings. Positive leniency was indicated by the overall average rating being above 6 on the 9-point scale. This may not represent a serious problem, however, since we might expect such a displacement in the mean rating away from 5.0 (the theoretical average point on the scales) if the selection and training programs of the various departments are useful and valid. This displacement may particularly be expected—and indeed hoped for—when the referent anchors are behaviors and not other people performing the same job. The behaviorally anchored scales require the rater to assess the performance of an individual relative to job behaviors and *not* relative to other job incumbents. Thus, ratings for the typical incumbent may be above average in terms of the full range of possible job behaviors without necessarily indicating a positive leniency bias.

Rating halo was examined by intercorrelating the performance dimension ratings. The typical intercorrelation was high, averaging about .62 for the peer scales and about .64 for the supervisory scales. The proper interpretation of the halo data requires that we also examine the estimated reliabilities for the scales. The average reliability of the peer scales (estimated by the analysis of variance method of Ebel, 1951) was about .60 and of the supervisory scales about .65. If the scale intercorrelations are squared (to represent shared variance) and subtracted from the reliability estimates (already in terms of variance), the resulting difference suggested the amount of unique, systematic variance contributed by the scale. Although a simplification, this process suggests that each of the scales has the potential for providing unique, reliable, and useful information about performance.

As noted before, sampling distributions of the various scale indexes were obtained ($N = 37$ departments for peer scales and $N = 48$ departments for supervisory scales). An examination of these distributions suggests considerable department-to-department variability in the psychometric properties of the scales. Although some variability in these indexes would be expected, the extreme amount of variability found in some measures, particularly the reliability estimates, suggests the need for research on factors within a police department that may be systematically related to such psychometric properties of the rating distributions.

Factor Analysis of Performance Scales

A principal-components factor analysis was performed separately for the peer and supervisory scales, followed by an oblique (biquartimin) rotation. Three factors emerged from each analysis, accounting for 78% of the total variance in the peer scales and 81% in the supervisory scales. For the peer scales, factor 1 appears to represent interpersonal orientation or skills (the performance evaluation scales of dealing with the public, compatibility, communication, and work attitude load most strongly on this factor). Factor 2 appears to be technical adequacy in job performance (job knowledge, judgment, use of equipment, communication), and factor 3 is demeanor.

For the supervisory scales, factor 1 seems also to represent interpersonal orientation or skills (relations with others, dependability, attitude), but there are some differences from the similarly labeled peer component. Factor 2 represents technical adequacy, but again the specifics seem different from the related component of the peer scales. The performance scales loading strongly on factor 2 are job knowledge, judgment, initiative, and communication. Factor 3 also represents demeanor.

Although the labels for the peer and supervisory scale components are identical, the various performance scales and their definitions, which determine the operational definition of the performance factors, are not so similar as to suggest that one source of rating information (e.g., the supervisor) could be substituted for the other without loss of performance information. Nevertheless, the results do suggest that both peers and supervisors generally focus on similar patterns of performance when evaluating the performance of police patrol officers.

A recent factor analysis of supervisory ratings of the job performance of 101 minority officers in one police department showed few differences from the analysis just described (Freytag, Note 2). There was some tendency for interpersonal relations scales and dependability to load on two factors rather than on a single factor. The various performance scales were slightly more correlated for this minority sample than for the total sample previously described.

Relationship of BAS to Other Measures of Job Performance

Data were available in several cities, and this permitted an examination of the relationship between the BAS ratings and various other measures of performance. The other measures of performance included objective data (number of arrests, arrest-conviction ratios, etc.), and ratings on other performance appraisal instruments used by the various departments. The sample sizes in these studies are generally small, but the correlations between the BAS and the other performance measures have been positive if not large. The data as a whole suggest a convergence between the BAS measure of performance and other performance indexes.

IMPLEMENTATION OF THE BAS EVALUATION SYSTEM

The BAS evaluation procedures that have been just described cannot be properly implemented by any police department without a prior consideration of their possible uses within the department's personnel system. The uses of any evaluation procedure can be classified into one of three categories: administrative, counseling, and personnel research.

Administrative uses of personnel evaluation information identify performance appraisal data as input for such personnel decisions as promotion, transfer, merit pay increases, and retention. Traditionally, these administrative uses have been the primary ones. There has been a recent trend, however, toward an increased use of performance appraisal information for counseling, that is, for developing the individual employee's job-related skills. Evaluation results are discussed with the employee as a means of identifying strengths and weaknesses in his or her job performance so that positive job behaviors may be maintained and less favorable ones improved.

The final way in which an organization may use performance evaluation data is for *personnel research*. To be properly conducted, personnel research studies, such as the validation of selection standards or the evaluation of training programs, require a measure of job performance.

The way in which performance appraisal data of any kind will be used determines which characteristics of the information are necessary and desirable. The following discussion is directed toward an examination of the BAS evaluation system in relation to the three categories of uses.

The BAS system data can be used as input to administrative decisions regarding retention of an officer following the probationary period, transfer to a special-duty assignment, promotion, appropriate discipline, and merit pay increases. Many departments may find it difficult to implement peer evaluations in the administrative decision process. Many officers are reluctant to evaluate their peers, especially if the performance of their fellow officers is less than satisfactory. A department should ascertain whether its patrol officers view peer ratings as appropriate input for administrative decisions. If they do not, it would be better to exclude this source of information from such decisions than to try forcing officers to rate their peers. It is likely under this circumstance that any resulting ratings would be highly skewed in a lenient direction.

Supervisory ratings using the BAS do not present the legitimacy problem. It is generally accepted that evaluation of subordinates is a duty of the supervisory position. However, there are still several important considerations concerning the use of supervisory ratings for administrative decisions. An important consideration is whether the available evaluation information is appropriate for the role requirements of the job that the officer will perform following the personnel decision. For some decisions, as on simple merit pay increases, this is not a problem because the prior and subsequent performance requirements are identical. However, personnel decisions on such issues as promotion or special-duty assignments will usually involve a change of role requirements. One must match the role requirements of the future assignment or job with the relevant evaluation data that are available for the individual.

Relevance refers here to whether the new job duties require performance on a particular performance dimension of the old job. Only the performance ratings on those BAS dimensions that are common to the old and new jobs or assignments should be used as input for the transfer or promotion decision. It is not sufficient to specify that the individual's "quality of work" is satisfactory and therefore decide that he or she should do well in the new position. It is obvious that the nature of the work roles is likely to be different and that a general, global performance dimension such as quality or quantity of work is seriously deficient information on which to base a transfer or promotion decision. Only when the tasks represented in each of the positions are identified, when the individual in question is appropriately evaluated on each of these dimensions, and when individual characteristics are compared with work role requirements can a successful transfer or promotion be effectively assured.

Thus BAS information should not be uncritically used in a personnel decision without a prior determination of its relevance for that particular decision. The BAS system, with its emphasis on multiple, behavior-based performance dimensions, does avoid many of the relevance problems of other, more global rating scales.

While administrative uses of performance evaluation information are important, perhaps even more important for the effective operation of any organization is the use of appraisal data in the counseling of employees. Performance feedback as a means of aiding employees in the development of improved job skills is often given lip service in organizations, but rarely is it made as effective a device as it could be. The reason for this is usually that supervisors find it a difficult and not very rewarding experience. Subordinates are often quite defensive about less than excellent performance, and the whole counseling session may regress to an experience dreaded by both individuals.

Over the years the sign-off procedure has been the major mechanism for ensuring performance feedback to subordinates. This mechanism has not fulfilled its purpose. While it does ensure that the patrol officer sees a performance evaluation, it does little else. It does not relieve the extreme discomfort experienced by both supervisor and subordinate when negative feedback is required. As a matter of fact, this procedure might even serve to exaggerate the discomfort. We propose that a mechanism similar to the one presented in Figure 2 might be a more adequate one. Figure 2 presents a computer-generated performance profile that the subordinate and supervisor can use as a vehicle for discussing the individual patrol officer's performance. It plots the officer's performance scores against profiles of appropriate norm groups (as determined by the department). This norm group might be all officers who have been on the department for two years or less, those with more than five years' seniority, all traffic officers, or all officers in some other category. The top 10% and the bottom 10% of the norm group can be determined by some ranking procedure. Then the average profiles of these two

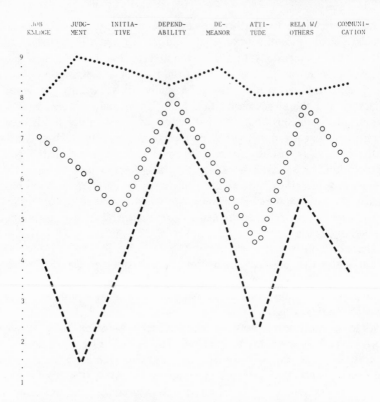

FIGURE 2   Computer-generated performance profile for purposes of performance feedback: . . . ., indicates performance scores of the top 10% of the department's (5 yr.; traffic; etc.) patrol officers; – – –, indicates performance scores of the bottom 10% of the department's (5 yr.; traffic; etc.) patrol officers; ○ ○ ○, indicates the performance scores of the individual patrol officer. (Adapted from Landy & Farr, 1976, p. 96.)

groups can be calculated and superimposed on the feedback sheet along with the individual officer's profile. This provides an anonymous yet relevant basis for performance comparison. By referring to the performance appraisal scales, the supervisor can indicate the strengths and weaknesses of the officer in comparison to the norm group. Furthermore, these comparisons can be made in behavioral terms, by referring to the behavioral anchors on the scales. This procedure might be interfaced with an existing management information system. If no such computerized system exists in the agency, it can be done rather easily by hand. This feedback system has the advantage of providing the officer with comparative data about weaknesses and strengths. It has the further advantage of freeing the supervisor from the burden of comparing the performance of officers who have varying amounts of experience.

Performance data obtained from patrol officers on the peer BAS could also be incorporated into the feedback process. Potential resistance to peer evaluations may be reduced by assuring the patrol officers that their evaluations of their fellow officers will not be used for administrative purposes. However, it may prove difficult to convince officers that their ratings will not at least indirectly affect later supervisory evaluations of the officers. A possible solution to this situation would be to have the peer evaluations directed to a staff personnel officer who would conduct individual feedback sessions based on the peer evaluations. Of course, if the patrol officers view peer appraisals as appropriate input for administrative decisions and counseling, then no problems should be created by the supervisor's receiving the evaluations and counseling the officers on that basis. Another possibility would be peer counseling in which fellow officers review one another's job performance. However, for such sessions to prove useful, officers would have to be trained both to give and to take such criticism. Again, patrol officers may not wish to be a part of the counseling process. The implementation of a peer evaluation system for any purpose probably requires careful planning and systematic gathering of officer preferences for such a system. Otherwise, officer resistance is likely to defeat the purpose of the proposed evaluation data uses.

The final category of uses of performance evaluation information is that of personnel research. Good job performance data are necessary before any element of the personnel system can be properly evaluated. For example, we cannot decide whether a selection test is valid for the prediction of job performance or whether a training program is instructing officers in the proper way to perform their jobs unless we have some means of measuring the job performance of the officers. All too often the primary emphasis is placed on choosing the selection test or developing training procedures without a comparable amount of attention to the measure of job performance. This is equivalent to putting the cart before the horse. Until we can specify what we consider to be good job performance, we cannot choose tests that should predict good performance. Neither can we design training programs to teach officers how to perform their jobs well.

The BAS evaluation system has many characteristics that have been cited as desirable for research purposes by authorities in the personnel research area (e.g., Dunnette, 1966; Guion, 1965). The BAS system provides for ratings on specific dimensions of job performance, uses multiple sources of rating information, and is behaviorally based. If the performance ratings are to be used for research purposes, it is usually advantageous to tell the raters that the evaluation information will be used only for research and *not* for any administrative use.

The training of raters is an important part of the performance evaluation process. Raters need to be instructed in the avoidance of common rating errors (i.e., halo, central tendency, and leniency). They should also receive training in the use of the specific appraisal system to be utilized by the department. Practice sessions should be run to ensure that the raters understand the task. It is possible to create scenarios describing the job behaviors of hypothetical officers whose performance on various job dimensions is at known and varied levels. In this way any rater who gives discrepant ratings can be identified and further instructed in the proper use of the scales. It is simply not enough to give a rater an instruction booklet and assume that this will qualify him or her to evaluate performance.

ADAPTING THE BAS TO A PARTICULAR POLICE DEPARTMENT

One of the purposes of the development of the BAS evaluation system was to end up with an appraisal system that could be used in a wide number and variety of municipal police departments. We feel that we realized this aim. However, it may be necessary for a particular police department to make some changes in the BAS in order to use it in the most effective manner. Obviously, one part of the BAS that may require some modification is the set of behavioral examples appearing in the instructional booklet. The examples in the booklet are generally applicable to police departments, but any single example is likely to be irrelevant in some department or to be scaled inappropriately regarding the favorability of job performance due to local laws or procedures. There may also exist at the local level better examples of job performance that will be more meaningful to the raters in that department.

As an aid to modifying the behavioral anchors, a list of potential behavioral examples are available in Landy and Farr (1976). These potential examples are grouped by dimension, and each includes a first approximation to a scale value. A department wishing to incorporate any of these examples as scale anchors could submit the potential anchors to its officers for favorability scaling and dimension allocation, as we described earlier, in the discussion of the development of the BAS. This procedure would identify additional examples that could be included as scale anchors for the various dimensions of job performance. It would also serve as a way of increasing the commitment that raters have in the appraisal system by involving them in the modification procedures.

FEASIBILITY OF COOPERATIVE RESEARCH EFFORTS

An important implication of this performance appraisal project has been the demonstrated feasibility of personnel research conducted with the cooperation of many police departments. An oft-cited reason for the paucity of good personnel research is its expense in time, human resources, and dollars. Efforts such as this one suggest that the expense to any single department can be made quite tolerable if multiple agencies are involved in the project. The main obstacle to such cooperative efforts would appear to be the coordination of such activities into a coherent research program. It is hoped that universities and regional governmental bodies will take the initiative to develop a framework and structure for coordinating these badly needed research endeavors.

REFERENCES

Campbell, J. P., Dunnette, M. D., Arvey, R. D., & Hellervik, L. W. The development and evaluation of behaviorally based rating scales. *Journal of Applied Psychology*, 1973, *57*, 15–22.

Dunnette, M. D. *Personnel selection and placement.* Belmont, Calif.: Wadsworth, 1966.

Ebel, R. L. Estimation of reliability of ratings. *Psychometrika*, 1951, *16*, 407–424.

Guion, R. M. *Personnel testing.* New York: McGraw-Hill, 1965.

Landy, F. J., & Farr, J. L. Police performance appraisal. *JSAS Catalog of Selected Documents in Psychology*, 1976, *6*, 83. (Ms. No. 1315)

Landy, F. J., Farr, J. L., Saal, F. E., & Freytag, W. R. Behaviorally anchored scales for rating the performance of police officers. *Journal of Applied Psychology*, 1976, *61*, 750–758.

Landy, F. J., & Trumbo, D. A. *Psychology of work behavior.* Homewood, Ill.: Dorsey, 1976.

Smith, P. C. Behaviors, results, and organizational effectiveness: The problem of criteria. In M. D. Dunnette (Ed.), *Handbook of industrial and organizational psychology.* Chicago: Rand McNally, 1976.

Smith, P. C., & Kendall, L. M. Retranslation of expectations: An approach to the construction of unambiguous anchors for rating scales. *Journal of Applied Psychology*, 1963, *47*, 149–155.

REFERENCE NOTES

1. Landy, F. J., & Farr, J. L. *Police performance appraisal* (Tech. Rep. NI-71-063-G). University Park, Pa.: Pennsylvania State University, 1973. (Available from Law Enforcement Assistance Administration, Washington, D.C.)

2. Freytag, W. R. *The validity of the oral board interview in police officer selection: A comparative analysis between minority-group members and white males.* Unpublished manuscript, 1976.

5

PREENTRY ASSESSMENT AND TRAINING
Performance Evaluation of Police Officers

Joseph M. Fabricatore
Kearney: Management Consultants, Los Angeles, California

This chapter discusses current issues and policies that pertain to evaluating police applicants for both psychological suitability at entry and performance during training. Although these two evaluation areas have been quite separate in the past, recent concerns over nondiscriminatory, effective screening and job-valid academy training suggest that preemployment and training evaluation procedures could be merged into a unitary and continuous system.

PREEMPLOYMENT EVALUATION

Over the years psychology has contributed to police screening and evaluation decisions (Kent & Eisenberg, 1972), but how this input can best be used depends on the philosophy underlying the selection procedure. In preemployment evaluation a basic distinction can be made between policies that "screen out" unsuitable or unfit applicants and those that "select in" individuals who appear most likely to best meet the stresses and demands of police work. This distinction is reflected in the typical, "successive hurdles" municipal selection process, in which written and medical examinations screen out those who fail to meet some minimal criteria and an oral interview

The opinions expressed in this chapter are entirely those of the author and do not necessarily reflect the views and policies of the Los Angeles Police Department or those of the Department of Personnel, City of Los Angeles.

purports to select in, qualified applicants by means of averaged subjective ratings.

The screen-out/select-in distinction also appears in the underlying philosophies of those parties most concerned with hiring and police personnel decisions—the federal government and the municipal police department. The government, concerned with civil rights issues, may be said to lean toward a screen-out-only approach, in which only the most obviously unfit and inappropriate applicants (on whatever basis) are denied police employment consideration. Police personnel departments, on the other hand, would appear to endorse the select-in approach, typified by the dictum "only the best shall serve." The potential for conflict between the former, which at the extreme becomes an open or even random selection policy, and the latter, which at its extreme becomes restrictively selective and possibly discriminatory, is obviously great and probably irresolvable at the level of argument. These two selection philosophies may, in fact, have no common ground in the typical selection systems that are currently used by most police agencies.

What may be needed is a radical restructuring of police selection policy that starts with the consideration of equal availability for all individuals while ensuring that only the most qualified shall continue. The situation involving these two adversary selection policies can be depicted as a normal curve (see Figure 1), with applicants identified as unsuitable grouped at one tail and applicants judged preferred (by whatever criteria) at the other. Individuals neither screened out nor selected in populate the middle and present the problems in selection policy. Should they all be considered equally likely to become competent police officers?

Ultimately, a number of variables interact and affect the performance of police officers after the hiring decision. In view of these variables—for example, academy training, unrelated life events, personal motivation, chance, and so forth—the "equally likely" argument appears to have merit. On the other hand, average individuals may be considered more likely to be lower, or

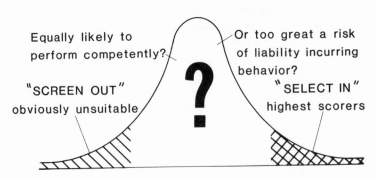

FIGURE 1 Normal distribution depiction of two selection policies for police applicants.

even potentially deficient, performers in comparison with the select-in group. While several investigations have identified the psychological attributes of superiorly performing police officers (Fabricatore, Azen, Boothe, & Snibbe, 1977; Hogan & Kurtines, 1975; Hogan, Note 2), these studies are generally based on already "screened" populations and reflect concurrent rather than predictive validity.

Colarelli and Siegel (1964) report a study showing better predictive validity for extremely "good" and "poor" groups of Kansas state highway patrol officers than for "average" applicants. With reference to the issues raised above, these authors note, "It is within the middle range, i.e., for the man predicted to be average, that the predictions hold up least well" (p. 289).

Colarelli and Siegel's research was unusual in two respects. First, this was a predictive validity study. Second, officer applicants designated as "poor" by the psychological screening were actually hired to evaluate the validity of the selection instruments. According to the researchers, "with one exception, every man predicted to be a 'poor' patrolman has either been terminated or is seen by his supervisor as poor or marginal in his job performance" (p. 289).

An additional complicating factor that influences police selection policies is the increased concern on the part of municipalities over legal liability for negligent selection and retention of psychologically unfit officers. A recent court decision ruled that a municipality may be responsible for ascertaining the potential for dangerous behavior of any police officer that it employs (*Allen* v. *City of Los Angeles*, Note 1). Now, if the federal government mandates equal availability of employment for individuals, such an employment policy will contribute more to continuing questionable or borderline police applicants than a police department policy that, for reasons of legal liability, gives priority to the exclusion of such applicants. The judgment against the city of Los Angeles in the above-cited case was $980,000. Thus the costs of making a selection error in the direction of accepting questionable applicants can be prohibitive.

Can psychological input to the conflict between screening out and selecting in models for police selection contribute to its resolution? This is doubtful, because the basic issues go beyond the identification of potentially high-risk applicants. While psychology cannot lay claim to infallibility in predicting the future, it offers considerable potential for identifying liability-prone individuals. The issue then becomes one of what should be done with the information provided by selection instruments, and this a matter of policy.

At present there is a latent period between the unanticipated effects of past emphasis on equal job opportunity and more recent concerns about hiring borderline police officers, who are likely to incur liability problems. Economic considerations in the form of huge court awards to the victims of psychologically unfit police officers may ultimately force a reconsideration of selection procedures and the compulsory requirement that all applicants for positions in law enforcement receive comprehensive initial psychological evaluations.

The role of psychology in police applicant screening and evaluation involves the very practical problem of integrating the psychological assessment with other parts of the selection process. Where in the successive-hurdles array does the psychological evaluation best fit? Since intensive psychological evaluation may be costly, making it the final step seems appealing, but this could raise serious time-pressure problems if the psychological staff is small and there is a large pool of applicants.

Depending on the selection policy of the police agency, the psychological evaluation could be relatively brief, involving a short interview and mental status examination to determine that the applicant has no obvious emotional problems, or the evaluation could be more extensive, involving testing, review of background information, assessment center exercises, an in-depth interview, and so forth. While the latter approach involves much more time, expense, and expertise, it would be preferred by departments that choose to minimize the number of high-risk or liability-prone police officers.

A question that may arise in the course of screening, as information is developed on applicants, is whether an evaluation report should be developed on *all* applicants or on only those who are evaluated as inappropriate. A related question is whether this report should be made available to departmental training personnel or kept strictly confidential. A full report is absolutely essential because rejected applicants may wish to contest that decision, and an appeals procedure will be necessary. There may be some advantage in having the municipality's or the department's legal counsel work with the psychologist to establish policy for handling confidential psychological information and appeals procedures.

In general, preemployment selection information is not made available to personnel at the police training academy. However, preemployment psychological evaluations would be helpful in predicting areas of outstanding performance, as well as in anticipating training problems. This would be especially useful for training programs that employ self-paced or individually determined instruction. Personality or behavioral problems observed by academy staff take on different meaning and require different responses if viewed in the context of a prior psychological evaluation, especially if these observations are reviewed with the help of the selection psychologist.

TRAINING EVALUATION

Once the decision is made to admit an applicant to the training academy, the evaluation issues shift from concerns with policy and legality to performance appraisal. But concerns about civil rights issues and safe, effective police behavior must be taken into account in evaluating academy performance, as well as in the preemployment evaluation.

Performance evaluation during police academy training has changed dramatically over the past ten years. Innovations include the behavioral specification of training goals, the use of performance and situational tests in evaluation, and individualized curricula incorporating programmed textbooks, behavioral simulations, and video and audio tape presentations. Attention to minority and sex discrimination issues has resulted in academy training that increasingly emphasizes behavioral, job-related skills rather than isolated academic and cognitive abilities. Specification of behavioral goals has enabled evaluation to focus more precisely on valid, job-related performance criteria.

Curriculum changes at the Los Angeles Police Department (LAPD) Academy have progressively reflected societal perspectives on minority and women's issues, as well as innovations in educational technology. Around 1969, training content was divided into "need to know" and "nice to know" categories on the basis of a field survey. Need-to-know content was subsequently reformulated by behavior specification into terminal performance objectives (TPOs). Today some 200 TPOs comprise the goals of academy training for the LAPD.

In 1972 the LAPD Academy training staff began to reexamine TPOs from the stance of "criticality," or job-relatedness, because of concerns about sex discrimination and the safety of newly graduated field officers. The question was asked, "What kinds of real job demands of a critical or life-threatening nature should the rookie field officer be able to respond to as successfully as an experienced field officer?" A survey of the 200 TPOs revealed unanimous agreement that 10 TPOs were critical.

The 10 critical TPOs included response to explosive-device call, first-aid assistance, suspect apprehension, and so forth, and they were designated for assessment prior to academy graduation by performance test. Since the performance tests require demonstration of criterion, or on-the-job behaviors, critical TPOs became job valid and were thus relevant to the concerns about discrimination and safety.

At present, training and evaluation at the LAPD Academy are based on traditional content that is presented in a contemporary training format, with emphasis on performance training and testing. The recruit officer gains necessary information and prepares for performance tests by active, self-paced participation in a curriculum called Multimedia Instruction for Law Enforcement (MILE).

A comprehensive assembly of instructional materials, MILE covers the conceptual and behavioral components of police work as they relate to the patrol function. The MILE program includes videotape and audiotape presentations, lectures, programmed workbooks, performance training, and situation simulations. Other areas in which behavioral training is provided are driving, shooting, and physical strength and endurance. Evaluation of recruits is done by graded reports, instructors' ratings according to well-defined scales, behavior checklists, paper-and-pencil examinations, peer evaluations, and evaluations of performance on simulated-situation tasks.

Much training and evaluation takes place through the use of situation simulations or performance training tasks. Such simulations were used in the 1930s by German military psychologists (Simoneit, 1940, 1944). An "extended interview" was used by the War Office Selection Board to select officer candidates for the British army during World War II (Garforth, 1945). Simulations were also used in World War II by Henry Murray and the Office of Strategic Services (OSS) assessment staff (1948) to evaluate individuals for assignment to irregular warfare activities.

The OSS procedures are the model for the situation simulations currently employed by most training programs and assessment centers. Briefly, individuals perform a number of tasks in group settings while a staff of assessors observes. The resulting scores, ratings, and impressions are pooled to arrive as some final evaluation or prediction based on each individual's performance.

Simulations are now used by police agencies for purposes of training, as well as for testing and assessment, and the psychodynamic theoretical framework of the OSS staff has been largely replaced by a behavioral orientation, with greater emphasis on statistical comparisons.

At the end of 1976, 23 scenarios were being used for simulations at the LAPD Training Academy. One example of a situation simulation performance test is used for training recruits to cope with explosive devices. The recruit must display critical behaviors in responding to a call involving a possibly explosive device. In addition to evaluating safe and unsafe behaviors in performing this task, the instructor-grader can also assess other performance objectives, for example, the officer's approach, of proper interview techniques; ability to discriminate various kinds of explosive devices; and proper behavior in handling, booking, and communicating.

Although recruit officers can prepare for these performance simulations by viewing related MILE materials and using videotape and workbook exercises, the actual details of the simulation are unknown. Thus, while recruit officers can create alternative scenarios and can plan and mentally rehearse their responses to various contingencies, they never know exactly what will happen in the simulation situation.

This uncertainty pays off. First, unpredictability increases the sense of realism in the test situation, since what will actually happen in the field almost always defies prediction. Second, unpredictability increases the involvement of the recruit officer, heightens the impact of the simulation, and intensifies the learning. Third, unpredictability permits the instructor to assess not only complex skills and responses to learned expectancies but ability to deal with unique or infrequent events—a capacity that is vital to an officer's safety and difficult to assess in any other way. The dramatic realism and emotionally involving demands of the situation can also reveal the potential for poorly controlled or liability-prone behavior.

In the performance test situation, each recruit officer must demonstrate the ability to perform the TPO successfully. However, in a performance training situation, it is generally not possible for all the persons in a squad actually to role-play the simulated task, and some members of the group must make use of observational learning and group discussion. The overall rating of each recruit in the training simulation is based on independently prepared field reports submitted by the recruit. These reports are graded, commented on by instructors, and returned to the recruits.

There are some disadvantages to performance training and testing. Expense and time are obvious drawbacks, and the personnel and equipment needed to properly carry out a realistic simulation can be extensive. There is also the need to create scenarios with sufficient impact and realism to encompass the critical TPO performance dimensions and to elicit the behaviors that must be assessed.

On the basis of this review of the recent history of academy evaluation and training, it should be apparent that there have been a number of significant changes in curriculum and testing at the LAPD academy. These changes derive from an effort on the part of training officers to provide sophisticated, up-to-date field preparation, so that when the recruit officer enters the field, he or she will be prepared and ready to confront critical situations.

Departments and training officers must continue to modify selection and evaluation policy, as changes are required by societal trends. The overall process is, essentially, a negative-feedback loop model in which job-performance demands increasingly define what academy curriculum and training will be. In the future we will probably see an increased blurring and more intimate linkage among preselection variables, academy success variables, and field performance success variables. Each of these sets of variables should be examined in the context of performance, be it test or training, and this will require a continuing refinement of measurement techniques.

It is interesting that situational tests and simulations originally used primarily for selection are now being widely used for training and certifying. The next logical step would be to bring back the situation test and use it as a selection device. Some recent preliminary efforts have been made by Gavin and Hamilton (1975). Other earlier attempts to use situational tests at the preentry level have also been reported (Chenoweth, 1961; Mills, McDevitt, & Tonkin, 1966), but systematic use of these tests has not yet occurred, and this will require a unique and critical mix of federal, state, and local resources.

Because of the costs for personnel and equipment, it is unlikely that selection of applicants by means of behavioral and situational tests could be done on anything less than a state or large-agency level. However, at present there appears to be no other strategy that can simultaneously meet selection, training, and certification requirements and also minimize bias against minorities and women in the selection process.

In place of the successive-hurdles approach so common in the selection of police officers, a contemporary assessment center approach has many advantages. This latter approach combines scores and ratings on diverse tests and simulated tasks into a complex set that yields a far more complete and valid evaluation. As envisioned here, this procedure is essentially the same as the original OSS procedure, which included psychological tests, interviews, behavioral observations, peer nominations, and performance tests.

Ideally, a police assessment center would combine the previously separated functions of screening, training, and providing field performance experience into an integrated set of situation test exercises. There would be feedback sessions designed to communicate and discuss every applicant's unique behavioral responses to the assessment, and to clarify the implications of the recruit's performance for his or her future career as a police officer. For the applicants who are selected specific areas for training concentration could be recommended. For rejected applicants significant information that determined the "reject" decision could be discussed, along with implications for alternative employment opportunities in other fields.

Although the costs for the assessment center approach to police selection may appear high, this is the only strategy that promises to meet the requirements of the federal government and the recruiting police agency, as well as the need of individual applicants. From an equal employment opportunity perspective the selection center approach is job valid. From the municipal police agency's point of view the assessment center has the potential for providing a comprehensive evaluation and selection system that meshes neatly with training. For the individual the possibility of a beneficial self-selection decision is greatly enhanced because applicants have a chance to test themselves against actual job requirements and to learn how evaluators and peers perceive their performance. In short, the selection center approach, by providing a refined and updated version of the OSS situational test, integrates psychological assessments and field performance data in evaluating both preemployment liability proneness and training dimensions.

SUMMARY

The impact of federal equal employment opportunity policies and concerns over municipal liability for the behavior of psychologically unfit police officers are discussed in the context of preemployment screening and academy training. The importance of taking job performance requirements into account in structuring entry-level screening and academy evaluation was emphasized, and several examples were given of how "critical" performance dimensions are already used to certify police recruit proficiency by means of situational tests. An assessment center approach to police selection based on the refinement of OSS-type situational tests was proposed to replace the current successive-hurdles screening process.

REFERENCES

Chenoweth, J. H. Situational tests–A new attempt at assessing police candidates. *Journal of Criminal Law, Criminology, and Police Science,* 1961, *52,* 232–238.

Colarelli, N. J., & Siegel, S. M. A method of police personnel selection. *Journal of Criminal Law, Criminology, and Police Science,* 1964, *55,* 287–289.

Fabricatore, J. M., Azen, S., Boothe, S., & Snibbe, H. Predicting performance of police officers using the 16 PF. *American Journal of Community Psychology,* 1978, *6,* 63–70.

Garforth, F. I., de la P. War Office Selection Boards. *Occupational Psychology,* 1945, *19,* 97–108.

Gavin, J. F., & Hamilton, J. W. Selecting police using assessment center methodology. *Journal of Police Science and Administration,* 1975, *3,* 166–176.

Hogan, R., & Kurtines, W. Personological correlates of police effectiveness. *Journal of Psychology,* 1975, *91,* 289–295.

Kent, D. A., & Eisenberg, T. The selection and promotion of police officers: A selected review of recent literature. *The Police Chief,* 1972, *39,* 20–29.

Mills, R. B., McDevitt, R. J., & Tonkin, S. Situational tests in metropolitan police recruit selection. *Journal of Criminal Law, Criminology, and Police Science,* 1969, *60,* 238–241.

Office of Strategic Services Assessment Staff. *The assessment of men.* New York: Rinehart, 1948.

Simoneit, M. Deutsches Soldatentum, 1914–1939. Berlin: Junker and Beunnhaupt, 1940.

Simoneit, M. *Grundriss der Characterlogischen Diagnostic.* Leipzig: Teubner, 1944.

REFERENCE NOTES

1. *Allen* v. *City of Los Angeles,* 1976. Unpublished legal case.
2. Hogan, R. A study of police effectiveness. Experimental Publication System, American Psychological Association, 1970, *6,* Ms. No. 195c.

6

OBJECTIVE AND SUBJECTIVE MEASURES OF POLICE OFFICER PERFORMANCE

Ernest C. Froemel
Industrial Relations Center, The University of Chicago, Chicago, Illinois

The reliable and valid measurement of police officer job performance is a goal that has long been pursued but at best only partially realized. The complexity of the job itself, the great diversity of work situations, the intangibility of the "work product," the public service aspects of the job, and the largely self-supervised status of the individual police officer are but a few of the factors contributing to measurement difficulties. Much of the present measurement attempts involve traditional trait-rating scales, with their vulnerability to rating biases and constant errors. It is no wonder, then, that any new approaches in this field are met with considerable suspicion by those who have to use them.

The use of so-called objective measurements of police officer job performance is frequently offered as a solution to this problem. Such measurements are usually counts or tabulations of discernible events. However, they too are met with opposition. One concern is the meaningfulness of any measure as an indicator of overall performance. Another concern is the danger of reawakening the "quota" approach to police performance measurement. In general, objective measures have the advantage of being impartial and relatively easy to collect, since they are usually on file in the organization,

The author wishes to thank Melany Baehr and John Furcon for their encouragement to write this chapter and for their constructive comments on the initial drafts. Thanks are also due to Frances Burns for her editorial assistance.

anyway. But they also have the disadvantages of (a) oversimplifying or overlooking important areas found in the complexities of the police officer's job; (b) being unexplored or unknown in terms of their technical characteristics, such as reliability or validity; and (c) requiring statistical adjustments across different units to permit individual comparability.

The research team at the Industrial Relations Center IRC has had a long-standing interest in measurements of job performance. This interest has usually centered around the search for a relevant and predictable criterion for the validation of selection test batteries. Additionally, the results of many job analyses have reinforced the belief that job performance is a complex phenomenon. Therefore pains have been taken to make use of as many different types of scales as have been available for the research studies. These scales have usually included a variety of objective measures, the organization's service rating, if any, and the IRC's version of the paired-comparison (PC) performance appraisal, which is described by Baehr (1968).

This same approach was employed in the team's first major study with a police department (Baehr, Furcon, & Froemel, 1969). About 160 performance-related measures were screened and examined before eight were finally selected for use in the study. Those eight included the PC rating, the 1966 departmental rating, and six objective measures, namely, tenure, awards, citizen complaints, disciplinary actions, number of arrests, and absences or sick days. The low intercorrelations between those variables supported the view that several different facets of plice performance were being measured.

A later factor analysis of those eight measures revealed two factors. One was composed of positive performance measures, and the other consisted of the negative performance measures. These were described as follows:

> In general, Factor 1 represents overall good performance as measured by the PC and CPD [departmental] ratings and the specific positive indicators of performance represented by awards. By contrast, the two highest loadings on Factor 2 are for the negative aspects of performance represented by disciplinary actions and sustained complaints. There is a weaker association of number of absences. Interestingly, the number of arrests made has about an equal loading on each factor. One could theorize that arrests made can be either a positive or a negative indicator of performance, depending on judgment employed in making them. (Baehr & Froemel, Note 1)

The results of a follow-up study in the same department were reported by Furcon, Froemel, Franczak, and Baehr (1971). In that study, the PC rating, originally administered in 1966, was repeated in 1969, and measures comparable to the original seven departmental measures were abstracted for 1967, 1968, and 1969. Hence, data were available for the examination of the relationships between the variables across several years. Furcon et al. concluded:

> With a few exceptions, primarily where the CPD rating shows a hitherto unestablished correlation with various "objective" performance measures, these results replicate and reconfirm the pattern of relationships observed in the initial project. The direction and strength of the associations reported in this section in general conformed to our expectations, verifying the anticipated relationships between some of the indices and the anticipated statistical independence of others. (p. 50)

The same study reports the intercorrelations for the performance variables across years. Table 1, an abstraction from Table 5 of that report, shows a strong relationship between any 2 consecutive years for any variable. Additionally, the correlation holds across 4 years for the PC rating, the departmental rating, awards, and arrests, although not for citizen complaints, disciplinary actions or absences. On the whole, however, these results point to the temporal stability or reliability of measurements and could have important implications for the use of those measurements in assessing police officer performance.

TABLE 1 Intercorrelations of performance measures for uniformed patrol officers across years

Performance measures		Year		
PC rating		1966–1967	1969–1970	
1966–1967		–	258	
1969–1970		.60	–	
Department rating	1966	1967	1968	1969
1966	–	511	492	470
1967	.61	–	500	478
1968	.43	.52	–	477
1969	.36	.45	.60	–
Awards	1966	1967	1968	1969
1966	–	516	504	489
1967	.54	–	510	494
1968	.41	.63	–	494
1969	.28	.43	.67	–

TABLE 1 Intercorrelations of performance measures for uniformed patrol officers across years (*Continued*)

Performance measures	Year			
Citizen complaints	1966	1967	1968	1969
1966	–	519	507	492
1967	.33	–	510	494
1968	.25	.36	–	494
1969	.18	.20	.34	–
Disciplinary actions		1961–1966	1967–1969	
1961–1966		–	516	
1967–1969		.31	–	
Arrests	1966	1967	1968	1969
1966	–	515	504	491
1967	.68	–	503	488
1968	.47	.70	–	486
1969	.36	.53	.72	–
Absences	1966	1967	1968	1969
1966	–	516	502	486
1967	.36	–	508	491
1968	.25	.46	–	490
1969	.15	.42	.42	–

Note. From Table 5 in Furcon et al., 1971. The numbers above the diagonal are the count of cases for each correlation. For statistical significance at $N = 500$, for $p < .05$, $r > .074$; for $p < .01$, $r > .104$.

The present study attempts to (1) replicate and expand earlier findings, (2) examine the effects of career cycle on objective measures, and (3) examine the factorial structure of a set of police officer job performance measures.

RESEARCH PROCEDURES

The primary objective of the study within the second major police agency was to develop a validated selection test battery for the entry-level police officer. As a part of this study, investigation of police performance measures was continued in order to serve two purposes: first, to provide an adequate criterion for the test validation and, second, to provide a better understanding of police officer performance measures. This report deals with that second purpose.

Performance-related data were collected from the department files across several years. The yearly measurements were intercorrelated to determine temporal stability. Additionally, the structure of the variables was examined, using factor analysis on the data from the final year.

Sample

The IRC was provided with the names of all police officers in the department, along with other identifying information, such as badge number and precinct assignment. On the basis of this information a random sample of about 600 uniformed patrol officers was asked to volunteer for the study. In the end 509 officers from this random list volunteered for and completed the testing phase. The performance data from the files of these officers was abstracted by department personnel for this study.

Variables

Performance measures and the time intervals used in the data collection are listed below.

I. Variables collected monthly
   1. Number of arrests made for felony offenses
   2. Number of arrests made for misdemeanor offenses
   3. Number of traffic citations issued
   4. Number of accident reports taken
   5. Number of other reports taken
   6. Number of nontraffic cases in court
   7. Number of convictions on court cases
   8. Number of transfers made between units
   9. Number of letters of commendation from the public
   10. Number of trial-board hearings
   11. Number of written reprimands
   12. Number of sick days used
II. Variables collected semiannually
   1. Department service rating
III. Variables collected one time only
   1. Years of service
   2. Years of education on entry to department
   3. Years of education on record in 1972
   4. Final police academy grade
   5. Percentile standing in academy class
   6. Latest 1972 marksmanship score

IV. Variables collected as a total for January–July 1972
1. Number of precinct citations
2. Number of department citations
3. Number of shots fired in the line of duty
4. Number of citizen complaints
5. Number of citizen complaints sustained
6. Number of chargeable accidents

Any data collected for more than one time point was limited to the period from January 1966 to July 1972. Of course, for any person who entered the department after January 1966 the data collection began with their first recorded entry.

In addition, the PC rating (Baehr, 1968) and the Job Performance Description Scales for precinct patrol officers (JPDS) from Heckman, Groner, Dunnette, and Johnson (1972) were used to assess the current level of performance for these officers. Supervisors were asked to identify those officers whom they knew well enough to rate. The supervisors understood that these ratings were being collected for research purposes only and would not be disclosed to the department.

The implementation of the PC rating has been detailed elsewhere (Baehr, Furcon, & Froemel, 1969; Furcon & Froemel, 1973; Furcon et al., 1971). However, a general description is included here. In brief, each supervisor is presented with the names of officers arranged in random pairs. For each pair the supervisor indicates which of the two officers is doing the better job. The technique provides an index to check each rater's consistency of judgment and an index to check for similarity of judgment across raters. These two indexes are examined to ensure that the rating score is not adversely affected by supervisor biases. The composite rating score, obtained by averaging the ratings across supervisors, is thought to measure a general level of performance.

The JPDS consists of 1 scale for each of 11 specific and defined performance dimensions. Following each definition there are up to 9 related behaviors described. The supervisor is to indicate the behavior closest to the typical behavior of the officer being rated. The 11 scales are named as follows:

JPDS01. Handling domestic disputes
JPDS02. Investigating, detecting, and following up on criminal activity
JPDS03. Crime prevention
JPDS04. Maintaining public safety and giving first aid
JPDS05. Using force appropriately
JPDS06. Commitment, dedication, conscientiousness
JPDS07. Integrity and professional ethics
JPDS08. Dealing constructively with the public

JPDS09. Teamwork
JPDS10. Report writing
JPDS11. Traffic maintenance and control

RESULTS

Data Preparation

After preliminary investigations of the monthly data it was decided to create yearly totals by combining the months from August through July. This would remove the seasonal effects seen in some of the data and would allow the use of the most recent information (August 1971 through July 1972). The department's service rating was averaged for the August 1971 to July 1972 periods.

At the same time several variables were deleted from the study due to lack of variability. The following variables had over 90% zero values: departmental citations, number of shots fired, citizen complaints sustained, trial board hearings (1966-1972), and written reprimands (1966-1972). The number of transfers (1966-1972) was also deleted since the values zero and one accounted for over 97% of the cases.

The variables describing the sample of 509 officers are shown in Table 2. Additionally, 26% of the sample was black and most were currently married. Note that only two officers had less than two years of service, which accounts for the low minimum values for age and tenure.

Correlations across Years

The intercorrelations for variables measured at yearly intervals across 6 years are presented in Table 3, along with their means and standard deviations. The number of cases with nonmissing data is shown in the column headed N, while the number of cases contributing to each correlation is shown in the cells above the diagonal.

Although there are some unusual patterns for some variables within

TABLE 2 Descriptive variables for uniformed patrol officers in sample

Variable	N	Mean	SD	Min.	Max.
Current education	507	12.5	1.1	10.0	16.0
Current age	508	30.4	6.5	22.0	53.0
Academy grade	434	85.5	3.9	74.0	94.2
Academy standing	417	52.4	26.9	1.8	98.4
Years of service	508	6.2	5.7	0.0	25.0

TABLE 3 Police performance measures across years

				Intercorrelations					
Year	N	Mean	SD	1967	1968	1969	1970	1971	1972

Number of felony arrests										
1967	136	57.60	85.40	–	134	134	133	131	132
1968	172	50.54	73.04	.88	–	172	170	165	166
1969	224	47.08	41.40	.50	.51	–	221	215	215
1970	330	60.44	61.97	.16	.19	.53	–	323	322
1971	429	63.42	64.23	.12	.20	.48	.73	–	426
1972	487	60.76	57.61	.17	.22	.49	.54	.78	–

Number of misdemeanor arrests										
1967	136	67.01	71.53	–	134	134	133	131	132
1968	172	58.64	58.34	.80	–	172	170	165	166
1969	224	65.31	94.84	.76	.85	–	221	215	215
1970	330	51.27	51.09	.49	.59	.44	–	323	322
1971	430	47.59	49.30	.29	.26	.20	.56	–	427
1972	487	48.63	53.79	.17	.08	.10	.23	.68	–

Number of traffic citations issued										
1967	136	338.02	439.23	–	134	134	133	131	132
1968	172	164.51	171.80	.76	–	172	170	165	166
1969	224	206.01	315.40	.77	.81	–	221	215	215
1970	330	210.86	293.57	.72	.70	.89	–	323	322
1971	429	192.55	273.75	.56	.52	.66	.81	–	426
1972	487	212.29	329.16	.51	.48	.62	.67	.81	–

Number of accident reports taken										
1967	136	29.36	41.74	–	134	134	133	131	132
1968	172	33.37	26.13	.30	–	172	170	165	166
1969	224	29.35	24.13	.18	.73	–	221	215	215
1970	330	34.27	32.15	.09	.44	.55	–	323	322
1971	429	29.30	29.02	.10	.42	.49	.64	–	426
1972	487	27.44	31.75	.11	.31	.29	.40	.51	–

Number of other reports taken										
1967	136	197.18	125.66	–	134	134	133	131	132
1968	172	209.19	119.30	.80	–	172	170	165	166
1969	224	184.38	118.44	.62	.72	–	221	215	215

TABLE 3　Police performance measures across years (*Continued*)

Year	N	Mean	SD	Intercorrelations					
				1967	1968	1969	1970	1971	1972
Number of other reports taken (*Continued*)									
1970	330	217.50	138.38	.52	.54	.75	—	323	322
1971	430	219.25	125.27	.48	.47	.62	.75	—	427
1972	487	189.16	117.72	.34	.39	.51	.54	.66	—
Number of nontraffic cases in court									
1967	136	29.24	65.74	—	134	134	133	131	132
1968	172	24.84	61.29	.84	—	172	170	165	166
1969	224	19.38	55.52	.88	.87	—	221	215	215
1970	330	17.36	44.76	.83	.78	.92	—	323	322
1971	429	17.09	41.05	.53	.51	.57	.60	—	426
1972	486	23.19	68.32	.27	.25	.30	.33	.63	—
Number of convictions on court cases									
1967	136	32.87	110.57	—	134	134	133	131	132
1968	172	25.69	84.81	.89	—	172	170	165	166
1969	224	15.70	54.27	.62	.76	—	221	215	215
1970	330	14.68	56.48	.46	.52	.61	—	323	322
1971	429	12.71	36.94	.34	.45	.56	.69	—	426
1972	486	16.08	45.81	.25	.32	.45	.36	.84	—
Number of letters of commendation									
1967	144	.32	.82	—	144	144	143	142	143
1968	182	.70	1.75	.53	—	182	181	180	181
1969	230	.98	1.77	.41	.51	—	228	227	227
1970	336	.97	1.63	.28	.36	.30	—	335	334
1971	443	1.18	1.98	.27	.14	.17	.43	—	442
1972	500	1.47	2.49	.18	.05	.07	.31	.57	—
Department service rating									
1967	143	86.15	5.17	—	140	143	142	141	141
1968	165	86.18	5.24	.93	—	165	164	163	162
1969	260	84.90	5.92	.80	.89	—	259	254	257
1970	351	85.75	5.67	.56	.70	.85	—	346	348
1971	463	86.11	5.81	.37	.55	.65	.89	—	460
1972	504	88.11	5.16	.26	.42	.51	.70	.89	—

TABLE 3 Police performance measures across years (*Continued*)

				Intercorrelations					
Year	N	Mean	SD	1967	1968	1969	1970	1971	1972
				Number of sick days used					
1967	144	6.20	6.19	–	144	144	143	142	143
1968	182	6.10	6.06	.30	–	182	181	180	181
1969	230	6.10	6.32	.31	.51	–	228	227	227
1970	336	5.40	10.76	.02	.01	.18	–	335	334
1971	443	5.74	6.23	.19	.22	.18	.21	–	442
1972	500	6.94	8.37	.14	.18	.11	–.01	.26	–

Note. The numbers above the diagonal are the count of cases for each correlation.

Size of correlation needed for significance:

	Number of cases for correlation				
Level of significance	127	152	202	302	402
$p < .05$	.174	.159	.138	.113	.098
$p < .01$	.228	.208	.181	.148	.128

different years, there is a general pattern of declining correlation as years intervene, with most variables showing a strong correlation between consecutive years. This is in agreement with the results reported by Furcon et al. (1971).

The subjective measure, department service rating, maintains fairly strong correlations across four to five years. The awards-related measure, letters of commendation, holds across two or three years. Unfortunately, there are no negative performance variables to compare with the results for citizen complaints and disciplinary actions. The arrest type measures also show consistent patterns. The traffic citations variable is the most stable, tending to correlate strongly over 5 or 6 years. Felony arrests hold for about 3 years, and misdemeanor arrests hold for about 2 years. Absences or sick days do not appear to be related from year to year.

The measures having no directly comparable variable in the Furcon et al. (1971) study also show strong stability across time. The number of accident reports and other reports taken, court cases, and convictions generally remain stable over 4 years.

An examination of the means and standard deviations of the variables for each year indicated no general pattern of increase or decrease across years. In order to investigate the relationship between these measures and years of service, the 6-year data was recombined according to each officer's tenure. For this part of the analysis the 2 officers with under 2 years of service were deleted.

Since tenure ranged from 2 to 25 years, there were 24 tenure cohorts, each with up to 6 years of longitudinal data. The data describing measures for the first year on the job resulted from combining the data from the first 5 tenure cohorts. For years 2 through 20 the measures resulted from pooling successive sets of 6 tenure cohorts, and points beyond 20 years were discarded because of the small numbers of officers with that much service.

In order to clarify the pooling procedure, the composition of the first tenure point will be described. Data representing measures for 1 year of service resulted from combining the 1971 data from the group with 2 years of service, the 1970 data from the group with 3 years of service, the 1969 data from the group with 4 years of service, the 1968 data from the group with 5 years of service, and the 1967 data from the cohort having 6 years of service. Figures 1 through 10 show the mean values for each variable plotted by years of service.

Relationships with Tenure

These figures show some apparently random fluctuations, but there is some interpretable degree of regularity, as well. For officers with 1 to 10 years of service, the average number of felony arrests (Figure 1) remains in the 60-70 range. It then shows a decline with tenure for officers with over 10 years of service. Arrests for misdemeanors (Figure 2) also starts high, in the 50-60 range, for officers with up to 7 years on the job. There is then a drop to an average of about 40 arrests per year, where it remains until the peak, shown by officers in their 18th year of service. On the other hand, the average number of traffic citations issued (Figure 3) stays low for officers at 1 to 7 years and then fluctuates about a higher level thereafter.

The taking of reports, both accident (Figure 4) and other (Figure 5), appears to be generally decreasing with tenure cohorts until the 17th year, where both averages increase abruptly.

The number of cases in court, as shown in Figure 6, is fairly steady until the 15th year cohort, where it begins to increase, peaking for officers at 18 years of service. The number of convictions (Figure 7) is similar, in that it remains steady for officers with up to 12 years' service, then increases to a peak at the 18-year cohort.

Figure 8 shows a fluctuating curve that stays above an average of one letter of commendation per year for the officers in the first 10 years of service and then drops to a lower level.

The department's service rating, shown in Figure 9, starts very low, as the officers enter the department, rises sharply for the officers in their first 7 years, and then levels off. After the 11th year cohort there may be a very slight downward trend, which is more pronounced for officers with over 16 years of service.

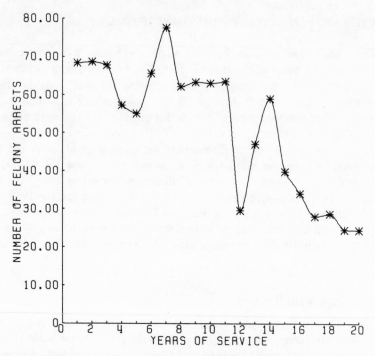

FIGURE 1 Mean number of felony arrests, by years of service.

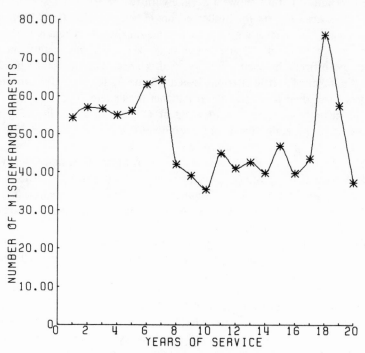

FIGURE 2 Mean number of misdemeanor arrests, by years of service.

98

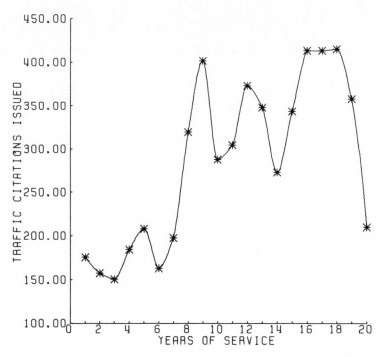

FIGURE 3 Mean number of traffic citations issued, by years of service.

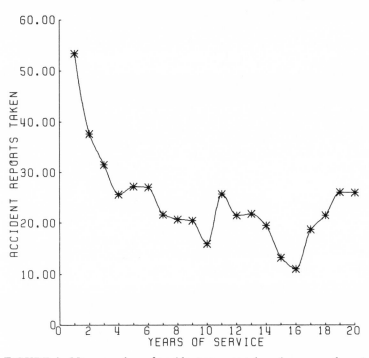

FIGURE 4 Mean number of accident reports taken, by years of service.

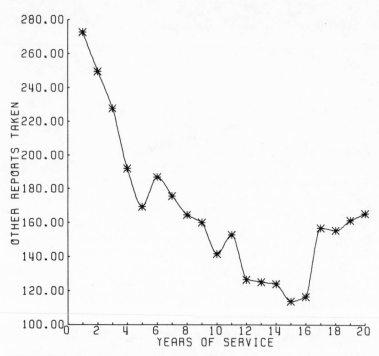

FIGURE 5 Mean number of other reports taken, by years of service.

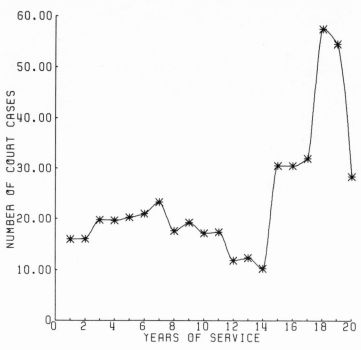

FIGURE 6 Mean number of court cases, by years of service.

100

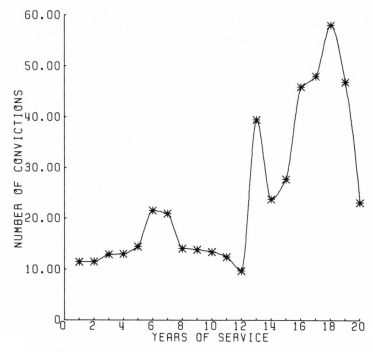

FIGURE 7   Mean number of convictions, by years of service.

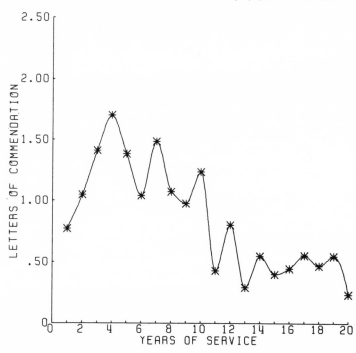

FIGURE 8   Mean number of letters of commendation, by years of service.

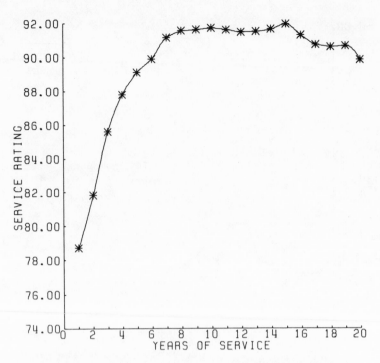

FIGURE 9 Mean department service rating, by years of service.

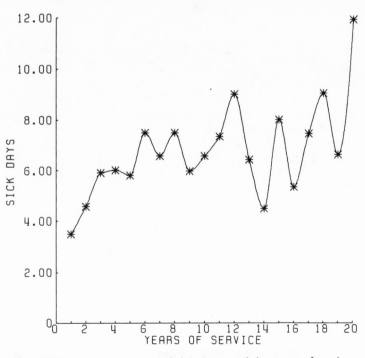

FIGURE 10 Mean number of sick days used, by years of service.

The number of sick days used shows little variation, as seen in Figure 10. After the first 2 years the general level of the curve appears to be constant.

Factor Analysis of Performance Measures

The variables tallied for 1972 and the one-time measures were factor analyzed as planned. All factor analyses were performed using the Statistical Package for the Social Sciences (SPSS) principal factor model, with iteration for communalities (Nie, Hull, Jenkins, Steinbrenner, & Bent, 1975). The rotation used was the direct oblimin, an oblique rotation. An examination of the latent roots led to the decision to extract and rotate six factors, which accounted for 55.77% of the total variance.

The variables used, their means and standard deviations, as well as the communalities, latent roots, and factor pattern matrix, are shown in Table 4. The intercorrelations between the factors are fairly low, as can be seen in Table 5. Variables with a factor loading less than .30 were not considered in the interpretation of the factor.

The first factor is composed of the subjective measures especially administered for the validation study, that is, the JPDS and PC rating. Note that for the JPDS a value of 1 represents the highest level of performance, with successively higher values reflecting lower performance. That is why the PC rating on factor 1 has a different sign from that of the JPDS variables. All these variables, then, are measuring the same facet of police performance.

Factor 2 concentrates on arrest-related activities. Its loadings include number of felony and misdemeanor arrests, court cases, convictions, and letters of commendation. It is obvious that these variables form a consistent police performance pattern.

Tenure and the department service rating dominate the third factor, with additional loadings for precinct citations and the PC rating. The factor indicates those variables with a strong tenure component.

The remaining three factors are composed of one or two variables, and thus are not so strong as the previous three. Academy grade and Academy rank form factor 4. Factor 5 consists of the number of acident reports and other reports. The number of traffic citations issued forms the lone loading for factor 6. Citizen complaints, charageable accidents, and sick days do not load onto any factor. These last three variables and the last three factors represent elements of police performance not contained in the first three factors but not represented by enough variables to form comprehensive factors.

DISCUSSION

The First Factor

It is interesting to find that the JPDS and the PC are measuring one common factor, which is probably global, or overall, performance. Although

TABLE 4 Performance measures used in the factor analysis ($N = 350$)

Variables	Mean	SD	h^2	Factor loadings					
				1	2	3	4	5	6
Job performance scales									
Handling domestic disputes	2.58	1.06	.59	.75	.09	-.01	.04	.04	.18
Investigating, etc.	2.58	1.25	.71	.82	-.02	-.16	.04	-.11	-.02
Crime prevention	3.57	1.44	.56	.72	-.03	-.05	-.02	.01	.06
Maintaining public safety	3.60	1.33	.65	.78	-.02	-.04	-.04	.02	.05
Using force appropriately	3.20	.87	.51	.61	.11	.10	-.05	.15	.24
Commitment, etc.	2.82	1.65	.65	.77	-.12	.07	-.02	-.05	-.14
Integrity, professional ethics	3.18	1.15	.58	.77	-.01	.05	.01	-.01	-.08
Dealing with public	3.40	1.16	.60	.74	-.04	.06	.09	.12	.13
Teamwork	2.35	.88	.49	.71	-.01	.05	.03	-.06	-.14
Report writing	3.06	1.12	.64	.72	-.09	-.11	-.12	-.09	-.01
Traffic maintenance	3.17	1.42	.74	.88	.02	-.01	.02	-.02	-.14
PC rating	50.87	7.65	.69	-.68	.02	.33	.10	.07	-.11

	Mean	SD	h²					
Years of service	4.36	2.73	.61	.01	-.17	.76	.07	-.07	.03
Academy grade	85.51	3.94	.85	.06	.02	.15	.92	.04	.02
Academy standing	52.88	27.13	.77	.07	.001	-.06	.90	.06	-.03
Precinct citations	1.69	3.10	.38	-.04	.06	.58	-.06	-.08	.03
Citizen complaints	.27	.45	.11	.02	.11	.22	.02	.16	.18
Chargeable accidents	.37	.48	.07	.07	-.01	.04	-.13	.03	.18
Felony arrests	65.43	54.37	.46	-.04	.56	.13	-.06	.20	-.18
Misdemeanor arrests	48.29	35.14	.37	.12	.45	-.17	-.003	.22	.20
Traffic citations issued	190.05	269.06	.19	-.04	-.09	.03	.03	-.11	.40
Accident reports taken	30.05	33.32	.36	.01	-.18	-.18	.02	.53	.01
Other reports taken	204.43	112.40	.99	-.10	.15	-.05	-.01	.93	-.18
Court cases	18.87	23.88	.92	.04	.97	-.003	.08	-.03	-.04
Convictions	13.13	17.99	.83	.03	.92	.04	.05	-.03	-.05
Letters of commendation	1.64	2.65	.45	-.06	.67	-.03	-.03	-.19	-.01
Department service rating	87.71	5.01	.75	-.26	.09	.67	.10	-.22	-.08
Sick days used	6.13	5.57	.08	.17	-.02	.05	-.15	.09	-.07
Latent roots				7.82	2.79	2.17	1.51	.81	.51

TABLE 5   Factor intercorrelations

Factor	1	2	3	4	5
1	−.25				
2	−.11	.17			
3	−.28	.03	.06		
4	.12	.18	−.21	−.15	
5	.10	.02	.12	−.04	.02

both measures are based on supervisory ratings, they do not totally reflect a "methods" factor, since the service rating does not load on that factor but yet is determined by supervisory rating.

Guion (1965) has reported the results from industrial studies that showed that traditional rating scales tend to reflect a single factor that is independent from objective measures. However, the JPDS is based on a procedure designed to produce independent and multidimensional scales of performance. After reviewing several similarly based behaviorally anchored scales, Schwab, Heneman, and Decotiis (1975) expressed skepticism about the purported multidimensionality of the scales and discussed why multidimensionality is hard to achieve.

It appears that, in addition, the separate scales of the JPDS do not adequately differentiate between various aspects of performance. Differentiation could have been shown by JPDS scales loading with related objective measures. For example, JPDS11, traffic maintenance and control, could have loaded with traffic citations in factor 6; JPDS10, report writing, could have appeared in factor 5 with the two report counts; and JPDS05, crime prevention, could have loaded with the arrest measures in factor 2. However, the JPDS is too overwhelmed by the general performance factor for this differentiation to occur.

Furcon (Note 2) used several subsamples from a wider collection of data to report in detail the relationships between the scales of the JPDS and the PC rating. Stepwise multiple-regression analysis resulted in multiple correlations ranging from .65 to .76 and using from two to five scales from the JPDS to predict the PC rating. These results are not in conflict with the factor analysis. However, since there is only one factor, the interpretation of the regression results is affected. That is, each scale is not really asking about a separate aspect of performance but is rather asking about the same aspect in a different way. Thus, the scales of the JPDS are like the items in a one-factor ability test.

The Other Factors

The remainder of the factor analysis results are equally interesting. They show that "subjective" and "objective" measures are indeed measuring different performance factors. The strongest factor of objective measures, factor 2, deals with one of the most common conceptions of a police officer's job, namely, crime fighting. It shows the police part of the criminal-justice cycle from arrests, carried through the courts and possibly ending with a letter of commendation. However, there are other police duties besides making arrests.

What part of the police job is described by factor 3? This factor shows high tenure, high ratings, and high citations. From one perspective, this factor could be describing the administrative response to good, routine police work, carried out over a long period of time. A supervisor may wish to acknowledge, through ratings and citations, the value of continuous good work of a routine nature.

There is little that can be said about the remaining factors and the nonloading variables. It is clear that the academy performance measures, the taking of reports, and the issuing of traffic citations reflect aspects of police performance different from each other and different from the first three factors. It is probably true that accidents and sick days are really random events, and while they are headaches for administrators, they have little to do with individual police performance. On the other hand, citizen complaints deal with an important part of performance. It is unfortunate that there were not enough of the negative measures to replicate the negative factor, as reported by Baehr and Froemel (Note 1).

Patterns of Performance

An examination of the figures depicting the relationship between performance measures and tenure reveals some consistent changes in levels of performance. For officers at about 7 years of service there starts a pattern characterized by a decrease in misdemeanor arrests, an increase in traffic citations issued, a minor peak in court cases and convictions, and a stable service rating. Around the 11th year a pattern develops that shows a drop in felony arrests, a leveling of misdemeanor arrests, a surge in taking reports, and a decrease in letters of commendation. The 18th year of service shows peaks for misdemeanor arrests, traffic citations, court cases, and convictions.

The data are not definitive enough to explain these patterns. They may merely be artifacts of this sample. However, Baehr, Furcon, and Froemel (1969) report eight empirically derived patterns of patrol performance, characterized by differing years of service and levels of performance. Those patterns belonging to "newcomers" had mean tenures of 4.85, 6.36, and 4.54;

the "established" patrol officers showed mean tenures of 10.11, 9.62, and 9.00; and the "old-timers" served for means of 23.09 and 16.15 years.

The finding of tenure-based performance clusters in one set of data and the appearance of consistent performance levels in another suggest that there really is some systematic change akin to developmental stages in the police career. These changes may reflect formal changes in orientation, as when an assignment or emphasis in an assignment is shifted formally by the department. Or they may reflect informal changes resulting from the officers' readjustment of behavior, based on some self-directed re-evaluation of their careers. In any case, this is a topic worthy of further study, a topic that may have implications for career guidance and development in the police profession.

Best Measures

The results of this report do little to answer questions about the "best" performance measure to use. Since there are a variety of reasons for assessing performance, it is likely that what is best for one purpose is inappropriate for another. However, several cautions can be elaborated regarding the use of objective and subjective measures.

Objective measures

In the first place, the objective measures all deal with specific aspects of performance, and care must be exercised to ensure that all relevant aspects are considered. This requires attention to the officer's assigned duties. For an officer on desk duty the number of arrests would probably be irrelevant, whereas the number of reports would be relevant. However, the count of reports would also be relevant for patrol duty, albeit to a different degree. And how can a set of objective measures deal with an officer whose duties have changed within the assessment period?

In addition, the changes in external situations affecting the values of objective measures must be considered. The oscillation of mean values in Table 4 reflects this problem. The officer who made about 67 misdemeanor arrests in 1967 and then dropped to about 59 arrests in 1968 did not really suffer a decrease in performance level. Both values are averages for their respective years, and the correlation of .80 between years indicates that the officers who made many misdemeanor arrests in 1967 were still making many arrests in 1968. There was some change in the situation that affected the number of misdemeanor arrests between 1967 and 1968. Although it is not important to know what that change was, it is important to account for the effect it had on the number of arrests. Standardization of measures by assignment and within rating period could resolve some of these problems of interpretation.

Subjective measures

Subjective measures tend to deal with overall performance. Even a seemingly differentiated instrument like the JPDS is really measuring only one factor of performance.

The reliance on human judgment, which characterizes subjective measures, is both the strength and the weakness of the measurements. When the rater "takes into account" situational changes, the temporal stability is increased. That is, the assessment of performance holds up longer under a variety of circumstances. But when the rater lets irrelevant considerations influence judgments, the assessment of performance becomes invalid. It is extremely important to guard against such irrelevant influences. The training of raters and the selection of appropriate scaling techniques can do much to alleviate this problem. Even so, subjective measures should be examined for evidence of such rater effects prior to their use.

CONTINUING RESEARCH

There are currently several ongoing research efforts building on the results of these analyses. In the first place, the belief in the multidimensional quality of police performance has been again reinforced. Thus ongoing studies are once more examining a variety of performance measures. Newer police performance scales using both the behavioral anchoring technique, as does the JPDS, and the mixed standards technique (Blanz & Ghiselli, 1972) are being collected along with the usual array of objective measures and the PC rating.

The PC rating has not been a major part of this report, but there are several research efforts under way that deal specifically with this rating. A recently published study by Saunders, Baehr, and Froemel (1977) reports on methods for identifying and correcting the effects of racial bias and job tenure in PC ratings.

Another study is concerned with the "relativity" of the PC rating. It is well known that PC ratings are expressed on a scale relative to the rating group. Intergroup comparisons are now based on assumptions that generally hold but that make users uncomfortable. This research study is directed at developing a behaviorally anchored PC rating, which will remove this relative quality and allow direct intergroup comparisons. And finally, there is the opportunity to study the stability of the PC rating across time and across varying situations.

The problem of using multiple performance measures in prediction models is also being investigated. The technique of canonical correlations was devised by Hotelling (1935) to deal with this very issue. However, the method has been little used, probably because of the difficulty in interpreting the results. Recently these difficulties have received serious theoretical attention. Bock

(1975) has suggested one way to interpret results, and Cliff and Krus (1976) have suggested another. Sanders's (Note 3) resolution of the interpretation problem is a technique called interbattery factor analysis. These techniques should be examined for their practical applicability to multidimensional performance prediction.

Finally, there are plans to develop and test a structural model of police performance, using the various types of measures. Ghiselli (1956) identified three concepts of dimensionality: "static," which referred to simple multidimensionality at any one time; "dynamic," which referred to factorial changes occurring over time as a result of learning or development; and "individual," which considered factorial differences due to individual styles of performance. A structural model could begin to explore these concepts and lead to an increased understanding of police performance by showing the influence of these measures on each other.

SUMMARY

This chapter has presented the results from a study that was a part of a continuing research program aimed at a better understanding of police performance measures. Using data from a sample of 509 uniformed patrol officers, the study examined both objective and subjective measures for (a) their stability across six years, (b) their change in relation to years of service, and (c) their factorial structure or dimensionality.

Stability across time was shown to vary differently for the different measures. Some held for only 2 years, while others remained stable for over 4 years. The variables also exhibited differential change over years of service. The changes were fairly consistent and were thought to reflect the effects of learning or development on the job. Finally, the performance measures were shown to consist of six factors. The first three factors were clearly interpretable, while the last three were suggestive of other performance dimensions.

REFERENCES

Baehr, M. E. The appraisal of job performance (Occasional Paper No. 27-R1). Chicago: University of Chicago, Industrial Relations Center, 1968.

Baehr, M. E., Furcon, J. E., & Froemel, E. C. *Psychological assessment of patrolman qualifications in relation to field performance.* Washington, D.C.: U.S. Government Printing Office, 1969.

Blanz, F., & Ghiselli, E. E. The mixed standard scale: A new rating system. *Personnel Psychology*, 1972, *25*, 185–199.

Bock, R. D. *Multivariate statistical methods in behavioral research.* New York: McGraw-Hill, 1975.

Cliff, N., & Krus, D. J. Interpretation of canonical analysis: Rotated vs. unrotated solutions. *Psychometrika*, 1976, *41*, 35–42.

Furcon, J. E., & Fromel, E. C. *The relationship of selected psychological tests to measures of police officer job performance in the state of Illinois.* Chicago: University of Chicago, Industrial Relations Center, 1973.

Furcon, J. E., Froemel, E. C., Franczak, R. G., & Baehr, M. E. *A longitudinal study of psychological test predictors and assessments of patrolmen field performance.* Chicago: University of Chicago, Industrial Relations Center, 1971.

Ghiselli, E. E. Dimensional problems of criteria. *Journal of Applied Psychology,* 1956, *40,* 1–4.

Guion, R. M. *Personnel testing.* New York: McGraw-Hill, 1965.

Heckman, R. W., Groner, D. M., Dennette, M. D., & Johnson P. D. *Development of psychiatric standards for police selection.* Minneapolis: Personnel Decisions, Inc., 1972.

Hotelling, H. The most predictable criterion. *The Journal of Educational Psychology,* 1935, *26,* 139–143.

Nie, N. H., Hull, C. H., Jenkins, J. G., Steinbrenner, K., & Bent, D. H. *SPSS: Statistical Package for the Social Sciences* (2nd ed.). New York: McGraw-Hill, 1975.

Saunders, D. R., Baehr, M. E., & Froemel, E. C. Identification of, and correction for, effects of racial bias and job tenure on supervisory ratings of bus-operator performance. *Psychological Reports,* 1977, *40,*859–865.

Schwab, D. P., Heneman, H. G., III, & Decotiis, T. A. Behaviorally anchored rating scales: A review of the literature. *Personnel Psychology,* 1975, *28,* 549–562.

REFERENCE NOTES

1. Baehr, M. E., & Froemel, E. C. The Arrow-dot test as a predictor of police officer performance. *Perceptual Motor Skills,* 1977, *45,* 683–693.
2. Furcon, J. E. Behaviorally anchored job performance description scales as predictors of overall paired-comparison ratings of police officer success. In M. E. Baehr (Chair), *Job Performance Appraisal.* Symposium presented at the meeting of the Illinois Psychological Association, Chicago, November 1975.
3. Saunders, D. R. Personal communication, December 1975.

III

BIOGRAPHICAL FACTORS, APTITUDES, INTERESTS, AND VALUES IN POLICE SELECTION

7

THE CIVIL SERVICE EXAM HAS BEEN PASSED: NOW WHAT?

Wayne F. Cascio
School of Business and Organizational Sciences,
Florida International University, Miami, Florida

Leslie J. Real
Manager of Labor Relations, City of Memphis, Tennessee

In the best of all possible worlds, personnel selection decisions would be errorless. We would give each applicant a job tryout and then six months or a year later decide which applicants performed best on the job. Obviously, this kind of approach is totally unrealistic in police work, since the time, money, and hazards involved are too great. For this reason we need some accurate way of *forecasting* which applicants are likely to be more successful police officers than others so that we can select all or some portion of these applicants. This is the basic rationale underlying the use of tests and other predictive devices in personnel selection. But tests and other predictive devices are useful only to the extent that they help administrators/managers make decisions. The more accurate the decisions are (that is, the more of those selected on the basis of tests and other predictive devices who turn out to be successful performers) the more valuable these instruments of prediction become.

All other things being equal, personnel selection decisions are more accurate the longer the period of time we have to observe the candidates and the more job-related information we can collect about them. The typical police officer selection process capitalizes on both of these factors by using a multiple-hurdle approach to selection (see Figure 1).

In a multiple-hurdle approach each applicant must successfully pass all steps in the selection process before a final acceptance decision is made. This approach is noncompensatory in that failure at any one step in the selection

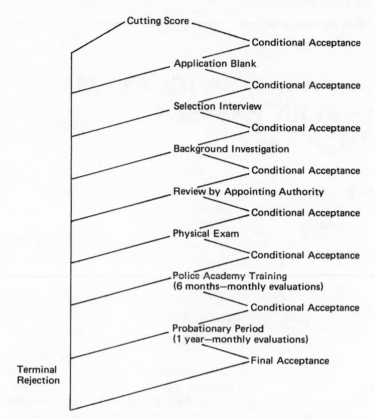

FIGURE 1 Typical police officer selection process—Civil Service Examination.

process cannot be compensated for by outstanding performance at another step. Thus, an applicant who fails the physical exam is terminally rejected regardless of how well he or she did on the previous hurdles (civil service exam, application blank, background investigation, etc.).

Assuming that each phase in the selection process contributes some unique and relevant information about later job performance as a police officer, the net result of requiring each applicant to clear eight hurdles and to be observed and rated for 18 months prior to final acceptance is that more accurate hiring decisions will be made and higher-quality police officers will result. We hasten to emphasize, however, that these positive benefits will only come about if each hurdle validly measures some ability, skill, or personal characteristic that is *in fact* important to successful job performance as a police officer.

The purpose of this chapter is to focus on four of the most widely used nontest methods for assessing candidates for police officer jobs: educational standards, selection interviews, background investigations, and application blanks (biographical predictors). While the application blank and, to a certain extent, the interview are based on the applicant's own statement of what he or she did in the past, educational standards and background investigations rely on the opinions of relevant others to help evaluate what and how well the applicant did in the past. The rationale underlying all four methods (with the exception of certain interview approaches) is that past behavior is the best predictor of future behavior. When properly validated, all four methods can be valuable police selection tools, as we shall see.

EDUCATIONAL STANDARDS FOR POLICE OFFICERS

The amount of formal education that is either necessary or desirable for police officers is a topic that has provoked considerable discussion among law enforcement personnel in recent years. Indeed, *The Police Chief* magazine devoted its August 1976 issue to critical areas of education and training. In short, is it true that better educated individuals do make better police officers and that less educated individuals tend to make poorer police officers? Federal law enforcement agencies think so, and they require a college degree as a minimum education prerequisite for employment (Cascio & Real, 1976).

In fact, all major studies that have dealt with the question of improving law enforcement have recommended higher education for police officers. Thus the American Bar Association, the Police Foundation's Task Force on Education and Training, the National Advisory Commission on Civil Disorders, and the President's Commission on Law Enforcement and Administration of Justice support higher education as a requirement for recruits. One reason for such emphasis may be the belief that a liberal education is required if police are to escape the rigid conservatism that seemed to characterize police thinking in the 1960s (Finnigan, 1976).

To be sure, law enforcement personnel encounter a broad spectrum of social conditions in their work. The modern police officer's daily job requires that he or she balance the sworn responsibility of upholding laws and maintaining the peace with the observance of acceptable social norms concerning professionalism and discretion.

In recent years there have been numerous complaints by the public that police officers are not sensitive to the problems of specialized groups. On one hand officers are expected to behave in many situations with tact, empathy, and understanding, and on the other hand, they are expected to be able to react and deal effectively with individuals who only respond to physical force. In short, police suffer from our society's many contradictory role demands. Perhaps the best way to cope with these apparent contradictions is by developing in police officers a broad conceptual base for understanding them. One method of doing this may be by encouraging officers to expand their formal educational experiences.

Support for this strategy comes from a comparison of behavioral styles of college graduate versus noncollege police officers (Trojanowicz & Nicholson, 1976). Noncollege officers prefer to follow schedules and daily routines; move against an aggressor or counterattack more rapidly when somebody acts toward them in a belligerent or aggressive manner; consider themselves to be practical and sensible, with both feet on the ground, as opposed to imaginative, ingenious, and having novel ideas; like to work closely with their supervisors rather than by themselves; would rather have their supervisors make decisions for them; and finally, value themselves according to how successfully they have conformed to the role requirements of the organization.

In contrast, college graduate officers are willing to experiment and try new things, as opposed to preferring the established and conventional way of doing things; prefer to assume leadership roles and like to direct and supervise the work of others; use a step-by-step method for processing information and reaching decisions; like to engage in work providing a lot of excitement and a great deal of variety, as opposed to work providing a stable and secure future; and finally, value themselves by their achievement of the status symbols established by their culture.

In short, college graduate officers are considerably different from their noncollege counterparts. The former like to have less direction from supervisors and like a job that is more challenging. This may in fact cause problems for the organization due to the graduate's reaction to the routine activities often found in police organizations, but such problems are beyond the scope of this chapter (cf. Trojanowicz & Nicholson). For our purposes, the key question is whether college graduate police officers perform more effectively on the street than noncollege officers do. If higher educational standards are to be used in police selection, then it is necessary to present evidence of superior performance that supports the higher educational requirements.

Until recently such evidence was scanty, but in 1976 two studies based on empirical evidence appeared. In one study the performance of 97 noncollege officers was compared to that of 113 college graduate officers in the Baltimore Police Department (Finnigan, 1976). After controlling experimentally for the effects of age, IQ, race, and military service, the college-educated officers were consistently rated significantly higher than the noncollege officers. The type of college degree (e.g., law enforcement, sociology, business) was irrelevant.

Rated performance in this study was divided into four main categories: (1) performance of various types of duties (regular duties, additional duties, administrative duties, supervision of subordinates/officers, handling citizens, evaluation of subordinates, training personnel, and tactical handling of officers), (2) exhibition of various traits and characteristics (endurance, personal appearance, dignity of demeanor, attention to duty, cooperation, initiative, judgment, presence of mind, force leadership, loyalty, personal relations, and economy in management), (3) overall general value to the department, and (4) the willingness of the rater to have the officer under his command based on actual or perceived judgments of the officer's ability in crisis situations.

In a different study Cascio and Real (1976) examined the relationship between amount of formal education and rated performance, as well as actual on-the-street performance (e.g., number of preventable accidents, injuries by assault and battery) of 940 police officers from the Dade County, Florida, Public Safety Department. Of these officers 825 were white, 60 were black, and 53 were Latin American.

Of the 44 criteria that were related to amount of education for each subgroup, 16 showed significant results for one or more subgroups. Although the magnitude of the correlations was small, a fairly consistent pattern developed. That is, higher levels of education tended to be associated with fewer total injuries, fewer injuries by assault and battery, fewer disciplinary actions from accidents, fewer preventable accidents, fewer sick times per year, fewer physical force allegations, and so forth. Common sense may well explain some of these statistical relationships between education and police officer performance. Fewer injuries as a result of assault and battery, for example, could be related to an individual's superior ability to understand and diagnose situations without having to resort to force. Fewer verbal discourtesy allegations may be the result of the individual's ability to speak clearly, forcefully, and articulately.

Attempts to relate supervisory ratings of job performance to amount of formal education did not show statistical significance in terms of any single area such as job knowledge, judgment, initiative, dependability, demeanor, attitude, relations with others, or communication. However, overall rated performance was significantly related to amount of formal education. These relationships held up even after the effects of age and length of service were statistically removed. Like the Finnigan (1976) study, major area of college study had no appreciable effect on either rated or actual on-the-street performance.

To illustrate further the value of education in terms of police performance, a composite performance index was constructed for each individual by simply adding together his standing on each of the 16 criteria found to be relevant for the entire group. On this composite index, scores ranged in value from 0 to 104. All officers whose performance scores fell below the median (the point on the performance scale that divides the upper 50% of the scores from the lower 50% of the scores) were defined as superior performers. Higher scores indicated more personnel complaints, legal investigations, use of force reports, etc. These relationships are presented graphically in Figure 2.

Figure 2 has been presented for all police officers, although similar charts could have been drawn for each subgroup. Results for whites, blacks, and Spanish-surnamed personnel were essentially equivalent. Figure 2 shows that,

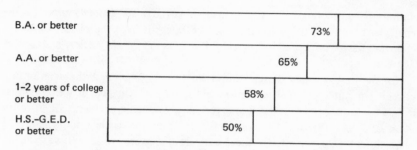

FIGURE 2 Institutional expectancy chart—all police officers
($N = 940$).

as the level of education increases, the level of performance also increases. Thus there appears to be a systematic relationship (at least in terms of the 16 criteria considered in this study) between police officer performance and amount of formal education.

In a follow-up study using the same group of officers, Cascio (1977) investigated the possibility that the effects of intelligence and motivation, rather than the level of education per se, differentiated effective from ineffective performers. Using path analysis (a statistical technique for testing causal hypotheses), Cascio demonstrated that while the *direct effect* of intelligence on performance was negligble, both motivation and formal education predicted police officer performance significantly. However, their effects were not confounded. That is, the *direct effect* of motivation on performance was significant, as was the *direct effect* of education on performance, but the correlation between motivation and education was only .09.

These results indicate that formal educational level does deserve serious consideration as a police officer selection variable. Motivational level is likewise important as a predictor of police performance in and of itself. Taken together, formal education and motivational level should both be considered in predicting police officer performance. The broad intellectual base, along with the diagnostic and logical skills that an individual tends to develop through college course work, could be decisive in his or her ability to handle the dynamics and complexities inherent in the job of a contemporary professional law enforcement officer.

THE SELECTION INTERVIEW

The selection interview has been a standard tool of personnel administration for some time. Its advantage is that it provides the hiring authority with firsthand information on the applicant. It gives the applicant a chance to perform and gives the hiring authority the opportunity to evaluate qualities that can only be elicited through a face-to-face meeting.

Unfortunately, until recently the validity of the selection interview in the prediction of police performance was not supported with evidence. However, Landy (1976) successfully validated a selection interview that was used with applicants for the position of patrol officer with the Dade County, Florida, Public Safety Department. All applicants had applied for positions between August 1972 and August 1973, and all applicants had previously passed a civil service examination.

Each applicant was interviewed by a panel of three individuals—two of whom were members of the personnel bureau of the police department and the third a police officer of a supervisory rank, usually a sergeant. The police officer was chosen from a pool of 40 line officers who had been trained in interviewing techniques by the personnel bureau. In the time period specified, 399 white male applicants were interviewed by both of the personnel officers, but the police officer interviewer changed periodically. For this reason, it might be better to think of the third member of the board as a composite or role rather than a single individual. Of the 399 applicants, 150 were ultimately hired and 249 were rejected.

Each applicant was interviewed for one hour, with a numerical score kept in nine areas. This score was determined independently by each panel member after the interview. The following areas were scored: appearance, communication skills, education, experience, employment history, social sensitivity, apparent emotional stability, responsibility/maturity, and sincerity of purpose. An average (mean) score was computed for each dimension, and these scores were then forwarded to the personnel department to be evaluated in addition to other selection factors. Since each of the panel members made independent ratings of each of the applicants on each of the traits, it was possible to compute indexes of reliability for each trait. The intraclass correlation coefficients for each of the traits were as follows: appearance = .87, communication skills = .82, education = .98, experience = .92, employment history = .82, social sensitivity = .81, apparent emotional stability = .80, responsibility/maturity = .83, sincerity of purpose = .87, and the final overall recommendation, suitability for position = .94. These data indicate a high degree of agreement among the three raters as a group.

Since it is not the purpose of this chapter to discuss performance criteria, suffice it to say that these ratings were related to eight behaviorally anchored rating scales of police officer performance (cf., Landy, Farr, Saal, & Freytag, 1976). The analysis indicated that the oral-board reliably predicted on-the-street behavior two years later. Probably the major reason for this was that specific areas to be evaluated in the interview were in fact relevant to police performance. (See Figure 3.)

Prediction of an applicant's probable future behavior in law enforcement

Name of Applicant _____ Date _____

Signature of Interviewer _____

FACTORS TO BE RATED		Score
Appearance Appropriateness of Dress, Neatness, Grooming, Physical Presence of Stature	**0** Unfavorable impression, unsuitable appearance **2** Unimpressive, untidy, negative impression **3 / 4** Clean, neat, in good taste, appropriate **5** Distinctly favorable impression; leaves positive image	
Communication skills Effectiveness of Expression, Voice Quality, Vocabulary, Grammar, Ability to Communicate	**0 / 1** Confused or involved explanations, speech slurred or indistinct **2 / 3** Poor presentation, vague, limited vocabulary, poor diction **4 / 5 / 6** Satisfactory presentation, adequate vocabulary, proper grammar, usage **7 / 8** Strong presentation, direct and relevant verbal response **9 / 10** Impressive clear presentation, high-verbal skills, well-organized thoughts	
Education Amount and Relationship to Position	**0** GED **1 / 2** High school **3** Associate degree **4** Bachelor's degree **5** Bathelor's degree in job-related field or any postgraduate work	
Experience Previous Work History, Public Contact and Military Experience in Relation to Requirements of Position	**0 / 1** Lacking sufficient experience for position **2 / 3** Little or no related experience **4 / 5** Good compatible experience **6 / 7 / 8** Well rounded in experience for job requirements **9 / 10 / 11 / 12** Outstanding overall experience record	
Employment Job Hopping, Dismissal, Progress, Career Development and Objectives, Responsible Positions Held	**0** Dismissals for cause, indiscriminate job hopping **2 / 3** Continuing history of poor performance or progress, short-term employment **5 / 6 / 7** Stability, progress, good performance **8 / 9 / 10** Evidence of career goals, stability, progress, responsible previous positions **11 / 12** Strong evidence of goals and progress, highly responsible positions held	
Social Sensitivity Interest and Understanding of Others, Concern for Community Welfare, Knowledge of Current Events	**0 / 1** Intolerant, highly prejudiced, no social awareness **2 / 3** Unresponsive, noncommittal, resentful **4 / 5 / 6** Responsive, tolerant, aware **7 / 8** Wholesome attitudes, knowledgable **9 / 10** Superior understanding of others, concern over community welfare, high degree of social awareness	

122

Apparent Emotional Stability
Degree of Composure, Self-Control, Confidence, Emotionalism, Awareness of Strengths and Weaknesses

- **0 / 1** — Timid, withdrawn, lacking self-control, belligerent
- **2 / 3** — Defensive, ill at ease, lacking restraint, unsure of self, unaware of own shortcomings
- **5 / 6 / 7** — Composed, good control, apparently even temperament, sufficiently confident for job
- **8 / 9 / 10** — Poised, well balanced, good self-control, at ease, aware of own shortcomings
- **11 / 12** — Exceptionally well balanced, excellent self-control, well adjusted

Responsibility—Maturity
Judgment, Dependability, Family and Marital Background, Financial Conditions, Moderation in Habits

- **0 / 1** — Strong evidence of poor judgment or immaturity
- **2 / 3** — Indication of poor judgment or immaturity
- **5 / 6 / 7** — Maturity and responsibility consistent with age and background
- **8 / 9 / 10** — Indication of good judgment and responsibility
- **11 / 12** — Strong evidence of good judgment and responsibility

Sincerity of Purpose
Police Interest, Desire, Preparation for Career Goals, Enthusiasm

- **0 / 1** — Minimum effort, apparently uninterested
- **2 / 3** — Little evidence of any long-term goals or interests
- **4 / 5 / 6** — Shows interest, adequate preparation and enthusiasm
- **7 / 8 / 9** — Indication of desire, preparation, and goals
- **10** — Strong evidence of desire, preparation, and goals

Suitability for Position
What Is Your Appraisal of Applicant?

- **0** — Not recommended, unacceptable
- **2** — Recommended with hesitancy
- **4 / 6 / 8** — Recommended, average risk
- **10** — Recommended with confidence, good candidate, well qualified
- **12** — Highly recommended, exceptional candidate

Comments: _____

Total Score: _____

FIGURE 3 Oral interviews rating form.

123

is based on the assumption that people tend to behave relatively consistently under similar circumstances and that a knowledge of present and past behavior will establish a basis for predicting future behavior. Knowledge of present behavior may be derived from observation during the interview situation. Knowledge of past behavior may be developed from an analysis of the application form, from skillful questioning during the interview, and from reference-check data. In the following sections we offer practical suggestions for conducting selection interviews.

Preparation for a selection interview involves two important steps:

1. Knowing as much as possible about the job to be filled and the requirements for good performance in that job. Consider what qualifications the person in this job needs in order to demonstrate effective performance.
2. Finding out as much as possible from the application form about the candidate's background.

A selection interview is face-to-face communication that is initiated for a specific purpose and focuses on specific content areas. It differs from mere conversation because of its explicit purpose. It is not an interrogation because it should feature free interchange between the people involved. Since few people are born with the ability to interview, departments should provide necessary training in the interviewing process.

No matter how good the system is, the key to the interview process will be the quality of those who do the interviewing. It is imperative, then, that only those with a keen interest in interviewing and the intellectual ability to do it well be selected as interviewers. Once selected, individuals must be trained in how to conduct the interview. The following is an outline of one format that may be used in such a training program.

Preparing for the Interview

The interviewer is seriously handicapped if he or she fails to study the available data on the applicant's background before the interview. These preliminary data provide a frame of reference for understanding the full significance of the candidate's responses.

Preparatory steps

The interviewer should be sure to read over the application form, carefully making notes of items to be followed up in the interview and examine test scores, reference letters, and background information, if available. When reading the application form, the interviewer should note the following:

1. Any gaps in background
2. Insufficient responses to items
3. Inconsistencies of any sort
4. Attitudes reflected in key statements regarding reasons for leaving previous jobs and plans for the future
5. The manner in which the application was filled out (correctness of spelling, level of word choice, completeness of answers, attention to detail, accuracy, neatness, etc.)

The interviewer should always review test results if there are any in the file. He or she should not attempt to use raw test scores unless the panel moderator or staff psychologist interprets the scores.

Conducting the Interview

The interviewer's first objective is to establish rapport. The candidate is naturally tense and anxious; it's up to the interviewer to relieve this tension. It is generally agreed that the way to establish rapport is to create a nonthreatening, permissive, and supportive atmosphere. The applicant must be made to feel he or she is among friends and that the interviewer has the applicant's best interests at heart—that the interviewer is an understanding person, trying hard to see the applicant's point of view.

It's good to engage in friendly conversation at the beginning of the interview. The interviewer can ask the applicant how he or she happened to apply for the job or can pick out some item of common interest from the application form to chat lightly about—the applicant's home town, mutual acquaintances from the town, anything of common interest. The interviewer should put life into his or her voice and facial expression, inject a bit of humor into the conversation if this comes naturally, indicate in every way that he or she is interested in the applicant as an individual.

Planning

It is a good idea to have an outline to follow—something brief and simple—but it is not necessary to stick to it religiously. The applicant may jump around from topic to topic, and the interviewer may find it advantageous to let him or her do that, within limits. Nevertheless, an outline such as the following may serve as a useful guide:

1. Introduction (put the applicant at ease, break ice)
2. Get the applicant to talk about himself or herself
   a. Work history (start with present job and work backward in time)
   b. Service experience
   c. Education (formal and special courses)

   d. Outside interests and activities (spare time activities)
   e. Family responsibilities and relationships
   f. Goals (immediate and long range)
3. Tell the applicant about the job and job requirements
4. Allow a period of questions and answers, encouraging the applicant to ask
   questions
5. Close the interview by telling the applicant what happens next in the
   hiring procedure

Open-ended questions

The interviewer should avoid asking questions that can be answered with a *yes* or *no*, instead posing open-ended questions that call for lengthy answers, answers that shed light on the applicant's opinions. If questions begin with *how, when,* or *why,* they are probably open-ended. Leading questions, which suggest a particular answer, are a bad idea because the applicant will be sure to give the answer he or she thinks the interviewer is looking for.

Regarding work history, for example, the interviewer might try leading off with a question like, "Tell me about your job at the XYZ Company." The way the applicant answers this question will indicate what he or she feels is important. If a job candidate is slow to get going, the interviewer can ask about likes and dislikes in a previous job; *why* that job was appealing in the first place. Then the interviewer can probe more deeply into such topics as the following:

level and complexity of work
extent of responsibilities
motivation
attitudes and feelings
effectiveness on the job
achievements
interpersonal relationships
level of authority

What the interviewer is looking for is an idea of the candidate's growth, direction, stability, achievement, and interpersonal skills. This involves examining several crucial areas.

   1. *Relevancy of previous work experience.* How relevant is past experience to the duties and responsibilities of a police officer? An interviewer should not insist on *identical* experience; similar experience, as a rule, is desirable.

   2. *Likes and dislikes.* What were the applicant's likes and dislikes in previous jobs with the same requirements as law enforcement?

   3. *Reasons for leaving.* These reasons are especially significant. If they are

honestly reported, they will help determine the probable level of job satisfaction that the candidate would experience if hired for the present opening. If there has been a succession of short-term jobs in the applicant's work history, this may raise doubts concerning the candidate's performance on past jobs and/or the possibility of pleasing him or her in any given job. Sometimes separations that are reported by candidates as resignations are, in truth, discharges. In summary, examine the applicant's overall job picture.

Personal background

Next the interviewer should explore the applicant's armed service background and go on to his or her formal education. Helpful information includes the candidate's major field, academic performance, attitudes about courses, reasons for attending a particular school and choosing a particular major, and nature of extracurricular activity. Then an interviewer will want to examine outside interests and leisure activities. Finally, he or she should look at family and personal material, including the applicant's personal goals.

What is the significance of exploring these areas of an applicant's background? In the following pages we will look at some examples.

Armed service record Experience in the armed services is similar in many respects to law enforcement. The service is an example (in most situations) of a highly structured environment where the individual's life is regulated and ordered. Also, in time of war a person in the service can be under a great deal of stress. The areas to be explored relative to service experience are similar to those described in the section on work experience. Special attention, however, should be paid to the applicant's attitudes and feelings about such a structured environment and about the stress that often accompanies it.

Education Choices in education, as well as amount of formal education, can shed light on an applicant's personality, motivation, character, and interests.

In what subjects was he or she best and poorest (or liked most and least)? If, for example, a candidate liked English, history, and languages, you can reasonably assume strength in verbal skills. If an applicant liked chemistry, biology, and physics, this probably indicates scientific interest and aptitude. Night school attendance or having worked one's way through school may indicate perserverance, energy, and industry. Likewise, academic performance (good grades) is an indicator of achievement, as well as of a sense of responsibility. Holding class offices would indicate not only leadership ability but favorable personal relationships.

In short, school performance can be an important indicator. The New York Telephone Company did an interesting study of hires from New York City high schools. They found that students with good attendance records were seven times more likely to succeed at work and five times more likely to succeed if they got excellent or good grades on character than students with poor attendance records.

Outside interests   Since a person has more freedom of choice in outside activities, these can be particularly revealing. Note how varied or restricted the applicant's outside activities are. Note whether they are solitary in nature or of a group type. Solitary activities might indicate that the person is a "loner." Extensive group activities can indicate an outgoing nature and might indicate an aptitude for leadership. Extensive participation in sports would indicate a high energy level and good physical health, as well as an ability to work closely with others on teams.

Personal goals and objectives   A discussion of what the applicant is aiming toward in terms of both immediate job and long-range objectives is often a good way to summarize the section of the interview dealing with an exploration of the applicant's history.

The foregoing material suggests that the questions likely to yield the greatest information are those dealing with significant decisions made by the applicant throughout his or her behavioral history. The interviewer should be certain to focus attention on such specific areas as the following:

choice of course in school and higher education
reasons for any changes in course of education
activity during summers while at school
choice of branch of armed service and length of tour of duty
choice of career, field of work
reasons for changes in career, field of work
choice of particular company and job at start of work
reasons for changes to subsequent companies and jobs
choice of location of home and reasons for any changes
timing of marriage and choice of spouse
reasons for wanting to make a job change at this time
extent and range of spare time activities
current relationship with family

Interviewing Techniques

Controlling the interview

A skillful interviewer controls the interview and keeps it on track—but without appearing to do so. The interviewer must be sure to cover all areas and to see that each gets its full quota of time. In particular, it is necessary to get an explanation for any inconsistencies, time gaps, and missing data noted in advance of the interview.

Digging for negatives

When probing for possible unfavorable information, it is important to be subtle. For example, an interviewer who has reason to believe that the applicant is a slow worker might phrase a statement as follows: "I get the impression that quality is especially important to you and that you will take whatever time is necessary to make sure that work is done right, even though it may mean sacrificing speed to do it." Statements like this suggest to the applicant the the interviewer is favorably impressed, and the way the applicant responds will often yield additional useful information. In those instances where a threatening question cannot be successfully disguised, it is advisable to ask it toward the close of the interview; otherwise, it will often affect overall rapport adversely. Near the end there will be less to lose because the bulk of the interview will have already been accomplished.

Nonverbal communication

During an interview the interviewer is continually evaluating the applicant's words, gestures, facial expressions, hesitations, actions, and reactions, but those who are truly skilled in the art do not show their own reactions in any way. The slightest nonverbal response by the interviewer to any of these things may make the applicant "clam up." Remember, he or she is watching the interviewer's face, too!

Encouraging the applicant to speak

Listen carefully throughout the interview, and don't interrupt except with encouraging noises like "Uh-huh" and "I see" and "Yes, I understand." Don't break the flow of the applicant's words and thoughts, as long as they are relevant.

This may sound obvious, but it is necessary to consider that applicants speak at an average rate of 150 to 200 words per minute, and most interviewers can comprehend, on the average, about 600 to 800 words per minute. An interviewer who allows his or her mind to wander while the applicant is talking may well miss significant information.

On statements that the interviewer would like the applicant to expand, the statement can be repeated to the applicant in another way. For example, if the applicant indicates a former boss was rough on the applicant the interviewer may echo, "Your boss was kind of hard-nosed, huh?" This approach is better than asking direct questions, and it eliminates the cross-examination feeling. Once in a while, the applicant will seem to run out of things to say; yet the interviewer wants him or her to continue. The interviewer may try letting the silence build up for a few moments. The applicant will find it uncomfortable and will start talking again. Finally, the interviewer should use language that the applicant will understand but should not talk above or below the applicant's level of comprehension.

Note taking

An interviewer should take notes, for some minor item of information may be important in connection with information that emerges later.

Abbreviated notes are fine, but the interviewer should not be constantly scribbling away with pencil and paper or writing down negative or sensitive material while the applicant is speaking. The sensitive information should be kept in mind and written down later when the applicant is on another topic.

Forming Hypotheses

Keeping job requirements in mind will help the interviewer form hypotheses on the applicant's suitability. It is necessary to seek out further information to substantiate or disprove these hypotheses. Individual behavior often tends to form patterns; look for them. Be careful about jumping to conclusions. A study by Springbett (1958) at McGill University indicated that interviewers tend to form biases that influence them either to accept or reject the applicant, depending on the direction of the bias. The bias induces the interviewer to seek out information that supports it.

Results of a related study showed that the interviewer is influenced to a greater extent by unfavorable than by favorable information (Bolster & Springbett, 1961). In addition, interviewers often develop a stereotyped image of a good applicant and subsequently try to match applicants to this stereotype (Webster, 1964). There are several practical implications from the McGill studies. Interviewers should

1. Discipline themselves to keep objective job specifications rather than stereotypes in mind
2. Try not to let biases form early
3. Realize that they are probably being unduly influenced by unfavorable impressions and try to compensate by carefully considering their relevance to the job.

Closing the Interview

When everything has been covered satisfactorily, the interviewer should encourage the applicant to ask questions about the job. It is a good idea to spend more time on this phase if the applicant looks especially strong. Moreover, the applicant's questions can be quite revealing as an added source of information on personal attitudes. Finally, when making a summary evaluation, the interviewer should decide whether the candidate is the kind of person who will fit into the department, if he or she has the capacity to grow in professional competence and stature, and if he or she is the kind of person the interviewer would want to work with and have as a representative of the department.

THE BACKGROUND INVESTIGATION

The background investigation, rooted in the premise that the best indicator of what a person will do in the future is what he or she did in the past, is potentially an accurate and useful tool in the selection process. It is accurate and useful as long as the investigation is conducted in a professional manner by trained, competent investigators who know what to look for and where to look. The background investigation is crucial to the police officer selection process, for it serves to maintain the integrity of a department by ensuring that only qualified and reputable candidates are selected.

The key to the success of the background investigation is the quality of the investigators. Investigators should have a thorough working knowledge of appropriate state and federal laws governing employment and selection procedures. He or she must also be knowledgable in interview techniques and in developing sources of information. In addition, investigators must be able to gather facts, determine their relevance, and transcribe this information into a logical, sequential report. Above all, the confidentiality of reports and sources of information must be maintained. The following, in abbreviated form, is a discussion of the areas that should be covered.

Confidential and Required Documents

The investigation should begin by examining the documents presented by the applicant. Ambiguities should be noted. Oral interview notes should be reviewed, for they may be a source of potential leads. In addition, the investigator should ensure that the applicant has provided all the information required of him.

Personal History and Interview

An interview with the applicant is mandatory and should (if possible) be conducted at the applicant's home. Note should be taken of the environment, its cleanliness, and the condition of the yard. These could be telling indications of the individual's life style. Police officers, even off duty, are under the eye of the public, and the way an individual conducts personal affairs can have a direct bearing on what to expect of that person on the job. Information about the candidate's spouse, past spouse, or future spouse should be elicited. A police officer's home life, especially ability to maintain stable home conditions, is important. Finally, information on an applicant's parents should be gathered, especially if they appear to have influenced him or her significantly.

Family History and Neighborhood Check

The applicant's spouse, parents, and close friends should be interviewed. Associations with potentially criminal elements should be thoroughly investigated.

A spouse should be asked why he or she thinks the applicant wants to be a police officer. Is the spouse aware of (and able to accept) shift rotations, callbacks, court time, and all the many inconveniences of the job?

Neighbors should also be questioned concerning the applicant, and an investigator should always carry a picture of the applicant when talking with them. The investigator needs to verify how long the neighbors have known the applicant and attempt to determine whether the applicant gets along with them and whether his or her children are well behaved. Information about drinking habits and the types of friends that come to the house should also be obtained. In his or her personal life a police officer must not consort with individuals who could put the officer into a compromising position on the job.

Information about family fights and driving habits can indicate the applicant's self-control and handling of personal affairs. One who cannot control one's personal life may well have difficulty assisting others with theirs. If the applicant is divorced the ex-spouse could be an excellent source of information. However, investigators should be cautioned not to be swayed by personal hard feelings that are not verified by facts.

Military Service

The military most closely approximates the strict environment found in most police departments. Such things as types of discharge, disciplinary actions taken, and promotions all relate to the individual's ability to adjust to the rigid conditions that he or she may be subjected to as a police officer. All military information should be verified with the National Personnel Records Center.

Education

Academic achievements can be directly related to the ability to achieve in the academy and may give some indication regarding proficiency in basic skills such as writing ability and the ability to comprehend complicated concepts (like those faced by an officer in a court of law).

Driving Record

An indication of the applicant's stability and respect for the law may be found in the driving record. Individuals who have had long-term, consistently poor driving records may present problems on the force. Automobile accidents are among the biggest causes of police injury—and the cost to the department for wrecked vehicles is extremely high. In addition, failure to obey traffic laws may be indicative of a fundamental lack of respect for the law.

Employment History

Employers, supervisors, and co-workers of the applicant can often provide valuable insights into personal characteristics, such as dependability, aptitude, and interpersonal competence. The frequency of job changes may be an indication of future tenure. However, real job changes should be carefully distinguished from part-time and summer employment changes. Supervisors often have valuable knowledge of an applicant's past job performance. Such things as job titles, dates of employment, disciplinary records, and reasons for leaving should be verified. To ensure accuracy, the investigator should also check the amount of sick time and number of injuries against the applicant's own statements.

Financial Status—Credit

One area that can cause undue pressure on an individual and possibly compromise his or her effectiveness is lack of competence in maintaining financial stability. Checks should be made with local credit bureaus, banks, and mortgage companies. Credit references should be conducted to verify timeliness of payments. Moreover, any large amounts of money in property holdings should be investigated.

Conviction Records

Most states prohibit employment of police officers who have been convicted of a felony or a misdemeanor involving moral turpitude. In addition to checking national and federal crime information centers, investigators should call police departments in the areas in which the candidate has resided. A history of a criminal past, particularly if there is a discernible criminal pattern, is significant information for the hiring authority.

Health and Medical Information

All records of any serious injuries sustained by an applicant, any psychiatric treatment, and any surgery should be documented. Special attention should be directed to any condition that may deter or prevent a police officer from meeting the physical requirements. Any serious medical problems of the applicant should be pursued with him or her and verified by a physician. Rapid weight loss, depression, or other similar medical information may be indicative of an individual's inability to perform successfully as a police officer.

Character References

The investigator should try to ascertain an applicant's character and values, as distinguished from his or her reputation. Character and reputation are not synonymous, and the investigator must be able to distinguish the two. Even though character references are generally favorable in nature, valuable information, verification of information, and secondary leads can all be obtained from these sources.

Membership in Organizations, Associations, and Clubs

It is important that the applicant's memberships in clubs, professional organizations, etc., be reviewed to ensure that a conflict of job and personal interests does not exist, as well as to provide unobtrusive information on the applicant's likes and dislikes.

This outline actually covers only a portion of the necessary information for the hiring decision. Of all selection tools, the background investigation is the one procedure that should have the full support of the top administrator. Only through the background investigation can opinions formed during the interview, scores on tests, and performance on other predictive instruments be substantiated.

BIOGRAPHICAL PREDICTORS OF POLICE PERFORMANCE

In September 1973 the Dade County Public Safety Department received a grant from the Police Foundation entitled "Police Officer Selection and Performance Appraisal." This two-year project had three objectives: (1) to develop a sensitive, relevant, and reliable performance appraisal system for police officers; (2) to develop a police personnel management information system as an aid in administrative decision making and as a research tool; and (3) to investigate the validity and selection fairness of biographical data as predictors of police performance. This section of the chapter summarizes our findings with respect to the biographical data portion of the project. The research to be reported was carried out by Dr. William Buel of Byron Harless, Schaffer, Reid, and Associates, Inc., of Tampa, Florida.

Biographical data have long been used in personnel selection, with considerable success. In fact, in a review of the personnel selection literature, Asher (1972) found that when appropriate procedures were followed (to include cross-validation) biographical data were superior to any known alternative selection methods. Of the biographical data studies reviewed by Asher for which job proficiency served as the criterion, 55% of the validity coefficients were .50 or higher, 74% were .40 or higher, and 97% were .30 or higher. These results generated considerable interest among police researchers, especially when coupled with the results in the New York City Police Department reported by Chaiken and Cohen (1973), which showed that biographical data relating to occupational mobility, education, and early responsibility significantly predicted both tenure and later performance.

Biographical data are based on the proposition that the best indicator of future behavior is past behavior, and they offer several advantages when used in selection. Since they often sample many different areas of personal background (e.g., early family history, academics, work history) they often contain all the elements of consequence to job success. Second, item-by-item validation guarantees that only items that do predict criterion behavior for various sex and ethnic subgroups will be included in the final scoring key. Third, analysis of those items in the personal backgrounds of the most highly successful officers can enhance considerably our understanding of what contributes to successful police performance.

With these potential advantages in mind we attempted to forecast road patrol officer performance. For ease of exposition the remainder of this summary will be divided into five sections: sample, predictors, criteria, results, and needed improvements.

Forecasting Road Patrol Officer Performance

Sample

As of December 1973, 377 road patrol officers were on duty in the Dade County Public Safety Department. This figure represents the maximum possible sample size that could be obtained if both predictor and criterion data were available for all officers. As it turned out, however, data on only 246 (65%) of the officers were available. Of this total, 204 officers were white American males, 11 were females, 12 were black males, and 19 were Spanish surnamed. Since the minority group samples were so small, they were held out for cross-validation against the scoring keys developed for the nonminority sample. The 204 nonminorities were divided into above-median and below-median performers and then further subdivided into validation and cross-validation groups, as shown in Table 1.

The nonminority group averaged about 29 years of age, with 3.5 to 4 years experience and with 13.5 years of education. The black officers were slightly older and slightly less educated on the average, but the female and Spanish-surnamed officers were comparable to the white American male officers in age and education.

TABLE 1 Sample breakdown for nonminority males

	Above median	Below median	Total
Validation	61	61	122
Cross validation	41	41	82
Total	102	102	204

Predictors

The questions within the biographical questionnaire covered the respondent's academic and familial experience, his or her hobbies, working career, interests, personal motives and values, ambitions, achievements, and a variety of related areas hypothesized to differentiate effective from ineffective job performance. The questionnaire contained 184 5-alternative multiple-choice questions and was to be answered by choosing the single alternative to each question that best described the respondent. For example:

A. How old were you when you joined the Dade County Public Safety Department?
   a. 20 or younger
   b. 21 to 25
   c. 26 to 30
   d. 31 to 35
   e. 36 or older
B. How old were you when you became completely independent of financial assistance from your family?
   a. 15 or younger
   b. 16 to 20
   c. 21 to 25
   d. 26 to 30
   e. 31 or older

Several types and levels of questions were included. For example, question A predates employment with the Dade County Public Safety Department, whereas question B examines the individual's early experience in a more general sense. Alternatives to each question were phrased so that even those individuals with experience atypical of the group could respond. The data were gathered between December 1973 and January 1974.

Criteria

The criteria to be predicted were supervisory ratings on nine behaviorally anchored rating-scale dimensions (eight plus a total): job knowledge, judgment, initiative, dependability, demeanor, attitude, relations with others, and communications. Since the characteristics of these scales have been described elsewhere (see Farr & Landy, chapter 4 of this volume), they will not be described in detail here. In general, however, ratings were positively lenient (the average score on each dimension was about 6.6, with a 1.4 standard deviation on a 9-point rating scale), with dimensions intercorrelating in the mid-.60s.

Interrater reliability was somewhat lower than expected, especially when a sergeant and a lieutenant rated the same officer. Under these conditions, reliabilities for each dimension ranged from .13 (relations with others) to .52 (judgment). When the interrater reliabilities of sergeants alone were estimated, however, reliabilities generally improved, and they ranged from .14 (relations with others) to .69 (judgment). Interviews with lieutenants indicated that they were too far removed from the individuals in their charge to be able to rate performance reliably. All criterion data were gathered on training days during a 1-month period in August 1974.

Results

All possible combinations of alternatives for each question were examined in relation to supervisory ratings for all nine behaviorally anchored rating scale dimensions. As an illustration of this process, Table 2 shows the alternative choice—criteria relationships for a sample question.

Scoring keys for each dimension were developed, with each scoring key containing the appropriate weights for those item alternatives that showed validity for the validation group. A portion of one such key is shown in Table 3. In terms of overall results in the validation sample, the numbers of valid questions by criterion dimension are shown in Table 4.

As might logically be expected, some questions were found valid for more than one criterion dimension. So far, so good. It appears that a reasonably large number of questions showed validity for one or more dimensions. However, when the scoring keys developed on the validation sample were used to predict the supervisory ratings of the cross-validation sample, none of the

TABLE 2 Alternative choice—criteria relationship: What is your weight? (a. 150 pounds or less; b. 151 to 170 pounds; c. 171 to 190 pounds; d. 191 to 210 pounds; e. 211 pounds and over)

Criteria	Alternatives[a]				
	a	b	c	d	e
Job knowledge					
Judgment					
Initiative		1	1	1	1
Dependability					
Demeanor					
Attitude					
Relations with others					
Communications		1	1	1	1
Total		1	1	1	1

[a]Alternatives are weighted as +1 if chosen by more of the individuals rated above the median on a criterion than those rated below the median.

TABLE 3 Biographical scoring key–job knowledge

6.[a]	62.	93.	120.	145.
a.	a. 1	a.	a.	a. 1
b.	b. 1	b.	b.	b. 1
c.	c. 1	c. 1	c.	c. 1
d. 1	d.	d. 1	d. 1	d. 1
e. 1	e.	e. 1	e.	e.

12.	65.	95.	128.	151.
a.	a.	a.	a.	a.
b. 1	b.	b. 1	b.	b.
c. 1	c.	c. 1	c. 1	c.
d.	d. 1	d. 1	d. 1	d. 1
e.	e. 1	e. 1	e. 1	e.

[a]In question 6, for example, if alternative d or e was chosen, +1 was added to the respondent's score; if alternative a, b, or c was chosen, the respondent received a 0 for that question.

dimension-specific biographical scoring keys significantly predicted the same dimension in the cross-validation group. When corrected for restriction of range in the criterion, however, several dimension-specific biographical scoring keys significantly predicted supervisory ratings on that same dimension. The results were somewhat more encouraging for the minority group holdout samples, with more dimension-specific keys predicting the same criterion dimension. But since the numbers of persons in these samples were small, little confidence can be placed in such results.

TABLE 4 Number of valid questions by criterion dimension

Criterion dimension	Number of valid questions
Job knowledge	25
Judgment	31
Initiative	30
Dependability	24
Demeanor	27
Attitude	26
Relations with others	35
Communications	29
Total	49

Needed Improvements

At this point the temptation is strong simply to write off biographical predictors of police performance and say they don't work. Yet there is danger in this approach, for we may well be throwing the baby out with the bathwater. Despite the fact that this study did not lead to a usable product, we did learn a great deal from it. These insights are the most valuable byproducts of the research, and other investigators should be well aware of them. With an eye toward the future, therefore, we offer the following suggestions.

1. Recognize the limitations of concurrent validity studies. First, when using currently employed officers rather than applicants, the effect of motivation is ignored; it is simply assumed that employees are motivated to respond as would job applicants. Second, the effect of job experience is ignored; an effect that may well influence certain responses. These assumptions are not particularly worrisome in the case of items dealing with historical, verifiable data, but they can be serious with items asking for values, preferences, attitudes, and situational judgment.

2. Use the maximum possible sample size available. In addition to increasing the power of statistical tests, you will also avoid the "volunteer" aspect of our study, where only 65% of the sample participated in the research. Volunteers often respond differently from the total group.

3. Police officer performance is complex and multidimensional. Indeed, there may not be a single pattern of background characteristics that reliably distinguishes marginal from satisfactory performance. On the other hand, perhaps different criteria (such as tenure, training academy performance, or objective criteria, such as injuries, accidents, or arrests) are more predictable. Try them out.

4. A final problem may lie with the form of criterion instrument used. Our study used an absolute rating system, in which each officer's performance was rated without reference to others. The range of performance ratings was restricted (positively lenient), thereby producing less predictable variance. The dimensions all intercorrelated reasonably highly, and interrater reliabilities were considerably lower than desired. While behaviorally anchored absolute ratings are extremely useful in performance counseling, they are probably less useful in validation studies. Perhaps a more appropriate criterion measure would be a relative rating system in which each officer is compared to relevant others, for example, a behaviorally anchored paired comparison format. Such a system would yield maximal criterion variance by spreading scores in a manner that would lead to more stable cross-validation results.

5. Always cross-validate! Since the development of biographical scoring keys represents raw empiricism, chance relationships are likely. Cross-validation and continual (e.g., annual) revalidation is an essential check on the stability of obtained results.

In sum, the potential of biographical data to predict police performance has yet to be realized in practice. To some extent this may be due to deficiencies in the methods used. It is to be hoped that, in future research, investigators will heed the suggestions made here, and thereby provide a more rigorous test of the usefulness of biographical data in police selection.

SUMMARY

Personnel selection decisions are implied predictions of future job behavior. One applicant is chosen in preference to others because of a belief that the first applicant will perform more effectively than those who were not chosen. A wide variety of instruments are available to help administrators make selection decisions, but it is essential that the instruments used are reliable and valid. In this chapter we have examined four nontest methods that can be useful components of police selection programs: educational standards, interviews, background investigations, and biographical information. When validated in the specific context in which they will be used, each of these methods can provide meaningful, although somewhat different, information for selection purposes. Educational standards and background investigations rely on information provided by others, while biographical and interview information is provided directly by the applicant. These four methods are generally based on the assumption that the best indicator of what a person will do in the future is what he or she did in the past. Sometimes, however, present behavior is the best indicator of future behavior. Both approaches can contribute to improving the caliber of police personnel selection.

REFERENCES

Asher, J. J. The biographical item: Can it be improved? *Personnel Psychology*, 1972, *25*, 251–269.
Bolster, B. I., & Springbett, B. M. The reaction of interviewers to favorable and unfavorable information. *Journal of Applied Psychology*, 1961, *45*, 97–103.
Cascio, W. F. Formal education and police officer performance. *Journal of Police Science and Administration*, 1977, *5*, 89–96.
Cascio, W. F., & Real, L. J. Educational standards for police officer personnel. *The Police Chief*, 1976, *43*(8), 54–55.
Chaiken, J. M., & Cohen, B. *Police Civil Service Selection procedures in New York City: Comparison of ethnic groups.* New York: Rand, 1973.
Finnigan, J. C. A study of relationships between college education and police performance in Baltimore, Maryland. *The Police Chief*, 1976, *43*(8), 60–62.
Landy, F. L. The validity of the interview in police officer selection. *Journal of Applied Psychology*, 1976, *61*, 193–198.

Landy, F. L., Farr, J. L., Saal, F. E., & Freytag, W. R. Behaviorally anchored scales for rating the performance of police officers. *Journal of Applied Psychology*, 1976, *61*, 750–758.

Springbett, B. M. Factors affecting the final decision in the employment interview. *Canadian Journal of Psychology*, 1958, *12*, 13–22.

Trojanowicz, R. C., & Nicholson, T. G. A comparison of behavioral styles of college graduate police officers v. noncollege-going police officers. *The Police Chief*, 1976, *43*(8), 56–59.

Webster, E. C. *Decision making in the employment interview*. Montreal: McGill University, 1964.

8

THE DEVELOPMENT OF A WRITTEN TEST FOR POLICE APPLICANT SELECTION

Andrew Crosby
International Association of Chiefs of Police, Gaithersburg, Maryland

Michael Rosenfeld and Richard F. Thornton
Educational Testing Service, Princeton, New Jersey

This chapter describes the development of a test of immediate, practical use to police departments in selecting individuals from the labor pool for training as police officers. In the uncertain context of equal opportunity law and standards in the mid-1970s, police management needed selection devices to replace those, commonly in use, that had been found discriminatory. While it was not clear what form a satisfactory substitute might take, both the International Association of Chiefs of Police (IACP) and the International Personnel Management Association (IPMA) developed proposals for a project to provide an instrument for use in the selection process. Funding was provided to these organizations from the Police Foundation, and a contract was negotiated with the Educational Testing Service (ETS) to develop an original test that would be fair, valid, job related, and of maximal use to a wide spectrum of police agencies in the United States.

THE PROJECT CONTEXT

This project was undertaken in a climate of challenge to police departments unprepared to respond and of court-imposed remedies that often resulted in chaotic hiring and training programs. Very often the scenario was as follows: A court or a state or federal agency with a civil rights enforcement mandate would say to the police administrator

We find that the minority representation on your force is nowhere near the proportions in your community. We believe this is due to the disparate effect of the standards you require regarding your written test, the height of officers, your physical agility test, and your background investigation. Since you have not conducted any long-term studies in which you have actually observed the performance of all kinds of officers and thereby demonstrated that these standards relate directly to a minimum acceptable level of police performance, you must now suspend these practices.

One immediate effect of this situation was to change the manner in which police agencies recruited their potential trainees. Intensive recruitment campaigns were mounted in minority communities. For many departments, this new and different labor pool was being tapped for the first time. It has been estimated that in 1973 white males made up 91% of municipal departments and 97% of state law enforcement agencies. The shift in the characteristics of those to be evaluated for police work presented many significant implications for the design of new selection devices and procedures.

A more pervasive effect of the move to increase minority representation in law enforcement was a new concern with personnel issues beyond selection, yet having an important bearing on the setting of entry standards. There had been a tendency in the past on the part of police management to think of selection as largely finished with the acceptance of applicants into the academy. This was due to an unwarranted faith in the assumption that the selection tools—tests, height requirements, interviews—were doing their job.

Candidates for positions in police work were usually selected by "skimming off the top," that is, by accepting in rank order those who excelled on the chosen measures. While there was little questioning as to whether relevant and valid measures were being used, there was concern that applicants show high scores on them. However, the new conditions seemed to demand that police management obtain a better estimate of the potential of all applicants before reducing their number. Furthermore, this "better" estimate had to be fairer and more job related, and this meant that more applicants would proceed farther along the selection sequence, providing a richer sample of behavior and personal characteristics. Ideally, decisions about selection should be occurring well into the training, probation, and early career periods.

Questions arose about the training experience in police academies. What constitutes a "proper" failure rate? On what kinds of academy performance measures should retention or termination decisions be based? To what extent can the academy afford to give remedial training to improve basic academic skills that many trainees already possess at adequate levels on arrival at the academy?

The probationary period also drew attention. Although there was a clear trend toward longer probationary periods during the 1960s, very few individuals were terminated as a result of failure to meet required performance standards. Probably a major reason for the retention of most probationary officers is that few departments used a sound and extensive performance appraisal system during probation. Consequently, data were not available on which to base selection decisions. Notable exceptions to these general conditions have been appearing in recent years, as more and more departments have assigned field-training officers to evaluate probationers and have begun to require frequent, exhaustive performance reports.

Career growth issues relate to selection as a factor in attracting and motivating minority applicants to enter the law enforcement field. This attraction will be lacking unless it is clear that, in addition to a fair and valid system for entry, promotions to supervisory and management positions are also made on the basis of demonstrated aptitudes and performance for the higher-level jobs. Also, the promotional system should include effective training to develop needed attitudes and skills for today's conditions inside and outside the department. Thus a new police selection project had to take into account many complex, system-wide factors relating to selection before any meaningful decisions could be made on the scope and form of the proposed product.

APPROACHES TO POLICE SELECTION

In conceiving the development of a test to be used in police selection, it was necessary to consider at what level of abstraction from the job itself the test was to be designed. The academy training course, viewed as a test, has a format and quality different from the job, in some cases markedly so, although some degree of job simulation is the usual goal. The probationary period, with extensive evaluation of performance on the job, is, or can be, a test given in terms very nearly identical to those of the job. A type of test gaining popularity is the assessment center, where candidates' behavior is observed in a series of job-related situations. In the direction of greater abstraction, tests of specific areas of job knowledge, skills, aptitudes, or other human traits can be given in paper-and-pencil format. Such tests could be developed in any of the following areas:

1. Personality, character, temperament, interests, and motivation.
2. Job-relevant aptitude and ability tests.
3. Achievement: measures of how well an individual has learned to perform, for example, in demonstrated knowledge of the law.
4. Other constructed measures. These may be useful in predicting behavior and, on this basis, can be considered a parallel category. An example is the biographical inventory measure, by which an individual is evaluated in terms such as marital status and work history that have been found to be related to job performance.

After the type of procedure or instrument has been decided on but before the format can be chosen, the conditions surrounding the use of the procedures must be considered. Some alternatives are individually or group-administered; paper-and-pencil or performance; language-oriented or non-language-oriented; and interview, observation, or self-report.

PROJECT DESIGN DECISIONS AND THE RESULTING PRODUCT

The goal of this project was to design a selection instrument capable of providing assistance to the maximum number of departments in meeting their equal opportunity employment needs. Several criteria had been proposed, and these were subsequently confirmed and adopted as work got underway. The new instrument must require little, if any, special expertise to administer. It must be appropriate for departments that vary in size and carry out a variety of law enforcement tasks. It must be suitable for applicants without law enforcement experience in an age range of 18 to 40 years. Aside from any other role it might take in the selection process, the instrument should serve as a replacement for disputed "intelligence type" tests, which were being widely used for preliminary screening of applicants for law enforcement positions.

These guidelines effectively ruled out instruments other than group-administered, paper-and-pencil tests. A further design decision was to address cognitive intellectual abilities rather than motivational or personality traits. It was felt that, without supplementary clinical input, the latter were less effective in a paper-and-pencil format than were measures of cognitive skills. Implicit in these decisions was the assumption that the test would always be used with additional selection devices, which would provide decision-making information in other relevant domains and supplement the written test scores.

The product that resulted is a multiple-choice test of 180 items that can be administered within a 3-hour time limit. A parallel form of the test was also developed to be used when needed for ensuring security or for retesting. When sufficient experience is accumulated using applicant populations, some inefficient items may be removed from the test. Early indications are that it may be possible to reduce the test to about 150 items and thus to shorten the administration time. The test is rented to user agencies and may be scored by them or returned to the supplier for confidential scoring.

As a special feature, the police applicant test makes use of a candidate preparation booklet that is distributed in advance of the test. This booklet is designed to reduce the impact of educational and reading level differences in the applicant population by providing an opportunity to prepare for certain portions of the examination. It was also felt that this process could provide an indication of an applicant's ability to learn the skills and knowledge required to be a police officer by actually providing an opportunity for such learning.

The preparation booklet contains a complete description of the abilities measured by the police applicant test and provides practice questions in each ability area. In addition, the booklet contains information on 4 of the 12 abilities that must be studied by applicants prior to taking the test.

TEST DEVELOPMENT PROCEDURE

Test development began with the formation of two advisory committees, one to represent law enforcement experience and the other to consult on test technology. The police committee was composed of 12 current or former police officers and supervisors, who developed and reviewed test materials at several key points during the project. Care was taken to select committee members from geographically dispersed jurisdictions so that black, white, Hispanic, and female subgroups were represented. The technical committee of five ETS test specialists was formed to review the project methods and data on a regular basis.

A substantial effort was devoted to an analysis of the police patrol job. It was felt that test development should be based on an accurate and timely description of the patrol function in several sites across the United States. Even though other studies that described the police job were available, all were judged to have some deficiency in scope, sample size, or documentation for test development purposes. Therefore, in preparing to answer possible challenges on both legal and technical grounds, it was felt that a thorough job analysis should be carried out under the control of project staff in order to be generally compatible with the project approach.

To produce a methodologically sound and comprehensive set of job analysis results was especially important because this was considered essential to establishing the content validity for the test. Prevailing professional opinion supported the decision that where feasible empirical criterion-related validation efforts should be pursued as a supplement to content validation.

Police job analyses from the literature and from departmental files were reviewed by project staff. Conducted over the past ten years, these studies (see for example Baehr, Furcon, & Froemel, 1968; Santa Clara County Sheriff's office, 1971) varied widely in format. Some were narrative descriptions by a single observer; others were methodical, large-scale studies. This review resulted in a decision to develop an officer self-report instrument for the job analysis. A preliminary list of over 100 tasks typically performed by police officers was compiled from the collected information and used by the police advisory committee as a working draft. This list was expanded, some items were revised or deleted, and a rating system was devised. The list of tasks was then divided into categories for administrative convenience. The final "checklist" instrument contained 141 items describing police tasks, to be rated in terms of how often they were performed, how important they were, the extent to which they must be learned on the job, and the extent to which they were performed better by competent officers than by marginally performing ones.

To secure checklist responses from a large and varied group of officers, nine departments agreed to provide the opportunity for testing a random stratified sample of officers and supervisors. Six of these departments served municipal jurisdictions, two were state police agencies, and one was a metropolitan county. A total of 960 questionnaires were analyzed; 16% were from supervisors; 15% were from black officers; and 9% were from other ethnic groups, mainly Chicanos.

To reduce the data for the 141 items to a number of interpretable variables, the ratings of "importance" were factor analyzed. The result was 14 clusters of tasks, or dimensions, which suggested the basic dimensions of the police patrol job. These dimensions are:

1. Responding to routine calls for police assistance
2. Search and seizure procedures
3. Vigilance and judgment in patrol activities
4. Booking of prisoners
5. Facilitating traffic flow
6. Making routine business and nonbusiness checks
7. Community relations
8. Crowd control
9. Prepared, evaluative response to dangerous situations
10. Oral court testimony
11. Gathering information and reporting
12. Interpersonal aspects of arrest procedures
13. Arrest reports and records
14. Work preparation

To investigate potential differences in the perception of the job by respondent subgroups, factor scores on the 14 dimensions were compared by jurisdiction, job level, and race of the respondent. The results showed substantial agreement throughout the comparisons. This outcome suggests that the types of important tasks for which police officers must be prepared are similar across police jurisdictions, even though different situational conditions may influence task patterns. These similarities in content are extremely important when one considers that these data will be used as a guide to help identify abilities needed by recruits in learning and performing police work. Given the consistency of the job analysis data, it seems reasonable to assume that similar abilities are needed to learn and perform the job of police officer whether it be in a state, county, or municipal setting.

The next step in development was the identification of the cognitive-intellectual abilities judged to be relevant to learning and to performing the job tasks, as defined. Previous work at ETS had identified 59 abilities across the affective, psychomotor, and cognitive domains for which clear and stable definitions were available through accumulated research (Ekstrom, 1973). The 22 cognitive abilities in this set were examined by the technical advisory committee in relation to each of the 14 job dimensions, according to instructions carefully explaining the intended use of the abilities. Then the police advisory committee reviewed thses results. Of the 22 abilities, 11 were retained in the matching matrix, and another was added as a result of the police committee's judgments. The final set of selected cognitive abilities can be described as follows:

1. The ability to understand the meaning of words or ideas (verbal comprehension)
2. The ability to recall a series of items after one or more presentations of that series (serial recall)
3. The ability to recall items of information that are arbitrarily paired (paired-associate memory)
4. The ability to remember logical connections and meaningful relationships among previously learned items of information (memory for relationships)
5. The ability to recall the essence of previously studied material (memory for ideas)
6. The ability to order semantic information into the most meaningful sequence (semantic ordering)
7. The ability to find general concepts that will explain available information (induction)
8. The ability to be sensitive to the consequences of given situations (problem sensitivity)
9. The ability to perceive relevant visual stimuli in the presence of distracting materials (flexibility of closure)
10. The ability to comprehend positions of visual objects in space (spatial orientation)
11. The ability to plan an efficient visual path (spatial scanning)
12. The ability to recognize objects after they have undergone physical change (visualization)

The next step was to write a number of test questions (items) for each ability. In developing the test items, specifications were written to guide the item-writers. The specifications and other instructions were intended to ensure that the test would contain adequate material to reliably measure each ability, have an appropriate balance of verbal and nonverbal items, be at an acceptable reading level, and appear to the applicants to be related to the police job.

A pool of items was reviewed by the two committees. After the resulting changes and deletions, and further changes based on item analyses of the trial administration data, 15 items were selected to test each ability. Approximately 50% of the final set of 180 test items consists of graphic material, such as maps, diagrams, scenes, data forms, and person identification sketches, on which the questions are based.

The reading level of the test was set generally at a 10th-grade standard. This decision was intended to make the test compatible with the reading performance of high school graduates and with the expected level to be met in much of the written material at the academy and on the job. However, surveys of that material revealed a vocabulary of terms, which, while not infrequently used in the general population, may be less familar to applicants from minority groups. After the test items were written, 368 words that were judged to be unfamiliar to minority group members were listed in the study guide so that applicants could become familiar with these words before taking the test. For example, the words in the list beginning with *B* are *bail, barricade, bay window, belligerent, bias, bona fide, burgle,* and *bystander.*

The study guide, a 38-page booklet, is made available to applicants one to three weeks before the test. The guide may be used for study in any way the applicant chooses, but it may not be used when taking the test. In addition to the vocabulary list, the guide contains advice on what the test is about and on how to approach questions and use the answer sheet; materials to study and memorize, with sample questions including typical police forms, typical police procedures, and "wanted" posters (some of this information must be recalled in order to answer some test questions); examples of other types of questions, involving the using of maps, exercising judgment, observing details, identifying common factors, and visualizing objects; and a sample answer sheet, with correct answers to the sample questions.

VALIDATION OF THE TEST

The police applicant test was designed to be content valid. Each development step provided observable, documented evidence to demonstrate validity of the test. In addition, criterion-related studies were planned, and four such studies were conducted at four different sites. The validity results obtained by comparing total test scores with performance ratings differed by site. The following paragraphs deal with the results by site.

Site 1. The sample consisted of 148 members of a state police department located in the eastern part of the United States. The sample consisted of 10 black officers and 137 white officers and included all black officers assigned to patrol duties. For the sample of 148 officers, the total test score was positively and significantly correlated with 10 of the 15 rating dimensions.

Site 2. The sample consisted of 116 members of a midwestern municipal police department; 51 were black officers and 64 were white officers. While 5 of the subtests were positively correlated with some of the criterion dimensions, the total test score failed to correlate with any of the 15 rating dimensions.

Site 3. The sample consisted of 84 members of a municipal police department in the southwest, including 26 Hispanic officers and 57 white officers. The total test score was positively and significantly correlated with all 15 criterion dimensions.

Site 4. The sample consisted of 170 members of a western municipal police department, and included 51 black officers, 62 white officers, and 49 Hispanic officers. The total test score had significant negative correlations with 3 of the 15 criterion dimensions.

The empirical results obtained in sites 1 and 3 present strong evidence of the concurrent validity of the test for the selection of police officers in these locations.

In site 2 the number of positive correlations obtained between subtest scores and criterion rating dimensions was only slightly higher than the number to be expected by chance. In addition, the total test score was not significantly correlated with any of the 15 rating dimensions. Practical limitations in the scope of the study prevented detailed investigation of variables that might have contributed to these results. However, the data indicate a consistent tendency for raters in this site to rate more leniently members of their own racial group.

Data on the length of service and level of education of the police officers participating in this study were also available. These data indicate that while level of education for blacks was not significantly correlated with test performance, there were significant negative correlations with 9 of the 15 criterion dimensions. Black officers with higher amounts of education tended to be given less favorable ratings. For white police officers, level of education was not significantly correlated with either test score or the criterion dimensions. The data also indicate that there were differing relationships by race between length of police service and several of the criterion dimensions. This situation makes it clear that further investigation into criteria is necessary in order to obtain a more accurate estimate of the validity of the pretest in site 2.

In site 4 the results based on the total group masked what appears to be differential validity by race. The data indicated that total test scores were positively correlated with 9 of the 15 criterion dimensions at either the .05 or .01 levels of significance for Hispanic police officers, for whom the correlation between total test score and overall rating was .57.

For black police officers there were no significant correlations between total test score and performance ratings, while significant negative correlations were obtained between total test scores and 9 of the 15 criterion dimensions for white police officers, for whom the correlation between total test scores and overall rating was −.37 (significantly different from 0 at the .01 level). The difference in the direction of the validity coefficients for Hispanic and white officers seemed to be related more to ratings of performance than to differences in the test scores of the two groups. The mean test scores for Hispanic and white officers were practically identical (Hispanics 158.43, whites 158.82). In site 4, as in site 2, further investigation into the criteria seemed to be required in order to obtain a more accurate estimate of the overall validity of the pretest at this site.

In summary, for two of the four sites there was clear evidence of the concurrent validity of the test. In the other two sites there was little or no evidence of the concurrent validity of the test, but the research findings suggested that the performance ratings might have been contaminated.

APPLICATION OF THE TEST

A substantial number of applicants have been tested with this instrument in the short period since it was constructed and reasearch is being implemented to follow up on the validity of the test. Jurisdictions using the test have been urged to conduct criterion-related validity studies.

On the basis of our findings in the development of the police applicant selection test, we make the following recommendations:

1. The final version of the test, containing measures of 12 abilities, should be used in the police selection program. Each of the 12 measures has been demonstrated to have content validity and to be statistically related to a measure of job performance in one or more sites. Considered as a whole, the test is highly reliable. At score points likely to be used in screening applicants, the test did not have adverse impact on black or Hispanic police officers in the concurrent validity samples.

2. The evaluation of candidates for positions as police officers, insofar as the test is concerned, should be done on the basis of total score. The concurrent validity study indicates that the total test score is reliable and predicts job performance in two of the four concurrent vlaidity sites. The content validity model used in the test development process and the concurrent validity demonstrated in research on the development of the test, provide sufficient evidence for users to consider differences in candidates' test scores employing the test as one basis for selecting police officers.

3. The descriptive booklet should be distributed to candidates sufficiently in advance of the test (1-3 weeks) to provide adequate opportunity for prep-aration. This booklet contains materials without which approximately 50% of the questions in the test could not be answered correctly. In addition, the booklet contains a complete description of the test and provides practice questions. The booklet is designed to give all applicants adequate opportunity to prepare for the examination.

4. A current, well-documented job description, if available, should be used

by jurisdictions to judge the correspondence between the job of police officer in a particular jurisdiction and the job dimensions that were used as the bases for test development in this project. If such job analysis information is not available, the verification-of-tasks instrument, available from the publishers, could be used to generate this information. The instrument can be administered to a representative sample of current police officers on patrol or to all police officers in small jurisdictions. Since the demonstration of the content relevance of the test for a particular jurisdiction is both an important and complex technical task, it is recommended that professionally qualified police and measurement personnel participate in the process.

5. Where feasible, criterion-related validity studies should be conducted by individual jurisdictions using the test. Such studies should be carried out by professionally trained personnel, and care must be taken to ensure that the criterion measures are as free as possible from contamination.

6. Since the test was designed to be only as difficult as necessary to assess minimum competency for the job of police officer, stringent test security is essential for effective use of the instrument.

It is assumed that further empirical validation data from this new test will be available soon to supplement existing evidence. These studies will approach as closely as possible the conditions of the predictive model, and the quality of the criterion measures will be substantially better than many current measures. Meanwhile, the test represents a useful contribution meeting the fair employment challenge at a time when there is an urgent need for objective data on which selection decisions can be based.

REFERENCES

Baehr, M. E., Furcon, J. E., & Froemel, E. C. *Psychological assessment of patrolman qualifications in relation to field performance.* Washington, D.C.: U.S. Government Printing Office, 1968.

Ekstrom, R. B. *Cognitive factors: Some recent literature* (Tech. Rep. No. 2, PR73-30). Princeton, N.J.: Educational Testing Service, 1973.

Santa Clara County, Calif., Sheriff's Office, Personnel Department, *Deputy Sheriff Job Description.* Unpublished manuscript, 1971.

9

USING THE STRONG-CAMPBELL INTEREST INVENTORY IN POLICE SELECTION

Robert T. Flint
Student Counseling Bureau, University of Minnesota,
Minneapolis, Minnesota

On the basis of 10 years of study, Cronbach (1975) concluded that higher order—and therefore extremely subtle—interaction effects seem to account for most psychological phenomena. Siskind (1976) mildly chided him:

> Why did it take so many years . . . to realize that the real world is far more complex than the laboratory? Any able practitioner of the behavioral sciences, however meager his reputation, knows that he is constantly working with higher order interactions, modifying generalizations, and identifying the significant characteristics of ever-changing phenomena. (p. 740)

Psychologists who work in mental health centers, academic settings, and private practice daily face the challenges implicit in both sets of remarks. Nowhere are these comments more pertinent than in the field of police selection. Psychologists, like myself, who are not attached to police departments nor extensively engaged in research are constantly challenged to assist with personal decisions about an occupation for which there are few norms, solid criteria, or proven psychometric conclusions.

We are often handicapped by our ignorance about police work. There are probably more myths, misconceptions, and erroneous stereotypes concerning law enforcement than any other field—except, perhaps, psychology. Moreover, psychologists often bring antipolice biases and prejudices to their first contact with police candidates. Consequently, we have to rely on general population norms, our own field observations, and the literature to help us with our task.

The practitioner who conducts even a cursory literature review, from Vollmer's early work on intelligence testing to Kent and Eisenberg's (1972) landmark study, soon discovers the futility of the quest for quick and uncomplicated assessment approaches. This is a literature of negative results.

Baehr and Furcon (1968) have shown the utility of multivariate analysis in this area, but few of us are equipped to pursue this approach. We labor under the Catch 22 constraints placed on us by managers with modest budgets: "Make the most accurate predictions possible about ability, aptitude, intelligence, motivation, personality, probability of tenure, and self-control, but"—Catch 22—"don't spend too much money or take too much of the candidate's time."

We who are primarily consumers, not producers, of research await the fulfillment of the promise that the research described in this book holds. But we cannot wait for the ultimate regression equation. Our clients, the police administrators of the land, need to make decisions today. We face a problem that is as old as applied psychology: how to optimize our contributions to the decision-making process with our limited instruments while waiting for research to catch up with our needs.

Learning to use an old instrument in a new way is one approach to this dilemma. I want to describe what the SCII has to offer to the psychologist who must assist in today's decisions while awaiting tomorrow's research. Many industrial and clinical psychologists think of the SCII as useful only in vocational counseling. I will describe how it can supplement tests of intelligence, academic aptitude, and personality in police selection. I will also discuss its use in promotional and career development contexts.

Holland (1966) has commented on the use of interest tests as follows:

> Because of our repeated failure to define *interests* conceptually, they have come to mean no more than the scales of the Kuder Preference Record and the Strong Vocational Interest Blank. That is, we have accepted methods of assessment in place of definitions. . . . And because interest scales have lacked "surplus" meaning, these studies fail to indicate that "interests" are an expression of personality and personal development. The accumulation of many such studies has led to a relatively independent literature known as "interest measurement." (p. 7)

I will not report outcome studies but will share with you some of the so-called surplus meanings that I obtain from the SCII in my police officer assessments. I will focus especially on its utility in answering the global question *Does this candidate's interest pattern suggest that he or she will enjoy the work and be motivated to achieve?* I will also comment on the more specific question *Is this candidate's mix of interests compatible with the needs of this police department?*

TECHNICAL INFORMATION ABOUT THE SCII

The following brief history of the SCII includes information on the Holland themes, the latest addition to an old test. Those who are familiar with the instrument may wish to proceed directly to the next section. However, an understanding of Holland's typology is essential for the most effective use of the SCII, and therefore those unfamiliar with his work are urged to read on.

The SCII is the latest revision of an empirically developed and standardized test that celebrated its semicentennial in 1977. The Strong Vocational Interest Blank (SVIB), the prototype, antedates most tests commonly used today. Its basic concept is generally familiar to psychologists: people who share patterns of similar likes and dislikes enjoy similar occupational activities. A corollary is that people who enjoy doing similar work display similar patterns of likes and dislikes. A particular interest pattern does not, of course, assess a person's skills or ability to do a particular job. Interest scores indicate only the degree to which a person is likely to enjoy working in a particular field.

Strong's original hypothesis, that people do not seek occupations randomly but are motivated to fulfill their interests, has long since been confirmed. The technical details of how he elaborated his concepts, developed his scales, validated them, and so forth, have been described by Campbell (1977). The SVIB originally indicated only whether one's interest pattern matched that of people in specific occupations. This format prevailed until 1969, when the Basic Interest Scales were added (Campbell, Borgen, Eastes, Johannson, & Peterson, 1968). According to Campbell (1977), they "were constructed by gathering together clusters of statistically related items; this technique generated homogeneous scales . . . with items highly consistent in content."

The 23 scales are broad focuses around which patterns of distinct but related interests cluster. They are clearly labeled as to content—for example, agriculture, art, and business management—and range in length from 5 to 24 items, with a median length of 11 items. Thirty-day test-retest correlations for reliability range from .79 (social service) to .93 (music/dramatics), with a median correlation of .88.

The SCII resulted from Campbell's (1977) incorporation of Holland's general occupational typology into the SVIB. Holland (1966) has reported the technical aspects of his work. Suffice it to say that Holland's typology was empirically derived, and his findings overlap with Guilford's (1954) factor analysis of human interests, as well as with the groupings commonly found in research studies of the SVIB.

Holland's typology is divided into general "themes": realistic, investigative, artistic, social, enterprising, and conventional. As with most typologies, there are relatively few pure examples of any one type. Only 25% of the 124 occupations covered by the SCII belong to a single typology. Examples are: skilled craftsman (realistic); mathematician (investigative); musician (artistic); social worker (social); lawyer (enterprising); and female secretary (conventional). Of the remainder, 37% are characterized by high scores on 2 of the 6 scales, and 38% score high on 3 of the scales.

INTERESTS OF POLICE OFFICERS

Police and highway patrol officers score high on the realistic, enterprising, and social themes. While both groups score highest on realistic, they rank differently on social. Police officers are realistic-enterprising-social (RES) while highway patrol officers are realistic-social-enterprising (RSE). A common-sense analysis of the two occupations supports this differentiation when the meaning of the themes is examined. Their utility in attitude assessment also becomes apparent. The following descriptions of the realistic, enterprising, and social types are taken from Campbell's (1977) comprehensive manual for the test:

> *Realistic type*: Persons of this type are robust, rugged, practical, and physically strong; somewhat uncomfortable in social settings; have good motor coordination and skills but lack verbal and interpersonal skills; usually perceive themselves as mechanically and athletically inclined; are practical, stable, natural, and persistent; prefer concrete to abstract problems; see themselves as aggressive; have conventional political and economic goals; and rarely perform creatively in the arts or sciences, but do like to build things with tools. Realistic types prefer such occupations as mechanic, engineer, electrician, fish and wildlife specialist, crane operator, tool designer, and various technician positions. (pp. 31–32)

People scoring high on the realistic theme also indicate a liking for, among other activities and occupations, building contracting, ranching, industrial arts, operating machinery, and reading popular mechanics magazines.

> *Enterprising type*: Persons of this type have verbal skills suited to selling, dominating, and leading; prefer to be strong leaders; have strong desire to attain organizational goals or economic aims; tend to avoid work situations requiring long periods of intellectual effort; differ from conventional types in having a greater preference for ambiguous social tasks and an even greater concern for power, status, and leadership; see themselves as aggressive, popular, self-confident, cheerful and sociable; generally have high energy level; and show an

aversion to scientific activities. Vocational preferences include business executive, political campaign manager, real estate sales, stock and bond sales, television producer, and retail merchandising. (p. 32)

The score on the enterprising theme is increased by a positive response to items such as auctioneer, auto salesperson, life insurance salesperson, sales manager, interviewer for sales prospects, and merchandise buyer for a store.

Social type: Persons of this type are sociable, responsible, humanistic, and religious; like to work in groups, and enjoy being central in the group; have verbal and interpersonal skills; avoid intellectual problem solving, physical exertion, and highly ordered activities; prefer to solve problems through feelings and interpersonal manipulation of others; enjoy activities that involve informing, training, developing, curing, or enlightening others; perceive themselves as understanding, responsible, idealistic, and helpful. Vocational preferences include clinical psychologist, missionary, high-school teacher, marriage counselor, and speech therapist. (p. 32)

The score on the social theme is elevated by endorsements of the following items: playground director, social worker, YMCA/YWCA staff member, churchgoer, schoolteacher, and giver of first aid assistance.

THE SCII POLICE OFFICER OCCUPATIONAL SCALE

The Police Officer Scale was developed in 1969 on a sample of 196 male sworn officers in all assignments except clerical in the Minneapolis Police Department. As with all samples selected for scale development, the criteria for inclusion in the normative group were at least three years of experience and a reported liking for the job. When the sample's responses were compared to those of men in the general population, 74 items differentiated policemen from men in other occupations.

The police officer scale was cross-validated against various samples previously tested with the SVIB. These included three classes of Minneapolis Police Department recruits tested and retested during their first year of service, 111 Utah sheriff's deputies, 288 Minnesota highway patrol officers, 44 Racine, Wisconsin, police officers, and 38 University of Missouri police officers. All these samples had mean scores close to the mean standard score of 50, established for the original sample. This finding is not surprising, in light of the data on the stability of the test across both time and groups within the same occupation. Campbell (1977) discusses in detail the data leading to the conclusion that people in the same occupation express highly similar interests at different times and in different locations.

Johansson and Flint (1973) found that the 74 items on the police officer scale fell into three broad categories: "militaristic," "risky," and "mechanical." The subjects indicated that they liked being military officers, participating in military drills, being with military persons, and drilling soldiers. They said they would like to be auto racers, airplane pilots, and secret service agents. They also said they would like to pursue bandits in a sheriff's posse and to engage in thrilling, dangerous activities. They felt they had mechanical ingenuity and expressed more interest in mechanical avocations than did the people-in-general group. Two significant social service items differentiated the subjects from people-in-general: giving first aid assistance and being able to smooth out tangles and disagreements between people.

The officers stated few dislikes. The ones they did state included poets, ballet dancers, outspoken people with new ideas, nonconformists, people who believe in evolution, college professors, writing one-act plays, and attending music and art events.

We found changes in SVIB scores on retesting two classes of Minneapolis Police Department recruits. The first group showed a gain on the police officer scale of $\frac{1}{2}$ standard deviation after 21 months; the second showed a drop of less than $\frac{4}{10}$ of a standard deviation after 17 months. Both groups initially scored less than 1 standard deviation below the mean of the normative group. This suggests that Sterling's (1972) finding that the personality and expressed attitudes of new officers are affected by the occupational socialization process does not apply so clearly to interests.

RACE AND SEX DIFFERENCES ON THE SCII

Borgen and Harper (1973) reported data that are relevant to the issue of equal employment opportunity. They compared the SVIB's predictive accuracy for both white and black winners of National Achievement and National Merit scholarships. They concluded, "Membership in career groups was predicted at least as well for blacks as it was for whites" (p. 26). Barnette and McCall (1964) also reported an absence of racial differences. Campbell (1977) made the following observation about these studies.

Even if undetected racial differences exist, the validity of interest inventories might still be constant for the races. If, for example, the members of one race express more artistic interest than those of another race do, more of the former might well end up in artistic occupations. If this were so, the validity of the inventory, and its practical usefulness, would be comparable in the two populations. (p. 67)

Unfortunately, the same assurance does not exist with regard to sex differences. While some occupations are sought out by men and women with similar Holland-theme rankings, gender clearly makes a difference in others. The SCII has separate norms for men and women, even for occupations that employ people of both genders. Campbell (1977) reports that men and women respond differently to about half the items on the inventory.

Sex differences in the SCII do not disappear when men and women who have made the same occupational choice are compared. For example, male and female mathematicians are both pure cases of the investigative theme, and male and female college professors alike receive the code of investigative-artistic. However, male physicians are coded investigative-realistic-social, while female physicians score high only on investigative. Male army officers are realistic-investigative-conventional, but female army officers are realistic-enterprising. As the numbers of women on patrol increase, enough experienced female police officers who enjoy their work will be available for the development of a female police officer scale.

USING THE SCII IN POLICE SELECTION

The descriptions of the realistic, enterprising, and social types contain many contradictory elements, yet also describe many activities in which police officers engage. This clustering of these scales highlights one of the problems frequently encountered in police selection—finding people who are equally interested in law enforcement, community relations, and crime prevention. The minimal relationships among the three scales emphasize the broad span of interests that police officers must have if they are to enjoy their work. The realistic and social themes correlate .31 and .45, respectively, with the enterprising theme but only .12 with each other. Only 5 of the remaining 122 occupational scales show an R-S configuration.

The theme descriptions contain information about attitudes toward various elements of police work. A review of the themes suggests that the realistic and social themes must be balanced if officers are to display positive attitudes toward both the enforcement and service aspects of the job. As we have seen, high scores on the realistic theme are attained by people who are "somewhat uncomfortable in social settings," who "lack verbal and interpersonal skills," "prefer concrete to abstract problems," and "see themselves as aggressive." People high on the social theme, on the other hand, "are sociable, . . . humanistic, and religious"; they "have verbal and inter-personal skills; avoid intellectual problem-solving, physical exertion, and highly ordered activities"; and they "perceive themselves as understand-ing, . . . idealistic, and helpful."

The attitudes and preferences expressed by a high score on the enterprising theme may be the bridge between the other two. High enterprising scores are obtained by people who enjoy leading others and taking on ambiguous social tasks. They possess persuasive verbal skills and enjoy jobs that have an administrative component. They do not like to spend long periods in intellectual effort, for they are pragmatic and seek quick results. Some interest in administration is desirable in police officers, and persuasive interests lend appeal to crime prevention and other community relations duties.

People who score low on the social theme and high on the realistic theme may be highly task-oriented. They may be seen as "hard-nosed," or callous. A reversal of those elevations may indicate a candidate who has too large an investment in the social service aspects of the job. Such a person may do well on service calls but avoid making arrests.

The difference between interests and attitudes may be more a matter of semantics than of reality. As was noted earlier, some attitudinal measures are built into the Holland themes. Moreover, a knowledge of people's preferred activities allows some educated guesses about attitudes in other areas. The following examples illustrate this point.

An applicant for a suburban police department had an excellent record as a military intelligence investigator. His skills and his motivation were both high. His personality test scores were well within normal limits, although they did suggest more rigidity than is displayed by the average candidate. He scored high on the SCII police officer scale and on the realistic theme. His enterprising theme score was in the high average range, but his social theme score was slightly below average. The interview revealed that his focus in police work was completely on the tactical and investigative aspects of the job. He had little interest in the service aspects of police work. He wanted to catch criminals and did not want to spend time on preventing crime, assisting victims, or developing community relations programs.

Less experienced candidates for the same position showed a better balance in their scores on the three police-oriented themes than did the former military intelligence officer. The administration decided to hire someone who had more interest in community service, which was strongly emphasized in that department. A socially oriented (in the Holland sense) candidate with strong realistic and enterprising interests was seen as more likely to be motivated to learn the technical skills necessary to perform tactical duties. It was judged unlikely that a candidate without positive social attitudes (interests) would perform service duties well, even with the best of training. A department with different priorities might have found the experienced candidate more attractive.

Another department reviewed the performance of a veteran officer and called for a psychological evaluation. His record was marginal; he rarely initiated action that produced arrests, he wrote poor reports, and in general, he paid little attention to his law enforcement duties. However, he enjoyed working with problems that his colleagues often disliked: family disputes, psychiatric cases, rowdy juveniles, and so forth. He had been reprimanded for spending too much time counseling and not enough time patrolling. Nonetheless, his personnel file was filled with letters from grateful citizens.

This officer was highly intelligent, and his personality profile scores were all within normal limits. He scored in the average range on all the SCII themes except social, where he was high, but scored substantially below the average policeman on the police officer scale. His highest scores were on the occupational scales of public adminstrator, school superintendent, social worker, priest, and elementary-school teacher.

The officer's performance was clearly linked to his interest pattern. He focused his energy on the tasks he enjoyed most and avoided the rest of his duties. His problems could not be attributed to lack of intelligence or to personality disorder. Early detection of his interest pattern would have given the administration many more options, including special assignments or more careful supervision, than were available after a pattern was established over several years.

The SCII basic interest and occupational scales indicate whether an individual is most likely to enjoy administrative, tactical, investigative, or research functions. Given the potential for specialization in modern police departments, this information can help the officer, as well as the administration. Special schools, formal education, and job experiences can be planned more effectively when a particular long-range occupational specialty has been selected.

A final example illustrates how interest pattern affects job performance— and how the SCII can be used in career development programs. This application of the instrument is closely related to its use in promotional situations. Consider two patrol officers who were promoted to sergeant. Positions were available for these men either in administration or in field supervision. Both men had proved themselves in the field. Supervisors judged that either man would be competent in either job, and the administration wanted to know the optimal placement for each. The SCII data made the decision far easier. It also facilitated career-planning discussions between the men and their chief.

One man scored moderately high on the realistic and social themes but moderately low on the enterprising theme. The realistic and social scores suggested that he enjoyed the traditional activities of police officers. His low score on the enterprising theme indicated a lack of interest in administrative and persuasive public relations activities. This hypothesis was supported by his high scores on the Basic Interest Scales of adventure, military activities, mechanical activities, athletics, public speaking, and law/politics. He scored as "very similar" on the highway patrol officer scale, and as "similar" on the police officer scale. This interest pattern strongly suggested that the officer would be most satisfied in a tactical position. He seemed unlikely to enjoy many of the activities associated with administration, although his record indicated that he was competent in that area.

The second officer scored moderately high on the social theme and was average on both the realistic and enterprising themes. These data suggested that he might encounter many of the problems of the marginally performing officer described earlier. However, certain demographic and psychometric data contradicted this conclusion. First, this officer had an excellent record of aggressive police work punctuated by many good arrests. Second, he scored high and moderately high, respectively, on the investigative and conventional themes. These themes suggest an interest in orderly, predictable work situations and in dealing with abstractions. People with strong investigative interests are often attracted to scientific pursuits, but an investigative urge can obviously serve a police officer well.

The second officer's pattern on the occupational scales was similar to that of people who work in administrative positions, despite his lack of elevation on the enterprising theme. His scores on the personnel director and public administrator scales were in the "very similar" range, and he scored as "similar" on several other scales associated with administration, as well as on the police officer scale. While certainly able to handle tactical duties, this officer would probably find an administrative or investigative position more interesting.

The two men were assigned according to the preferences shown on the SCII. At last report, each felt that he had made the right choice for him, and the supervisors of both reported that the officers were doing well. This case illustrates that the SCII, like all tests, must be interpreted in the context of demographic data, personal history, interview information, and other psychometric data. An individual's deviation from the pattern of the average police officer does not guarantee failure, any more than a good match is a warranty of success. Further, a deviation from the average interest pattern may be a signal to consider the officer (or candidate) for specialized duties or to groom him or her for a particular career path.

SUMMARY AND CONCLUSIONS

The SCII can stand by itself no more than any other assessment measure. It measures only interests, not intelligence, academic or any other aptitude, personality, or temperament. However, the SCII can complement tests that measure these attributes by tapping the nebulous but important areas of attitudes, world views, and interests.

The SCII is demonstrably free of racial bias. The development of a police officer scale for women will clearly increase the value of the SCII, but it can provide information about female candidates even in its present form. Its potential in career planning and in the placement of newly promoted officers is large.

If we take seriously Cronbach's conclusion about higher order interaction effects (1975), it behooves us to maximize the number of proved and familiar sources of information about candidates. The SCII has been neglected as such a source. It seems likely that we practitioners must continue to develop prediction equations on an intuitive basis for a long time, because the computers do not seem ready to provide us with the equations we seek. But we need to make sure that we have psychometrically sound instruments for each prediction, since anything less than the soundest of instruments will surely fall victim to the inadequacies of our clinical methods.

REFERENCES

Baehr, M. E., Furcon, J. E., & Froemel, E. C. *Psychological assessment of patrolman qualifications in relation to field performance.* Chicago: University of Chicago, Industrial Relations Center, 1968.

Barnette, W. L., Jr., McCall, J. N. Validation of the Minnesota Vocational Interest Inventory for vocational high school boys. *Journal of Applied Psychology,* 1964, *48,* 378–382.

Borgen, F. H., & Harper, G. T. Predictive validity of measured vocational interests with black and white college men. *Measurement and Evaluation in Guidance,* 1973, *6,* 19–27.

Campbell, D. P. *Manual for the Strong Vocational Interest Inventory.* Stanford, Calif.: Stanford University Press, 1977.

Campbell, D. P., Borgen, F. H., Eastes, S., Johansson, C. B., & Peterson, R. A. A set of Basic Interest Scales for the Strong Vocational Interest Blank for Men. *Journal of Applied Psychology Monographs,* 1968, *52,* (6, Pt. 2).

Cronbach, L. J. Beyond the two disciplines of scientific psychology. *American Psychologist,* 1975, *30,* 116–127.

Guilford, J. P., Christensen, P. R., Bond, N. A., Jr., & Sutton, M. A. A factor analysis study of human interests. *Psychological Monographs,* 1954, *68,* (4, Whole No. 375).

Holland, J. L. *The psychology of vocational choice.* Waltham, Mass.: Blaisdell, 1966.

Johansson, C. B., & Flint, R. T. Vocational preferences of policemen. *The Vocational Guidance Quarterly,* 1973, *22,* 40–42.

Kent, D. A., & Eisenberg, T. The selection and promotion of police officers. *The Police Chief,* 1972, *39,* 20–29.

Siskind, G. Personal reflections on reading Sarason's "Community psychology, networks, and Mr. Everyman." *American Psychologist,* 1976, *31,* 740–741.

Sterling, J. W. *Changes in role concepts of police officers.* Gaithersburg, Md.: International Association of Chief of Police, 1972.

10

CHANGING POLICE VALUES

Samuel D. Sherrid
Hudson Valley Community College, Troy, New York

Numerous researchers have explored various methods of screening out undesirable police recruits, but the results have been discouraging. For example, Rankin's psychiatric testing of Los Angeles police recruits (1959) could not effectively screen out unfit aspirants; nor was Hankey (1968) able to discover temperament traits that differentiated between successful and unsuccessful officers. Kent and Eisenberg (1972) surveyed police selection studies in which psychological tests, biographical information, situational tests, and civil service examinations were used as selection instruments, and these observers concluded that a valid and unbiased method for police selection has not yet been demonstrated.

Other studies have shown that, even when the selection process produces acceptable results, certain adverse attitudinal changes take place in police officers after appointment. Banton (1967), Niederhoffer (1963), Westley (1951), and Wilson (1970) all found that cynicism developed and increased in police officers as a function of length of service, especially, in the early years of police work. However, Wilb and Bannon (1976) found, at least for Detroit police officers, that Niederhoffer's (1963, 1967) cynicism findings were not related to job performance. McNamara (1967), in a study of New York City police recruits, discovered that democratic attitudes, developed through formal training at the police academy, tended subsequently to disappear or to be reversed during actual performance on the job.

More recently researchers have begun to look into behaviorally based rating scales in order to evaluate the job effectiveness of police officers after appointment. Eisenberg and Murray (1974) reviewed current practices in police recruit selection and pointed out that careful job analysis and better development of performance criteria were prerequisites for future success in developing procedures for police recruitment.

Dunnette and Motowidlo (1976) recently developed two procedures for evaluating candidates for positions in law enforcement. These tests, a police career index and a series of police job simulations, can be used in screening police recruits and in evaluating officers for promotion to detective, sergeant, or middle command positions. Only time will tell whether these new procedures will be more productive than previous attempts. In the interim there is much to be done with officers who are already on duty—or who will soon enter the system—to ensure that they perform satisfactorily and in accordance with the norms of a democratic society.

Numerous studies concerned with police *attitudes* (e.g., Knudten, 1970; Piliavan & Briar, 1968). Eisenberg, Fosen and Glickman, 1973; Kelly and Farber, 1974, have revealed that diverse and complex factors shape these attitudes. In commenting on the attitudes of police officers, Skolnick (1967) observes that many officers often find themselves facing the dilemma of preserving individual justice and maintaining social control. The officer may feel that his primary function is to control crime and that due process for an individual sometimes impedes such control.

No police selection method has as yet been tested sufficiently to demonstrate that it can effectively screen out undesirable applicants among police recruits. It has been found, however, that soon after even desirable candidates enter the police force, a process takes place that leads them to develop cynicism and undemocratic attitudes. Therefore, it is important to look for methods that will help officers already in the system to retain their wholesome attitudes and ideals; it is also necessary to attempt to change the value systems of officers with attitudes and behavior patterns that are not acceptable in a democratic society.

A police officer's value system often determines the kind of actions he or she will take when on the job. According to Chwast (1970), "Key determinants in the course the police pursue are the values underpinning these processes" (p. 113). It is therefore important and in the public interest that police officers adhere to a value system that is in harmony with democratic traditions.

The study described in this chapter attempted to reinforce democratic values already held by police officers and to change values that were not in conformity with a democratic society (Sherrid, 1973). The possibility of changing the value priorities of police officers was investigated. In order to bring the police officers' values into greater accord with those of society, dissonance and self-dissatisfaction were brought to the attention of the officers by exposure to inconsistencies in the beliefs expressed by police officers and the values they held. Rokeach (1971) had previously demonstrated that it was possible to change the values of college students.

Rokeach (1973) also developed a theoretical framework for predicting the influences that are most likely to lead to changes in values, attitudes, or behavior. He identified 10 subsystems, which varied along a continuum of centrality or importance, ranging from those that are most central (e.g., "cognitions about self,") to those that are least central (e.g., "cognitions about behavior of non-social objects"). In general, values follow cognitions about self in centrality of importance. Change is postulated when there is a conflict between self-conceptions and performance that creates a state of self-dissatisfaction. According to Rokeach (1973) "A contradiction within one's cognitive system engages self-conceptions and thus leads to self-dissatisfaction" (p. 228).

In investigating changes in values and attitudes, Rokeach (1973) developed a procedure whereby subjects were given information about their own values and attitudes, followed immediately by similar comparative information about other groups. The data were explained to the subjects in such a manner as to draw attention to contradictions between the subjects' attitudes and those of other groups, thus implying the possibility of contradictions within the subjects' own belief system.

In the study reported in this chapter an attempt was made to increase the importance that police officers placed on the value of equality. Officers were exposed to contradictions between their own self-concepts as tolerant persons and the low priority given by themselves and other police officers to the value of equality, as measured by the Rokeach Terminal Value Survey.

METHODOLOGY

Subjects

A total of 384 subjects originally participated in this study. Of these, 221 were New York City police officers, and the remaining 163 were officers from the New York metropolitan area who were enrolled in the police science curriculum at the State University of New York at Farmingdale. All the officers were randomly selected and assigned into a control or an experimental group.

Instruments

The two instruments used in the study were the Rokeach (1971) Terminal Value Survey and the Stouffer (1955) Nonconformist Tolerance Scale. The value survey contains a set of 18 terminal values that subjects are instructed to rank in order of importance. This instrument also contains a set of 18 instrumental, or means, values similarly ranked by subjects. The reliability and validity of these value sets have been demonstrated by a number of reasearchers (Cochrane & Rokeach, 1970; Feather, 1971; Homant, 1969; Penner, Homant, & Rokeach, 1968; Shotland & Berger, 1970).

The Stouffer scale contains 15 questionnaire items, with 3 items in each of the 5 sets. The items are arranged so that persons who indicate tolerance in their answers to the first set of 3 questions will most likely continue to do so in succeeding sets. A person can be ranked from 0 to 5, depending on the degree of tolerance expressed in the answers to the 5 sets of questions. A sample set of items from the tolerance scale is indicated below. For each item the subject's response choices are *yes, no,* or *don't know.*

1. Should an admitted Communist be put in jail, or not?
2. There are always some people whose ideas are considered bad or dangerous by other people. For instance, somebody who is against all churches and religion. If such a person wanted to make a speech in your city (town, community) against churches and religion, should he be allowed to speak or not?
3. If some people in your community suggested that a book he wrote against churches and religion be taken out of your public library, would you favor removing this book or not?

PROCEDURE

Pretest

The officers in both the experimental and the control groups were asked to rank the instrumental and terminal values in the value survey according to their own perceived importance. Both groups were then questioned, using Stouffer's tolerance scale, as to what they believed their attitudes or behavior would be in situations involving nonconformists.

The subjects were rated according to a scale devised by Stouffer, which classified them into six groups as follows: groups 5 and 4, who expressed tolerance in all five sets or in the last four sets, are considered tolerant; groups 3 and 2 are in between; and groups 1 and 0 are considered intolerant.

At the end of the pretest session, the control group members were dismissed after their answers were collected. The subjects in the experimental group were permitted to retain their answers to the value survey and the tolerance questionnaire and to refer to their own ratings as they viewed several charts showing previous results for groups of police officers and college students. One chart showed that the values of freedom and equality were ranked 3rd and 14th, respectively, by police officers in Michigan (Rokeach, Miller, & Snyder, 1971) and 3rd and 13th by the New York area officers (Sherrid, 1973).

A second chart showed how the college students had ranked these same values and how the rankings corresponded to expressed feelings toward civil rights issues. Students not in sympathy with civil rights ranked freedom very high and equality far lower. Students sympathetic to civil rights demonstrations ranked equality far higher and far closer to freedom. In commenting on the rankings, the investigator remarked that "the charts seemed to indicate that police officers and students, generally, are more interested in their own freedom than in other people's freedom" (Sherrid, 1973, p. 49).

Two additional charts were then placed on the screen. One of these charts showed how 16 metropolitan police officers rated on the Stouffer scale: 12 scored as tolerant, 2 were in between, and 2 were rated intolerant. The ratings of these officers were compared with the general public in terms of their willingness to tolerate nonconformists. In commenting on the charts, the researcher pointed out how favorably the officers' tolerance ratings compared to those of the general public.

The subjects were then asked to compare their own tolerance responses with those shown on the chart, and the investigator commented that officers testing as intolerant would be relatively unconcerned with other peoples' freedom but would care greatly about their own. In contrast, officers who scored as tolerant would want freedom both for themselves and for others. The investigator also read the following brief statement (Sherrid & Beech, 1976) about equality, which was generally familiar to most of the subjects.

1. Officers generally are aware that all persons should be treated equally before the law.
2. The constitution they swore to uphold protects the rights of all individuals on an equal basis.
3. The Declaration of Independence states that all persons are created equal.
4. Justice is depicted as being blindfolded, because justice, to remain just, must be blind to race, to religion, to sex, and to ethnic origin.
5. Although police officers have a strong awareness about *equality*, do they practice these principles? They indicate tolerance, but they seem to give equality a low value, which seems to be inconsistent. (p. 275)

The subjects were then asked to review the charts, their personal rankings of freedom and equality, and their responses to the Stouffer questionnaire, and to observe any inconsistencies between their value ratings and their tolerance statements. Finally, on a scale from 1 to 11, where 1 indicated most satisfied and 11 indicated least satisfied, each officer was asked to rate the degree of satisfaction he felt toward his own ranking of equality. The questionnaires were then collected from the experimental group, and the subjects were dismissed.

Posttest

A month to 6 weeks after the pretest session, the experimental and control groups were again asked to rank the 18 Rokeach values. Of the 384 officers in the original sample, 263 participated in the posttest session.

RESULTS

The Pearson product-moment correlation between individual differences in tolerance and pretest rankings of equality was .12 $(df = 383, p < .05,$ one-tailed t-test), indicating a minimal relation between these variables. The median pretest and posttest rankings of the 18 Rokeach values are reported in Table 1. The chi-square test of the difference between the experimental and control groups in the pretest median rank for equality was not statistically significant: χ^2 (1,1) = 1.83, $p > .05$.

After exposing the officers to the inconsistency between their self-concepts of tolerance and their low ratings of equality, the median ranking of equality increased to 10.25 for the experimental group, while the posttest control group ranking for this value was 13.72. The chi-square test of the difference between the experimental and control groups in their posttest ranking of equality was highly significant: χ^2 (1,1) = 11.50, $p < .001$.

The relation between the degree of dissatisfaction an officer reported and the extent to which he changed his ranking of equality from the pretest to the posttest was also examined. A total of 132 officers rated themselves on the satisfaction-dissatisfaction scale in the posttest session. The correlation between degree of dissatisfaction and the magnitude of change in the ranking of equality as a value was only .17, $df = 131, p < .05$, one-tailed t-test, indicating a minimal relationship between these variables. Thus it would appear that most officers tended to rate equality more favorably after exposure to the experimental manipulation, irrespective of how satisfied they were with their own initial ranking of equality.

A Spearman rank correlation of .79 was found between the ranked values of the 384 police officers originally pretested in this study and the ranked values of 153 East Lansing, Michigan, police officers tested by Rokeach et al. (1971). This finding provides evidence that the two populations were highly similar, especially since the present study was conducted more than four years after the Michigan study was completed.

DISCUSSION AND CONCLUSION

The findings of the present study provided evidence that the values held by police officers can be changed and that this can be accomplished by creating dissatisfaction through exposing officers to information about themselves that differs strongly from their concept of one who is tolerant.

TABLE 1 Pretest and posttest rankings on the Rokeach value survey

| | Pretest | | | | Posttest | | | |
| | Experimental | | Control | | Experimental | | Control | |
Values	Median	Rank	Median	Rank	Median	Rank	Median	Rank
Comfortable life	7.4	6	6.6	5	7.0	5	8.2	7
Exciting life	10.1	11	10.9	12	11.2	14	11.2	12
Sense of accomplishment	5.9	4	6.1	4	7.2	6	6.6	5
World at peace	10.7	12	10.3	11	9.3	9	10.5	11
World of beauty	14.6	18	14.8	18	15.4	18	15.6	18
Equality	13.0	16	13.5	16	10.2	11	13.7	17
Family security	1.5	1	1.5	1	1.4	1	1.5	1
Freedom	6.5	5	6.7	6	3.8	2	5.6	3
Happiness	4.7	2	5.2	3	5.1	3	5.6	4
Inner harmony	9.5	10	8.4	8	8.5	8	8.6	8
Mature love	8.1	8	9.0	9	10.3	12	8.6	9
National security	10.9	13	12.0	15	11.5	15	12.6	15
Pleasure	11.8	15	11.2	14	11.0	13	11.4	13
Salvation	14.5	17	14.2	17	14.3	17	12.9	16
Self-respect	5.2	3	4.9	2	6.3	4	5.1	2
Social recognition	11.5	14	11.1	13	12.1	16	12.0	14
True friendship	9.1	9	9.8	10	9.6	10	9.8	10
Wisdom	7.9	7	7.4	7	8.1	7	7.6	6

The importance of this finding is that, at least for the short term, the values of police officers become more positive when they become aware of the inconsistencies in their own values and beliefs.

Police departments should examine the values of recruits prior to hiring them and while they are still on probation. Furthermore, active members of a department should be tested periodically, as they are called back for special training and instruction. Monitoring the values of police officers is as important as ensuring their physical fitness, and such value testing would help to reverse the trend toward rejecting democratic values that was found by McNamara (1967).

The following are some implications of the findings of the present study for future research and operating policies.

1. College students enrolled in police science or criminal-justice curricula can be tested to determine what values they hold and whether their values are suitable for police work.
2. The assessment of values could be used for selection of personnel for special police tasks, such as (a) instructing in police academies, (b) community relations and juvenile work, (c) assignment to detective and investigative work for officers who rank high on imagination as a value.
3. The value-change procedures employed in this study could be used in human relations courses and in police community relations seminars.
4. The procedures of this study could be used for training and inservice training purposes for (a) corrections officers, (b) probation officers, (c) parole officers, (d) teachers, and (e) other community service workers.

SUMMARY

Researchers have explored a variety of methods for screening out unsuitable police recruits, but these attempts have not been so successful as desired. Furthermore, many police recruits who showed desirable traits on entry into the police force subsequently lose their democratic ideals and become cynical toward their work. To reverse this loss of idealism, the Rokeach Terminal Value Survey and Stouffer's Nonconformist Tolerance Scale were used in this study to change the values of police officers so that they would be more compatible with the standards of a democratic society.

REFERENCES

Banton, M. *The policeman in the community.* New York, N.Y.: Basic Books, Inc., 1967.
Chwast, J. Value conflicts in law enforcement. In A. Niederhoffer & A. S. Blumberg (Eds.), *The ambivalent force: Perspectives on the police.* Waltham, Mass.: Ginn & Company, a Xerox Company, 1970.

Cochrane, R., & Rokeach, M. Rokeach's value survey: A methodological note. *Journal of Experimental Research in Personality*, 1970, *4*, 159–161.

Dunnette, M. D., & Motowidlo, S. J. *Police selection and career assessment.* Washington, D.C.: U.S. Department of Justice, National Institute of Law Enforcement and Criminal Justice, Law Enforcement Assistance Administration, 1976.

Eisenberg, T., Fosen, R. H., & Glickman, A. S. *Police-community action: A program for change in police-community behavior patterns.* New York: Praeger, 1973.

Eisenberg, T., & Murray, J. M. Selection. In O. G. Stahl and R. A. Staufenberger (Eds.), *Police personnel administration.* Washington, D.C.: Police Foundation, 1974.

Feather, N. T. Test-retest reliability of individual values and value systems. *Australian Psychology*, 1971, *6*, 181–188.

Hankey, R. O. *Personality correlates in a role of authority–the police.* Unpublished doctoral dissertation for the C.P.A., University of Southern California, 1968.

Homant, R. Semantic differential ratings and the rank-ordering of values. *Education and Psychological Measurement*, 1969, *29*, 885–889.

Kelly, R. M., & Farber, M. G. Identifying responsive inner-city policemen. *Journal of Applied Psychology*, 1974, *59*, 259–264.

Kent, D. A., & Eisenberg, T. The selection and promoting of police officers: A selected review of recent literature. *The Police Chief*, 1972, *39*, 20–22, 24–29.

Knudten, R. D. *Crime in a complex society.* Homewood, Ill.: Dorsey Press, 1970.

McNamara, J. H. *Role learning for police recruits–Some problems in the preparation for the uncertainties of police work.* Unpublished doctoral dissertation, University of California, Los Angeles, 1967.

Niederhoffer, A. *A study of police cynicism.* Unpublished doctoral dissertation, New York University, 1963.

Niederhoffer, A. *Behind the shield: The police in urban society.* Garden City, N.Y.: Doubleday, 1967.

Penner, L., Homant, R., & Rokeach, M. Comparison of rank-order and paired-comparison methods for measuring value systems. *Perceptual and Motor Skills*, 1968, *27*, 417–418.

Piliavan, I., & Briar, S. Police encounter with juveniles. In J. A. Winter, J. Rabow, & M. Chesler (Eds.), *Problems in American society.* New York: Random House, 1968.

Rankin, J. H. Psychiatric screening of police recruits. *Public Personnel Review*, 1959, *20*, 191–196.

Rokeach, M. Persuasion that persists. *Psychology Today*, September 1971, pp. 68–71.

Rokeach, M. *The nature of human values.* New York: Free Press, 1973.

Rokeach, M., Miller, M. G., & Snyder, J. A. The value gap between police and policed. *Journal of Social Issues*, 1971, *27*(2), 155–171.

Sherrid, S. D. *The effects of cognitive dissonance upon values held by police.* Unpublished doctoral dissertation, New York University, 1973.

Sherrid, S. D. & Beech, R. P. Self-dissatisfaction as a determinant of change in police values. *Journal of Applied Psychology*, 1976, *61*, 273–278.

Shotland R. L., & Berger, W. G. Behavioral validations of several values from the Rokeach Value Scale as an index of honesty. *Journal of Applied Psychology*, 1970, *54*, 433–435.

Skolnick, J. H. *Justice without trial: Law enforcement in a democratic society*. New York: John Wiley & Sons, 1967.

Stouffer, S. A. *Communism, conformity and civil liberties: A cross section of the nation speaks its mind*. Garden City, N.Y.: Doubleday, 1955.

Westley, W. A. *The police: A sociological study of law, custom, and morality*. Unpublished doctoral dissertation, University of Chicago, 1951.

Wilb, G. M. & Bannon, J. D. Cynicism or realism: A critique of Niederhoffer's research into police attitudes. *Journal of Police Science and Administration*, 1976, *9*, 38–45.

Wilson, J. Q. *Varieties of police behavior*. New York: Atheneum, 1970.

IV

THE USE OF PSYCHOLOGICAL TESTS IN POLICE SELECTION

11

CRITERION-RELATED VALIDITY OF PERSONALITY AND APTITUDE SCALES
A Comparison of Validation Results under Voluntary and Actual Test Conditions

Norman D. Henderson
Department of Psychology, Oberlin College, Oberlin, Ohio

There are a number of advantages in supplementing police entrance examinations that measure cognitive abilities with tests that measure attitudes, interests, social skills, and basic personality characteristics. Clearly these dimensions come into play in on-the-job police performance, and a test ignoring all but intellectual skills can hardly be regarded as sampling the complete domain of behavioral characteristics required for effective police performance. Unfortunately, as robust predictors in most job situations, personality measures have not fared as well as have cognitive measures. Problems of faking and distortion during testing, along with interactions between various personality characteristics and the specific situations encountered on the job, probably contribute to lower validity of personality measures.

Of all procedures designed to assess the job relatedness of selection devices, criterion-related validation provides the strongest evidence for job relatedness. Because of practical constraints, most criterion validation studies of police selection procedures use a concurrent validation model—officers presently on the force are asked to take a battery of tests, and these tests are correlated with job performance ratings. While there are more limitations in

This work was supported in part by Grant # 75 DF-99-0037 from the Law Enforcement Assistance Administration to the city of Cleveland. I wish to thank Michael Marks and Marjorie Henderson for their assistance on this phase of the project.

the concurrent model than there are in a predictive validation model, the cost and time required to carry out the latter are so prohibitive that the concurrent validation model is likely to be the method of choice in the great majority of situations.

SOME PREVIOUS RESEARCH ON PERSONALITY AND APTITUDE MEASURES

A number of concurrent validation studies have been carried out to examine the predictive validity of various personality scales with respect to police performance. The test most frequently examined has been the MMPI. The results of these studies have been mixed. Blum (1964) found a number of significant correlations between MMPI scales and serious misconduct of police officers. Studying a very large group of Los Angeles deputy sheriffs, Marsh (1962) and later Azen, Snibbe, and Montgomery (1973) found modest but statistically significant relationships between frequency of auto accidents over 10- and 20-year periods and scores on the manic (MA) and depression (D) scales of the MMPI. A weak relationship between the MA and hypochondriasis (HY) scales and the performance ratings was also reported by Marsh, although studies in Cincinnati (Hess, 1972) and Salt Lake City (Mandel, 1970) both failed to find any significant correlations between MMPI scales and police performance. Overall, the results suggest that there are probably some weak relationships between scores on certain MMPI scales and some measures of police performance, but unless validation samples are exceedingly large, these relationships are likely to go undetected. Despite their statistical significance, the modest relationships that have been reported are quite small, throwing doubt on the practical validity of the MMPI as a predictor of job performance for police officers.

Marsh (1962) and Azen et al. (1973) also reported a modest but significant relationship between the activity scale of the Guilford-Martin Temperament Inventory and performance ratings and turnover. Again, however, the practical usefulness of such a weak relationship must be questioned.

Considerably more success has been reported by Hogan (1971) using the California Psychological Inventory (CPI). Several significant positive correlations were found between CPI scales and both ratings of cadets in the training academy and ratings of police officers by supervisors. The number of significant correlations obtained in these studies, as well as the magnitude of the correlations (several simple $rs > .50$), suggests that the CPI may be one of the more promising personality inventories for further research. Some success was also reported by Baehr, Furcon, and Froemel (1969) in a differential validation study of black and white officers carried out in the Chicago Police Department. Scattered significant correlations were reported between various performance ratings and several scales on the Edward's Personal Preference

Schedule (EPPS) and on the Temperament Comparator. Simple rs and weights in regression equations often differed considerably for various scales in different subsamples, however. Similar findings were obtained by Furcon, Froemel, Franczak, and Baehr (Note 1) in a follow-up study using the Temperament Comparator. While two scales showed consistency across both black and white officers, a number of additional scales showed highly inconsistent significant relationships with performance ratings for black and white patrol officers. In both of the previous studies, multiple-regression equations could be constructed separately for black and white officers, using a number of personality scales that together produced high multiple correlations with one or more criterion measures. In each case, however, regression weights for various personality scales differed considerably for blacks and whites. The importance of these differences with respect to the problem of differential validation cannot be underestimated, and this subject will be addressed later in this paper.

Specific aptitude and achievement tests and more general intelligence tests have fared somewhat better as predictors of subsequent police performance than have personality measures. Often, however, the criteria used in such validation studies center around police academy performance. Since most aptitude and intelligence measures tend to be good predictors of academic performance, it is not surprising that police academy performance is also reasonably well predicted by these measures. A number of studies using general intelligence tests, such as the AGCT, Wonderlic, and California Test of Mental Maturity, typically report correlations between test scores and academy grades in the .35 to .70 range, with the most frequent correlations around .50 (e.g., DuBois & Watson, 1950; Hess, 1972; Mills, McDevitt, & Tonkin, 1965; Mullineaux, 1955; Friedland, Note 2). Often, however, these same tests fare considerably less well as predictors of on-the-job performance; correlations of .10 to .20 are typical.

In addition to general personality traits and general intellectual skills, a wide variety of tests of more specific attitudes, interests, and abilities has also been subject to validation studies for police officers. While these are too diverse to describe here in detail, the general picture obtained from this research does not differ substantially from that described above. Specific ability tests, such as measures of mechanical aptitude or perceptual skills, tend to correlate moderately with police academy performance and less so with on-the-job ratings. Vocational preference tests and related measures tend to show scattered significant correlations with performance, with no clear pattern across groups. A review of much of this work can be found in Barrett, Alexander, O'Conner, Forbes, Balascoe, & Garver (Note 3).

In summary, many concurrent and predictive validation studies suggest that measures of personality traits or temperament tend to show inconsistent correlations with police performance across different groups, including racial groups. While considerably more consistent, measures of intellectual skills and ability fare less well as predictors of performance on the job than as predictors of police academy performance.

INTERNAL AND EXTERNAL VALIDITY
OF POLICE VALIDATION STUDIES

What about the validity of the validation studies themselves? Validity takes on a different meaning in this broader context. Unlike content, criterion, and construct validity, which deal with the measurements themselves, research using these measures can be examined from the point of view of internal and external validity. Internal validity refers to problems that are inherent in the research and that would allow alternate explanations for results obtained, while external validity deals with the generalizability of the research.

Certainly, there are some grounds for questioning whether results of concurrent validation studies—or even predictive validation studies using preselected groups—effectively generalize to a broader range of testing situations. Concurrent validation studies test individuals already performing on the job. Insofar as previous on-the-job experience, age, or other factors influence test performance, results from such studies may not generalize to a situation where younger and inexperienced applicants will be tested. Since most general aptitude or ability tests are relatively unaffected by such variables, problems of generalizing to new groups are probably less severe than for personality and attitude tests, which may shift over time, especially for a clearly defined occupational group such as police officers.

A closely related problem is that of restriction of range. Relationships between various test scores and job performance are likely to be greatly attenuated in a group that has already been preselected on similar measures. Officers on a police force who are selected largely on the basis of a civil service exam, which measures general aptitude, will show less variation on subsequent aptitude measures than would unselected applicants. In such cases the correlations obtained between various aptitude tests and subsequent performance measures are likely to underestimate the strength of relationship between test and performance that would actually be found in the general population of potential police applicants. While most screening exams do not include personality evaluations, a certain degree of self-selection results in police officers as a group being less variable on a number of temperament or attitude dimensions than would be the case in the general adult population. Whether police officers are more homogeneous on these personality dimensions than a group of applicants for police work is more difficult to ascertain. In any case, the general problem of restriction of range tends to have one clear result: We are likely to underestimate the predictive validity of our tests. This, in conjunction with problems of the reliability of job performance criterion measures, has led some authors to conclude that correlations between tests and job performance are likely to be so attenuated that empirical validity studies are technically feasible much less frequently than we assume (Schmidt, Hunter, & Urry, 1976).

A third difficulty with concurrent validation studies involves the problem of motivation during testing. The police officers taking tests on a voluntary basis as part of a concurrent validation study are under an entirely different motivational state than applicants vying for a position on the force. High or low grades play no role whatever in their careers. In fact, in most studies, complete anonymity is provided for such volunteers. Thus the voluntary test situation—as opposed to an actual examination on which promotions or other matters of employment status hinge—simply does not exert pressure to perform well. Because of this, volunteer officers are likely to give less than their best performance on the aptitude tests, but at the same time, they may perhaps respond more honestly to personality or attitude questions than they might if they felt that their answers would be used for selection purposes. It is plausible therefore that, even when validity is established for both aptitude and personality dimensions in concurrent validation procedures, the validity coefficients obtained will not be a fair representation of validity under true test conditions. We might expect, for example, that aptitude scores under true test conditions would more accurately reflect a candidate's ability, whereas anonymous "no stakes" conditions might produce more accurate measures of a candidate's attitude or personality. Validity coefficients obtained using traditional concurrent validation procedures may therefore be attenuated for aptitude measures and inflated for personality measures.

THE CLEVELAND PROJECT

The Cleveland Police Validation Project provided us with an opportunity to examine a number of the above questions. A brief description of the Cleveland project will be helpful. In conjunction with the development and administration of entrance and promotional exams for police officers, we were able to carry out a number of validation studies and related research in the Cleveland Police Department.

Figure 1 summarizes the basic structure of the project. Phase 1, in the spring of 1973, involved carrying out a traditional concurrent validation study. At this time approximately 400 patrol officers were rated by both their supervisors and fellow officers. From this group slightly over 100 white and 50 black officers completed a battery of tests measuring a number of aptitudes, interests, skills, and personality dimensions. Scores were subsequently correlated with various criterion measures, as well as with multiple-regression equations computed in the manner usually followed in developing selection batteries. The selection battery was then administered to 160 rookies just completing police academy training, to permit a predictive validation study to be completed in the future.

Approximately a year later, similar research was going on with respect to promotional examinations, and in December 1974 approximately 950 patrol officers took a 2-day promotional examination for the rank of sergeant. This

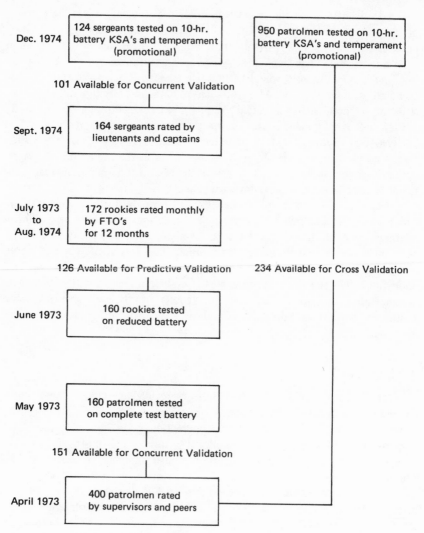

FIGURE 1   Data collected in the Cleveland Police Validation Project.

extensive promotional exam, requiring approximately 9 hours over the 2 days of testing, included a large number of measures of aptitude and personality, along with tests of knowledge of police work. Since several of these aptitude and personality scales represented parallel forms of scales used in the earlier entrance validation study and since 234 of the original patrol officers rated by supervisors and peers had taken this promotional exam, we had an opportunity to compare validity coefficients obtained under both our original no-stakes procedure and under true exam conditions.[1]

---

[1] Because of the anonymity involved in the original voluntary validation project, it

AN EXAMINATION OF EXTERNAL VALIDITY
OF VALIDATION PROCEDURES

A primary interest in the Cleveland project centered around the external validity of our original validation study. How well did the validation results using various personality and aptitude measures generalize to actual test situations with the same population? The correlations presented in Table 1 provide some insight into this question.

The 5 personality scales listed in the table were the only ones from the 16 PF Inventory that showed consistent relationships with both peer and supervisor ratings for both black and white officers. The reason for including just these scales will become evident later. Since a parallel form of the 16 PF was used during the actual promotional examination, a direct test of the robustness of our original findings was possible. The picture presented in Table 1 is not very encouraging. With respect to supervisory ratings, only a single scale (assertiveness) continued to show a correlation with performance ratings large enough to be useful. With respect to peer ratings, a roughly similar picture was found—most correlations decreased when the measures were taken under true exam conditions. Furthermore, no new personality dimensions emerged as predictors of either peer or supervisor ratings when the 16 PF was given as part of an actual exam. A composite measure based on the five personality scales is also presented in Table 1. In the case of both superior officer and peer ratings, the original correlations found between the composite personality measure and job ratings was cut in half during the actual test situation.

With respect to aptitude measures, Table 1 presents five measures for which there were parallel tests given in the voluntary and exam conditions. Each of these aptitude tests measured general ability in a somewhat different manner. The Cattell Culture Fair Test provided measures of fluid, nonverbal intelligence, whereas the Brightness Scale (B) on the 16 PF provided a more culturally loaded measure of general intelligence. Verbal reasoning and numerical ability were assessed by the Differential Aptitude Tests during the validation procedures and by the SRA Verbal (and quantitative) form during the promotional exams. From Table 1 we can see that these general ability measures fared considerably better than the personality scales listed above in the table. With respect to superior-officer, or supervisor, ratings, all correlations improved under actual exam conditions, with a substantial improvement in predictive validity for the composite aptitude measure. The

---

was impossible for us to know how many officers who participated in this project also took the promotional exams in 1974. Therefore significance tests between correlations taken under voluntary and exam conditions cannot be accurately computed. Significance tests based on independent samples provide the most conservative estimate of the significance levels involved. The greater the proportion of officers participating in both test situations the more conservative independent sample statistics become.

TABLE 1 Adjusted correlations between performance ratings of patrol officers and several personality traits and ability measures obtained under voluntary ($N = 151$) and actual exam conditions ($N = 234$)[a]

Test or scale	Correlation with superior officer ratings		Correlation with peer ratings	
	Voluntary	Exam[b]	Voluntary	Exam[b]
Responsibility (G)	.03	.03	.08	.05
Social boldness (H)	.07	−.01	.05	.08
Self-control (Q3)	.12	−.08	.10	.01
Anxiety (Q4)	.13	.00	.20	.07
Assertiveness (e)[c]	.08	.09	.12	.06
Composite personality	.20	.10	.27	.12
Culture fair intelligence	.17	.19	.03	.08
Crystallized intelligence	.11	.25	.11	.08
Verbal ability	.08	.09	.06	.03
Numerical ability	.18	.24	.16	.11
Composite ability	.22	.31	.17	.13

[a]Partial correlations controlling for years on force.
[b]Adjusted for reduced range on criterion measures.
[c]Nonmonotonic transformation.

results are less clear with respect to peer ratings, where the correlations between scores and ratings were not substantially different in the two conditions. Further evidence from the project suggests that peer ratings are less heavily influenced by cognitive skills than are supervisor ratings, and thus the modest correlation obtained between composite ability and peer ratings is not surprising.

Correlations corrected for restriction of range provide a better picture of the relative predictive power of different tests when used on a more unselected candidate pool. Table 2 presents these correlations between composite personality and ability measures and ratings under voluntary and exam conditions, corrected for restriction of range. Because of considerable preselection in the sample of police officers, ability measures can be expected to fare even better as predictors in a more general applicant pool, while personality measures show only minor increases in predictive power under these circumstances. The correlations presented in Table 2 provide an answer to our question concerning how well validation results obtained under voluntary conditions will generalize to actual test conditions. For both superior-officer and peer ratings, personality measures that looked at least reasonably promising after the original validation showed a drastic decline in predictive power when measured under actual exam conditions. Superior-

TABLE 2   Adjusted correlations between peer and superior-officer ratings with composite personality and ability measures under voluntary and actual exam conditions[a]

	Superior-officer ratings		Patrol officer ratings	
Composite	Voluntary	Exam	Voluntary	Exam
Personality	.21	.10	.29	.13
Ability	.27	.40	.20	.16

[a] Adjusted for restriction of range relative to general population, tenure partialled out.

officer ratings are typically used as an index of job performance. Thus, as is clear from Table 2, the results of our voluntary validation study would have been quite misleading with respect to the actual usefulness of both ability and personality measures. Under voluntary conditions, personality and ability factors seem to contribute about equally to ratings of job performance, but this was not the case when the measures were taken under true test conditions.

These results are not particularly surprising. Under true exam conditions the applicant is strongly motivated to achieve the highest possible score. With ability measures, a test-taker is undoubtedly putting forth more effort than would be the case under no-stakes conditions. Thus the true exam scores are likely to be better measures of a candidate's actual ability than are those obtained under conditions of low motivation. On the other hand, an applicant is less likely to engage in second-guessing the intent of questions on personality inventories in the no-stakes condition than he or she would under true test conditions. Because of this, personality profiles obtained under voluntary conditions are probably subject to less faking and are thus more valid assessments of true personality profiles than are those obtained under test conditions.

Table 3 presents data that suggest some possibility of faking and also indicate that the nature of shifts and responses under voluntary and actual test conditions can be rather subtle. The table lists means and standard deviations for each of the scales of the 16 PF given under the two conditions. Of the 16 scales 7 showed a significant difference in mean scores under voluntary and exam conditions. In support of the hypothesis that applicants try harder on aptitude measures during true exam conditions, there is a significant increase on the brightness, or intelligence, scale. With respect to personality dimensions, there tends to be some shift toward a "police image" on some scales—increases in maturity, shrewdness, conservatism, and compulsive behavior—and a shift toward the general population mean on others. Interestingly enough, three of the five scales found useful in the initial validation procedure showed no significant shifts in mean scores under exam

TABLE 3 16 PF scores for patrol officers obtained under voluntary test conditions and actual exam conditions[a]

	Voluntary[b]		Exam conditions[c]		Significance
16 PF Scale and description	Mean	SD	Mean	SD	p
A Outgoing, easygoing	5.6	1.8	5.4	2.0	ns
B Intelligent, bright	5.2	1.7	6.0	1.6	.01
C Stable, mature	5.8	1.6	6.0	2.0	ns
E Assertive, competitive	6.3	1.8	5.7	1.9	.01
F Enthusiastic, happy-go-lucky	5.8	1.5	5.6	1.9	ns
G Conscientious, persistent	6.2	1.4	6.3	1.7	ns
H Venturesome, uninhibited	5.9	1.8	5.9	1.9	ns
I Sensitive, tender-minded	4.8	1.5	5.4	1.8	.01
L Suspicious	5.7	1.9	4.9	1.9	.01
M Imaginative, absent-minded	4.8	1.8	5.1	1.8	ns
N Astute, shrewd	5.8	1.7	6.4	1.8	.01
O Apprehensive, insecure	5.2	1.8	5.2	1.8	ns
Q1 Liberal, experimental	5.2	1.8	4.6	1.9	.01
Q2 Self-sufficient, resourceful	5.5	1.7	5.3	1.9	ns
Q3 Controlled, compulsive	5.9	1.7	6.5	1.8	.01
Q4 Tense, frustrated	5.3	1.7	5.0	2.1	ns

[a]Sten scores based on general population norms with mean of 5.5 and standard deviation of 2.0.
[b]$N = 151$.
[c]$N = 905$.

conditions. There is also considerably more variability of response during actual exam conditions with 12 of the 15 scales showing a higher standard deviation. Clearly, while applicants may be answering personality questions differently under exam and voluntary conditions, shifts in their responses are not necessarily consistent or predictable.

The failure of personality measures to hold up substantially as predictors of police performance when given under test conditions is disappointing. Despite the desirability of sampling a wide range of behavioral characteristics related to police work, we can be reasonably confident of success only when we are measuring cognitive abilities. Possibly specific measures of attitudes, interests, social skills, and other "noncognitive" measures would fare better than general personality traits as job selectors. A considerable effort should be made to find such measures in order to allow a wider sampling of relevant behaviors on police entrance exams. The inclusion of such measures would also be of considerable usefulness in affirmative action hiring, since black-white differences on such measures tend to be smaller than those obtained on traditional paper-and-pencil aptitude tests.

INTERNAL VALIDITY OF VALIDATION PROCEDURES, WITH SPECIAL REFERENCE TO DIFFERENTIAL VALIDATION

If the results of validation studies of personality traits do not generalize to actual test situations, should we abandon the use of such scales altogether? I think not, since they may provide some insight into the internal validity of the results of validation research. The problem of finding adequate criterion measures for evaluating police performance is a serious one. Ideally, we would like to have a series of objective measures that could be applied in a standard manner for all officers. Unfortunately, most such objective measures are difficult to apply across an entire police force. Many measures, such as citations, disciplinary actions, law suits arising from citizens' complaints, accidents on the job, and similar events occur with such low frequency that they are not very useful for evaluating performance unless exceedingly long time spans are involved. Even data from events that occur frequently, such as arrests, subsequent convictions, complaints by citizens or detained suspects, number of calls answered, and similar measures, pose problems, since these measures tend to be influenced by a number of variables unrelated to the police officer's actual performance. Arrest records, for example, would have to be adjusted to take into account the officer's specific assignment, as well as the zone worked, the shift worked, the frequency of inappropriate arrests (as evidenced by dropped charges), and probably other extraneous factors influencing arrests frequency. Such adjustments would be nearly impossible to carry out accurately.

As a result of difficulties with objective measures, most validation studies use some form of subjective evaluation of performance by superior officers. Although a number of procedures have been developed to try to standardize such ratings, subjective elements are still likely to remain in the ratings. If subjectivity in judgments simply lowers the reliability of performance ratings, one can compensate for this unsystematic error by obtaining more ratings on each officer or by increasing sample sizes. If, however, there is a chance that systematic bias has occurred in subjective ratings, the internal validity of the results obtained may be in question.

Differential validation studies are particularly vulnerable to problems of systematic bias. In rating individuals from different subgroups, such as black and white or male and female patrol officers, an evaluator could systematically bias ratings in two ways. First, the evaluator might have a tendency to give lower performance rantings to one subgroup. The problem of true performance, as opposed to rated performance, becomes the issue in this case. Although no simple solution exists for this problem, carefully developed evaluation procedures can often minimize such effects, and if not, it might conceivably be possible to derive some standardized performance ratings based on different reference groups.

The second form of systematic bias is more subtle but equally serious. This bias involves rating job performance on the basis of differential expectations or behavioral stereotypes for different groups. While the average performance rating for black and white officers or male and female officers, may not differ, the behaviors that result in high or low ratings may differ between groups. The use of personality profiles could provide evidence for the existence of this type of bias in ratings.

Table 4 gives an example that lists correlations between a number of personality scales and performance ratings for a subgroup of black and white patrol officers who participated in the original police validation study in Cleveland. This subgroup completed both the EPPS and the 16 PF Inventory. A total of 9 of the EPPS scales and 4 of the 16 PF scales produced situations in which the correlation between scores and job ratings differed noticeably for blacks and whites. High scores on the EPPS deference, order, autonomy, affiliation/loyalty, and endurance/persistence scales were all positively related to high peer and officer ratings of blacks, while none of these showed

TABLE 4 Correlations of several personality factors with superior-officer and peer ratings of black and white patrol officers (Cleveland Police Department)

	Whites ($N = 75$)			Blacks ($N = 40$)		
	Officer	Peer	Mean[a]	Officer	Peer	Mean[a]
EPPS scales						
Deference	−.02	−.08	44	.23	.19	47
Order	−.11	−.05	44	.46	.43	44
Autonomy	−.07	−.03	44	.37	.30	49
Affiliation	.00	.06	41	.27	.21	32
Dominance	.00	.08	58	−.28	−.20	57
Abasement	.03	−.09	35	.05	.15	31
Endurance	−.13	−.20	49	.31	.23	43
Heterosexuality	.12	.11	74	−.55	−.45	72
Aggression	.00	.01	53	−.13	−.02	56
16 PF scales						
Outgoing, easygoing	.19	.14	5.6	−.25	−.22	5.5
Enthusiastic, happy-go-lucky	.00	.01	6.0	−.17	−.11	5.4
Liberal, free thinking	.21	.28	5.0	−.04	−.10	6.1
Self-sufficient, resourceful	.02	−.02	5.4	−.19	−.13	5.5

[a]EPPS based on percentile scores (general population mean = 50); 16 PF based on sten scores (general population mean = 5.5).

consistent relationships with ratings of whites. Conversely, high scores on dominance, heterosexuality, and aggression on the EPPS and 16 PF scores that suggested easy-going behavior, enthusiasm, and resourcefulness were negatively related to performance ratings for blacks, while the opposite was true for whites. It is not difficult to see that a stereotyped expectation or preference seemed to exist for at least some of the evaluators rating black and white officers. The black officers who were willing to receive suggestions from others, follow instructions, praise others, keep at a job until it was finished, and who demonstrated low levels of heterosexuality, aggression, and individual resourcefulness were rated higher than black officers who deviated from this pattern. The opposite was true for whites.

An examination of the mean scores for blacks and whites on each of these personality scales suggests that the differences in black-white correlations were not due to differences in the average level of expression of these traits. Despite nearly identical means on the heterosexuality measure, for example, pronounced negative correlations between scores and performance ratings exist for blacks, while a positive correlation exists for whites. Despite our precautions, superior officers, using a paired comparison rating procedure, and patrol officers, using rating scales, consistently had different expectations for blacks and whites. These expectations produced systematic differences in ratings of police behavior. Obviously such results could be different in other police departments and even in the same department over time. The results do demonstrate, however, that use of a personality scale in validation can provide some clues about the social dynamics contaminating the rating scheme being used.

The results presented in Table 4 have further important implications for differential validation research. It should be evident from the table that multiple-regression equations predicting police performance would be quite different for black and white candidates in terms of the relative weights of various personality scales used in selection. If these differential weights were actually used for a number of years in selecting entering officers, the force would begin to dichotomize along both racial and personality lines. Blacks who show retiring personality characteristics would be selected, while whites adhering to the tough, aggressive, "man's man" image would be favored. Such a selection strategy would of course represent blind empiricism at its worst—one that maximizes multiple correlations between tests and criterion measures for different subgroups with little regard for the internal validity of the process. Such a procedure would not necessarily maximize the predictive power of the test on true performance of future police officers but would simply maximize perceived performance tempered by stereotypes or differential expectations of various groups being evaluated.

It would appear that any predictor variable that works differentially for the subclasses in a validation study should be regarded with suspicion. In cases where predictor variables correlate in opposite directions for different subgroups or where there are substantial differences in predictor-criterion correlations for different subgroups the criterion variable itself should be suspect, at least with respect to the predictors being used.

The above considerations are also pertinent to situations where so-called objective criteria have been used for performance evaluation. As suggested earlier in this chapter, objective measures of police performance are often influenced by a number of extraneous variables, often related to a police officer's duty assignment. It is therefore incumbent on persons carrying out differential validation studies using objective criterion measures to demonstrate that duty assignments and other variables that may influence the criterion are randomly distributed among subgroups. It would probably be found that different subgroups are not equally represented in duty assignments. In Cleveland, for example, women were previously assigned to only a limited number of units within the force, and both precinct and duty assignments differed for black and white officers. In the Chicago police force at the time it was studied by Baehr et al. (1969), black officers were apparently assigned to higher crime areas than whites, and this fact resulted in a higher number of arrests by black officers and also in more complaints filed against them. Unless it can be shown that black and white officers or male and female officers are proportionally represented in all duty assignments under consideration, the criterion variable and subgroup membership become confounded. Under such circumstances differences in regression equations predicting the job criterion for different subgroups may simply indicate that the criterion measure itself differs among subgroups. The internal validity of the results of such a study is therefore severely in question.

Because of the problems associated with differential restriction of range or differential assignments among subgroups and because of problems of different types of systematic bias in ratings (or any combination of these), reports suggesting differential validity among subgroups must be examined closely for internal validity before being taken seriously.[2] Figure 2 summarizes the problem confronting a psychologist trying to find easily measurable traits or abilities that predict subsequent job performance. The upper portion of Figure 2 schematicizes the ideal situation: A given trait or ability directly influences job performance, and trait and job performance are reflected accurately in both a test score and a rating. In such a situation the test-rating correlation would provide a reasonable, although probably conservative, estimate of the true relationship between trait and job performance. Unfortunately, the lower

[2] The above arguments of course also apply when subgroup membership is used as a moderator variable in constructing the final prediction equation. The data presented in this chapter are largely in the form of correlation coefficients to provide clear examples illustrating some of the issues under discussion. Because of problems of restriction of range of both predictor and criterion variables across subgroups, in assessing differential validity it is more appropriate to focus on differences in standard errors of estimates of subgroups than on the correlations themselves. See Cole (1972), Einhorn and Bass (1971), and Barret, et al. (Note 3) for related issues pertaining to differential validation.

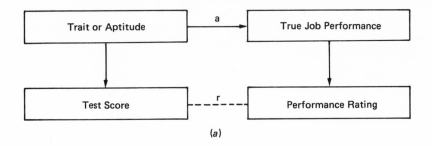

(a)

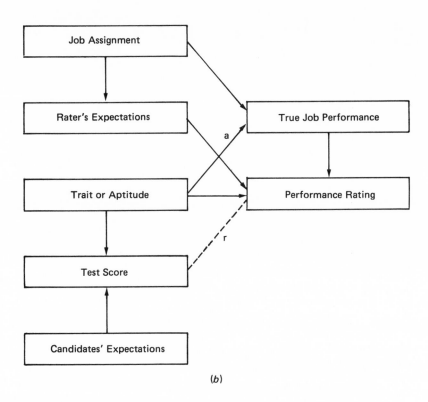

(b)

FIGURE 2 The relationships between tests, ratings, and behavior under
ideal (a) and actual (b) conditions. The relationship between a given
trait or aptitude and job performance (a) is estimated by the correlation
between a test score and performance rating (r).

portion of Figure 2 more accurately reflects the actual situation with the relationships between predictor and criterion variables. A given trait or ability may influence actual job performance, but at the same time it may independently influence the performance rating for non-job-related reasons. Actual job performance is influenced by the nature of the job assignment, and performance ratings are influenced by the raters' expectations. As we have shown, the candidates' expectations can also distort the test score designed to measure the underlying attribute. Under these circumstances the relationship between test and rating no longer accurately reflects the relationship between trait and performance. Of course, the strength of different influences shown in the figure would vary as a function of the validation circumstances.[3]

SUMMARY

The task of empirically validating selection devices for complex multidimensional jobs such as police work is far more complicated than we are often led to believe. The problems of sample size, range restriction, and test score and criterion contamination are severe for even the most basic validation procedures. In most situations more complex procedures, such as differential validation, may lose all internal validity because of these problems.

Results of research in the Cleveland Police Department, for example, indicated that the relationships between various personality dimensions and job performance obtained in a concurrent validation situation with volunteer subjects disappeared under actual test conditions, while relationships with aptitude measures increased slightly under true test conditions. Further analysis of personality profiles associated with high-rated black and white officers suggested that both supervisor and peer raters may be contaminating their judgments of police performance with racial stereotypes or differential expectations for blacks and whites. The results point out the importance of carefully examining validation studies in this area from the point of view of both internal and external validity.

REFERENCES

Azen, S. P., Snibbe, H. M. & Montgomery, H. R. A longitudinal predictive study of success and performance of law enforcement officers. *Journal of Applied Psychology*, 1973, *57*, 190–192.
Baehr, M. E., Furcon, J. E., & Froemel, E. C. *Psychological assessment of patrolmen qualifications in relation to field performance.* Washington, D.C.: U.S. Government Printing Office, 1969.

[3] One might argue that the relationships shown can be teased apart by using causal analysis techniques, such as path coefficients. Unfortunately, such procedures cannot be used effectively to clarify the situation because estimates of the strengths of relationships between most factors are difficult to obtain and because possible feedback loops may exist between some of the factors shown.

Blum, R. H., *Police selection.* Springfield, Ill.: Charles C Thomas, 1964.

Cole, N. S. *Bias in selection* (A.C.T. Research Rep. No. 51). American College Testing Program, 1972.

DuBois, P. H., & Watson, R. I. The selection of patrolmen. *Journal of Applied Psychology,* 1950, *34,* 90–95.

Einhorn, H. J. & Bass, A. R. Methodological considerations relevant to discrimination in employment testing. *Psychological Bulletin,* 1971, *75,* 261–269.

Hess, L. *Police entry tests and their predictability of score in police academy and subsequent job performance.* Unpublished doctoral dissertation, Marquette University, 1972.

Mandel, K. *The predictive validity of on-the-job performance of policemen from recruitment selection information.* Unpublished doctoral dissertation, University of Utah, 1970.

Marsh, S. H. Validating the selection of deputy sheriffs. *Public Personnel Review,* 1962, *23,* 41–44.

Mills, R. B., McDevitt, R. J., & Tonkin, S. Situational tests in metropolitan police recruit selection. *Proceedings of the American Psychological Association,* 1965, *1,* 243–244.

Mullineaux, J. E. An evaluation of the predictors used to select patrolmen. *Public Personnel Review,* 1955, *16,* 84–86.

Schmidt, F. L., Hunter, J. E., & Urry, V. W. Statistical power in criterion-related validity studies. *Journal of Applied Psychology,* 1976, *61,* 473–485.

REFERENCE NOTES

1. Furcon, J. E., Froemel, E. C., Franczak, R. G., & Baehr, M. E. *A longitudinal study of psychological test predictors and assessments of patrolmen field performance.* Report submitted to National Institute of Law Enforcement and Criminal Justice, Law Enforcement Assistance Administration, Grant # NI-0010, 1971.

2. Friedland, D. *Selection of police officers.* Unpublished study, City of Los Angeles Personnel Department, 1973.

3. Barrett, G. V., Alexander, R. A., O'Connor, E., Forbes, J. B., Balascoe, L., & Garver, T. *Technical report I: Public police and personnel selection: Development of a selection program for patrol officers.* Unpublished study, University of Akron, 1975.

12

POLICE CORRUPTION
Screening Out High-Risk Applicants

Allen E. Shealy
University of Alabama, Birmingham, Alabama

As Goldstein (1975) has pointed out, it is curious that police corruption, although widely if not universally acknowledged as a major policing problem, has not received more attention in the behavioral-science and criminal-justice literature in recent years. It is similarly curious that behavioral scientists involved in psychological screening of law enforcement applicants have also largely ignored this area, although there are exceptions to this, a major one being the Minneapolis group (Heckman, Grover, Dunnette, & Johnson, Note 1). Mills (1976) is another exception. He includes a "Serpico scene" in his simulated stress exercises, which are used with police applicants, but he does not include a specific rating scale for this area in his set of rating scales. Goldstein has suggested that the "blue curtain" of silence surrounding the subject has made it almost impossible to deal with the problem in a progressive way, and Patrick Murphy, the law enforcement profession's major advocate for implementation of anticorruption management methods has stated, "For too long corruption has been the skeleton in the police closet" (Goldstein, 1975, p. i).

There are many rationales for the lack of openness with regard to police corruption, ranging from realistic concerns for the protection of innocent law enforcement officials and organizations to more defensive attempts at denying, belittling, or justifying police corruption. An example of the last line of reasoning is the position that police are no more or less corrupt than the general society, that law enforcement officers are "human, like the rest of

197

us," and so there is bound to be a corrupt segment of the profession. Bracey (1976, p. 26), in a functional analysis of police corruption, concludes that "corruption should then not be viewed as a disease in itself, but rather as a symptom of problems in other areas of the social structure." Based on this reasoning, law enforcement officials feel scapegoated when the press exposes and "plays up" instances of detected police corruption.

A counterargument is that police corruption is a more important problem than corruption in other societal institutions in that the former undermines public confidence and may have a deleterious modeling effect on moral development of young people (Bahn, Note 2). Also, police corruption is like having the fox guarding the henhouse; in Goldstein's words, a police officer who accepts bribes is "like a fireman setting fires or a physician spreading disease" (p. 9).

There are a number of reasons why behavioral scientists involved in police selection have given relatively little attention to corruption. First, the application of behavioral science to police selection is a relatively recent addition to the screening process. Also, behavioral scientists are aware of the need to be diplomatic and nonthreatening in their work with law enforcement administrators in order to be able to continue to make a contribution, whether this be through research, consultation, clinical service liaisons, or as is becoming more prevalent, in the capacity of full-time staff in law enforcement organizations.

In addition, the definition of *corruption* is a problem for the selection researcher. In fact, there is little agreement among police administrators and researchers on the scope of the definition. Some see accepting a free cup of coffee as corrupt, or at least as the beginning of an "erosion process," leading to corruption (Bahn, Note 2). Fishman (Note 3), for example, includes this behavior in a scale designed for collecting epidemiological-type data on police corruption. (It is interesting that the title of this instrument is the Improbity Scale, *improbity* being a euphemism for *corruption*.) The definition problem is closely related to the criterion problem for test validation. The criterion problem is still the major difficulty in police selection, even with the variables that are better defined and less confounded by the problems of secrecy and defensiveness.

Another problem for the selection researcher involves the question of how much of corrupt behavior is situationally determined. Mischel (1968) has raised general questions about the ability of preemployment trait or character measures to predict later, on-the-job behavior. Fortier (1972), Mann (1973), Niederhoffer (1967), and Bahn (Note 2) have all emphasized the importance of situational variables and organizational dynamics in producing corrupt behavior of police officers. Swan (Note 4), based on his experience as a police officer, concludes that police corruption is a product of a "rotten barrel" rather than a few "rotten apples." Bahn's (Note 2) position is essentially that new recruits experience a corruption-fostering process of socialization to the police officer role. This socialization process involves organizational and peer pressures to conform to new values and standards of behavior that facilitate corrupt behavior. As a consequence of this view, emphasis is placed on developing an organizational climate that encourages integrity rather than on selecting recruits who have high resistance to these situational pressures.

The situationalists are undoubtedly correct in that more than half of the variance in behavior can be accounted for by situational, on-the-job variables. Saunders (Note 5) has stated that roughly 30% of the variance is the best we can hope to account for in preemployment predictions of on-the-job behavior. Police organizations seem to be "total institutions" that demand "total roles" (Goffman, 1961; Bahn, Note 2) because of the closed, tightly knit organizational dynamics and the homogeneity of personality characteristics of law enforcement applicants (Lefkowitz, 1975; Shealy, 1977). Thus it is likely that situational variables are even more important determinants of behavior in police departments than in other organizations. Even if a definition and criterion were agreed on and if there were more openness and willingness to allow research in this sensitive area, the importance of situational variables would make the task of predicting on-the-job corruption from the preemployment screening process quite difficult.

The purpose of this chapter is to demonstrate the openness of the administration of one police department to inquiry into the characteristics of officers judged by superiors to be corrupt. An additional intent is to outline one paradigm for validation of a measurement tool to be included as a part of the psychological screening process. In order to provide a context for discussing findings on corrupt police officers, it is necessary to briefly review theoretical approaches to moral development.

MORAL DEVELOPMENT

Hartshorne and May (1928-1930), in their classic studies of children's honesty, define moral character as resistance to temptation to break a rule when detection is unlikely. They include in their definition the traits of honesty, service and willingness for personal sacrifice for group benefit, and self-control. The investigators conclude that resistance to temptation is primarily determined by the situation, as they report low correlations between cheating in different types of situations. Burton (1963) has reanalyzed the Hartshorne and May data and through factor analysis has found a small, general factor, suggesting that there are stable, cross-situational consistencies in moral behavior.

Kohlberg (1964) lists 11 different aspects of moral judgment, suggested by Piaget's (1932) developmental studies. These constructs increase regularly with age in children, regardless of social class, nationality, religion, or type of situation in which subjects are studied. The conclusion from this work is that as children develop they move from an orientation of obedience, punishment, and explanations involving impersonal forces toward more internal and subjective processes. Kohlberg categorizes moral judgment in six types falling into three major levels of development:

1. Premoral (punishment and obedience orientation, instrumental hedonism)
2. Morality of conventional role conformity ("good boy" morality, morality maintained by authority)
3. Morality of self-accepted moral principles (morality of individual principles of conscience)

In summary, Piaget and Kohlberg view maturing moral judgment as movement away from control by external, situational variables and movement toward personal, introjected, internally controlled decision-making processes.

This autonomy of moral judgment has important implications for police selection, in light of the strong corruption-fostering socialization pressures on the police recruit, as outlined by Bahn (Note 2) and others. Kohlberg (1964) states, "The individual's direction by moral principles may often stand in opposition to social pressures by peers or adults." For police recruits, mature moral judgment would be a prerequisite for being able to resist pressures from other police officers or citizens to become involved in corruption.

MEASUREMENT OF MORAL JUDGMENT

Hogan's (1973) model of moral conduct and moral character appears to hold the most promise for use in police selection because of its development of measurement tools. This model builds on the work of Piaget and Kohlberg and organizes the dimensions of moral conduct into five areas: moral knowledge, socialization, empathy, moral judgment (that is, internalization of rules or maturity of moral judgment, as defined by Kohlberg), and autonomy. It is proposed (Hogan, 1973) that these five concepts, "when taken together, explain a considerable range of moral behavior and define certain important parameters of character development" (p. 220).

Considerable effort has been spent in developing methods of measuring these dimensions. The first dimension, moral knowledge, is important to the model because it is necessary for a person to know the rules of his or her society. Hogan assumes little correlation between moral knowledge and moral conduct because, given normal intelligence and training, everyone knows the basic rules or "rights" and "wrongs" of the culture. Since tests of moral knowledge are so highly correlated with general intelligence (Maller, 1944), measurement of moral knowledge is of little use in predicting moral conduct.

The second dimension, socialization, is defined as the extent to which a person internalizes the rules of conduct in his or her culture through socialization processes. Hogan advocates the use of the socialization scale of the California Psychological Inventory (Gough, 1969; Gough & Peterson, 1952) as a measure of this aspect of his model.

The third dimension, empathy, is defined as "the extent to which a person considers the implications of his conduct for the welfare of others, that is, the ability and extent to which a person 'puts himself in the other's shoes.'" Hogan (1969) has developed a scale to measure empathy as defined in his model.

The fourth dimension is called ethics of conscience vs. ethics of responsibility, and this dimension measures the extent to which a person bases his or her conduct on conforming to internal rules of "personal conscience," as contrasted with external rules of "social responsibility." This differs from socialization in that internalized moral judgment assumes an irrational, intuitive understanding of an ideal "higher" law. Persons with the social responsibility disposition have been described as rational, conventional, and resistant to change, while those with the personal conscience disposition have been described as independent, innovative, creative, and impulsive (Hogan, 1973). Hogan (1970) has developed two measures of this dimension, one a semiprojective technique (Hogan & Dickstein, 1972) and the other a checklist of attitudes.

The final dimension in Hogan's model is autonomy, which can be considered as the extent to which a person resists immoral conduct resulting from compliance with collective norms. Again, because of the strong organizational dynamics of the law enforcement profession, this dimension would seem important to consider in screening out police applicants who have low resistance to corruption-fostering group pressures. The Ego Strength Scale, developed by Barron (1953), is used by Hogan to measure this dimension of independence of moral judgment.

AN EMPIRICAL STUDY OF POLICE CORRUPTION

The author and his colleagues (Shealy, Deardorff, & Roberts, Note 6) were able to obtain the assistance of the administration of a relatively large police department in conducting a study to determine characteristics distinguishing between police officers identified as corrupt and those similarly identified as noncorrupt. There were internal investigations in progress of a number of patrol officers who were suspected of involvement in corrupt on-the-job conduct. More specifically, the administration was "certain" that it could correctly identify a sizable number of police officers who were accepting bribes. While these officers were under investigation, there was not sufficient objective evidence to justify job termination or to successfully bring criminal charges. For the purposes of this study we defined corruption as "acceptance of a bribe in return for unethical or illegal services."

As a beginning point in identifying corrupt and noncorrupt officers for the study, the police department administration compiled a list of officers who were "known" to be involved in corrupt conduct, as defined above, and a list of an equivalent number of officers who were believed to be of highest integrity. Next, two commanding officers who were believed by both the police administration and the researchers to be of high integrity were identified for use as raters to provide a reliability check on the dichotomous list of corrupt/noncorrupt officers and to convert this dichotomous measure into a continuous measure of corruption. Through the course of the study neither these officers nor the subjects themselves were informed of the nature of the study. The names of the officers in the two groups were combined into one randomly ordered list of names. In order to minimize halo error of the raters, this list was presented to each rater independently with instructions to rate each person on a 5-point scale as to (a) how long he had known the person and (b) how well he liked the person. Then the original groups were matched according to these two variables and the rank of the officers in each group.

A forced-choice paired comparisons technique was employed to develop a corruption score for each officer. A list of all possible pairs of names (the final list consisted of more than 2,700 pairs of names) arranged in random order was presented in small segments to each of the two raters independently. Each rater was asked to choose the member of the pair who was more likely to be the main character in the following vignette:

A police officer drives up to an illegal whiskey house on Saturday morning. He parks his patrol car and goes in. After exchanging greetings with the proprietor, the police officer accepts a $10.00 bill as a bribe and puts it into his pocket. No words are exchanged about the money, and the officer leaves.

A corruption score for each officer was calculated on the basis of the number of times an officer was chosen as the more likely of a pair to be the officer in the vignette. A score was computed for each person on each of the two ratings. There was high agreement between Rater A and Rater B ($r = .85$), between Rater A and the initial dichotomous measure ($r = .83$), and between Rater B and the initial measure ($r = .85$). As a further reliability check, artificial dichotomies were created by dividing each rater's scores at the median of the distribution. A comparison of the crossover frequency indicated minimal crossover, and this was near the median when it occurred. The final step in the identification and measurement of corruption was the combination of the three measures into one corruption score for each officer on the list.

The scales measuring the essential constructs of Hogan's model of moral judgment were administered to volunteers. Participation in the blind testing was strongly encouraged by the police chief, and with his help, test results were obtained on approximately 90% of the original subjects, evenly split across corrupt/noncorrupt groups. In addition, a biographical survey form was administered.

Of the five moral judgment measures, one discriminated significantly between the corrupt and noncorrupt officers. The scale measuring ethics of social responsibility versus ethics of personal conscience was the one variable in a multiple-regression equation that discriminated best between the two groups. This variable alone also discriminated significantly between the groups. The police officers who were identified as corrupt were more likely to use ethics of social responsibility while the noncorrupt officers were more likely to use ethics of personal conscience. In descriptive terms the test responses of the noncorrupt officers indicated that they were more likely to show concern for the sanctity of the individual, to use judgments based on the spirit of the law rather than on the letter of the law, to be concerned for the welfare of society as a whole, and to have the capacity to see both sides of an issue.

As for biographical differences, the corrupt officers were more likely to indicate that they had formally participated in more years of varsity athletics in high school, and that they had relatives in police work prior to their own employment as a police officer or currently had one or more relatives who were police officers. Perhaps participation in varsity sports is related to lower autonomy and resistance to peer presures in that motivation for participation may reflect need for peer approval. However, a number of equally reasonable explanations could be invoked to account for the biographical differences between corrupt and noncorrupt officers.

The weaknesses of this study are those usually associated with concurrent validation approaches, that is, the study does not answer the question of whether the differences between groups existed at the time of employment or whether they resulted from differing organizational experiences. Another problem is that only police officers were used in identifying corrupt and noncorrupt officers. An alternative approach that might be considered would be to have certain "in the know" citizens provide input to the identification process.

However, the study does provide some encouragement for screening applicants for resistance to corruption. First, it is quite encouraging that a police administration not only allowed such research to be conducted but supported it and was actively involved despite the risk of alienating some officers. It is also encouraging that differences were found between the groups and that these differences are largely congruent with moral judgment theory. It remains for ongoing and future research to determine the predictive validity of these variables.

FUTURE DIRECTIONS

It should be emphasized that the goal of the proposed screening is not to serve the same or similar function as the background investigation used by most police organizations (with or without a polygraph examination) as part of the in-house screening procedure. The background investigation and related techniques serve to identify persons whose past record indicates questionable incidents; these are measures of existing or previous unethical or illegal behavior patterns. Our goal as part of the psychological screening procedure is to identify correlates of a *predisposition* to become involved in behavior of dubious integrity after being hired as a law enforcement officer, since organization pressures of police work may provide a necessary catalyst for the manifestation of unethical conduct.

Measures of personality traits that are theoretically related to moral judgment may be helpful in screening and should be included in studies attempting to predict corrupt behavior. Kohlberg (1964) reports a correlation of $-.52$ between authoritarianism, as measured by the California F-scale (Sanford, 1959), and his moral judgment scale in the general population. While the question of authoritarian personality characteristics of police officers in general has received wide attention, an empirical analysis of the relationship between authoritarian attitudes and police corruption remains to be done.

Another personality construct that is theoretically related to moral development is locus of control. Kohlberg (1964) hypothesizes that internal locus of control is related to more mature moral judgment. While the author and several collaborators are currently investigating the relationship between locus of control and authoritarianism and numerous police performance measures, no corruption data are available from the particular organization involved in this research.

Autonomy is another personality construct that is theoretically relevant. Although we found no significant differences in ego strength scores between our corrupt and noncorrupt groups, we did find biographical differences suggesting differences in autonomy. We do have some information as to autonomy scores in a group of police applicants. Matarazzo, Allen, Saslow, and Wiens (1964) administered the Edwards Personal Preference Schedule (EPPS) to a group of police applicants and report that the subjects were below the mean of the general population in autonomy, one of the EPPS scales. This finding suggests that police applicants have a high base rate on at least one construct related to vulnerability to corrupt influences—and thus underscores the need for such screening as we are advocating.

A warm and positive relationship with one's parents is important for developing mature moral judgment (Kohlberg, 1964). This is sometimes tapped by clinical interviews of applicants and included in global impression ratings. In addition, many personality inventories contain items that tap this area. In the quest to find reasonable predictor variables for corruption risk, it would seem wise to include such character formation variables in our research.

Hogan (1973) hypothesizes that there should be "clear-cut personality correlates of the disposition to adopt the ethics of conscience or responsibility" (p. 225). Referring to correlations between the Myers-Briggs Type Indicator (Myers, 1973) and his moral judgment scales, he suggests that those who use ethics of personal conscience are characterized as independent, innovative, creative, impulsive, opportunistic, and irresponsible, while those using primarily ethics of social responsibility are considered resonable, helpful, dependable, conventional, and resistant to change. Our own findings of the Myers-Briggs Type Indicator typologies of 468 police applicants are that 45% of applicants have the extroverted, sensation, thinking, judgment (ESTJ) type (Shealy & Roberts, Note 7), which seems closely associated with Hogan's description of the personality correlates of the disposition to adopt the ethics of social responsibility. Myers' (1973) description of this type includes the statement, "He lives his life according to a definite set of rules" (p. A-1). The ESTJ type is further described as rational, nonintuitive, rigid and organized, and impersonal. These findings, when considered along with our finding that corrupt officers are more likely to use ethics of social responsibility, again suggest the great importance of screening applicants for the predisposition to corruption, since this predisposition may have a high frequency of occurrence in groups of police applicants. The 45% frequency of the ESTJ type in our studies of police applicants is three times greater than would be expected in a population of males with similar education levels (Myers, 1973). Again, we would suggest that this variable be included in future validation studies in corruption screening.

THE SCREENING PROCESS

Since completing the concurrent validity study described above, we have included the moral judgment scale measuring the disposition to adopt ethics of personal conscience versus ethics of social responsibility in our psychological screening battery. This measure is included both to provide data for future predictive validation studies and to provide additional data for current screening of applicants. It is administered in concert with the Minnesota Multiphasic Personality Inventory (MMPI), the Strong Vocational Interest Blank, the Myers-Briggs Type Indicator, and a biographical inventory. The psychological screening in this particular police department serves as an adjunct to the existing departmental screening procedures. In contrast to some psychological screening programs, which provide binary "go/no-go" hiring recommendations, our reports provide probability statements in six different areas of functioning. The sixth area is called "probability of this applicant's having high integrity as a police officer" and rated on a 1-to-7 scale.

To date, we have administered the moral judgment scale to 82 applicants.

It is encouraging that the mean of these applicants' moral judgment scale scores is more similar to the mean of the noncorrupt study sample than to the corrupt group mean. With the same scorer used in the concurrent validation study, the mean of applicants is very close to the mean of the noncorrupt sample of officers, with the applicants in fact scoring slightly higher. This suggests that our current sample of applicants are, as a group, low-risk candidates for corruption. However, this interpretation should be considered tenuous, since we have not ruled out the possibility that these scores will decrease after experience on the job and change in the direction of ethics of social responsibility. It should also be considered that the applicants were tested as part of the application process and were therefore more likely to respond to test items in a socially desirable way than were the subjects in the concurrent sample.

The range of moral judgment scale scores in our applicant sample is 7-25, with a relatively nonskewed distribution. This suggests that the scale is not very vulnerable to social desirability response set. It is quite encouraging to use a measure that does not obtain homogeneous results across applicants, since homogeneity of responses leads to low validity coefficients.

One caution should be made concerning the scoring of the moral judgment scale. The scale is composed of 15 items. Each item is a narrative statement, and the instructions to the subjects are to assume that another person has made this statement to the subject during a social conversation. The subject is asked to write what his or her response to the statement would be. Each of the responses is then scored on four content areas to determine if the response reflects (1) concern for the sanctity of an individual, (2) judgment based on the spirit rather than on the letter of the law, (3) concern for the welfare of society as a whole, and (4) the capacity to see both sides of an issue. Because the semiprojective technique uses such a subjective scoring system, it is vulnerable to constant rater "error," or rater tendencies.

In our concurrent validation study, we found an interscorer correlation coefficient of .80; however, one rater consistently rated subjects far lower than did the other. (Significant differences between the corrupt/noncorrupt group means on the moral judgment scale were found for each scorer.) In using the scale, then, it is important to establish rater norms, and in comparing scores to published research group norms or to locally developed norms, it is necessary to correct scores for the constant error of the particular scorer. In setting cutting scores for our probability statements, we use the concurrent validity norms established by the scorer who is the current scorer of applicants' test protocols. If we were to change scorers at some point, we would be obliged to change our cutting scores to reflect the tendency of the new scorer.

The interaction of moral judgment scores with the MMPI *Pd* (psychopathic deviate) scale leads to a positive interpretation of mild to moderate scores on the *Pd* scale. We have found that applicants who score more than one standard deviation below the mean of our study sample on the moral judgment scale (ethics of social responsibility, high-risk-of-corruption applicants) obtain MMPI profiles with no elevation above the mean on the *Pd* scale. Those scoring more than one standard deviation above the mean on the moral judgment scale (low-risk-of-corruption applicants) obtain moderate elevations on the *Pd* scale. This is consistent with Hogan's (1973) report that the peer description adjective with the highest correlation (.49) with the ethics of personal conscience was *rebellious.* We have found in a clinic patient population that persons who did not engage in a period of rebelliousness during adolescence were lower in autonomy as adults than those persons who reported in an interview that they were rebellious during adolescence (Klein & Shealy, 1974).

Since autonomy is one of the important dimensions of moral judgment, the rebelliousness reflected in mild to moderate elevations of the MMPI *Pd* scale may reflect autonomy and resistance to corruption. This is consistent with an earlier report (Shealy, Note 8) that the *Pd* scale alone did not discriminate between officers who were terminated for disciplinary reasons and those who are still active and that the *Ma* (hypomania) scale of the MMPI was a better discriminator.

It is interesting that our sample of applicants who are considered high-risk corruption candidates, while scoring lower than other applicants on the *Pd* scale, scored slightly higher than low-risk applicants on the *Ma* scale. Based on these tentative findings on applicants and on theoretical assumptions, we hypothesize a curvilinear relationship between the *Pd* scale and resistance to corruption, with extreme scores in either direction (as compared to other police applicants) being related to low resistance to corruption.

SUMMARY

Police corruption is very costly, both to the law enforcement profession and to society in general. Because of this it is one of the most important areas—perhaps *the* most important area—that should be considered in psychological screening of police applicants. Because of the "blue curtain" and the need of behavioral scientists working with the law enforcement profession to be nonthreatening, there has been relatively little emphasis on corruption research and application of research findings to psychological screening of police applicants. Psychological screening batteries that incorporate measures of maturity of moral judgment would tap the predisposition to succumb to organizational pressures that may foster corrupt conduct and would serve an adjunct to existing screening methods, such as the background investigation.

One phase of our research in this area has been presented in this chapter in the spirit of providing encouraging evidence that some police administrations are open to such inquiry. It is also encouraging that, when such cooperation develops, superiors' identification of corrupt officers is highly

208   A. E. SHEALY

reliable; in fact, findings on those officers judged to be corrupt suggest
validity for using police supervisors to identify corrupt and noncorrupt
officers.

Because of the small number of veteran female police officers, this
discussion has unfortunately been limited to males. Future research in the area
should—and undoubtedly will—be extended to include females.

In conclusion, it is hoped that the research discussed here will be viewed
as an optimistic beginning step toward developing meaningful and reliable
validation criteria and toward identifying predictor variables for future
research on screening for high-risk-of-corruption applicants.

REFERENCES

Barron, F. Some personality correlates of independence of judgment. *Journal of Personality*, 1953, *21*, 789–797.
Bracey, D. H. A functional approach to police corruption. *Criminal Justice Center Monographs*. New York: John Jay Press, 1976.
Burton, R. V. The generality of honesty reconsidered. *Psychological Review*, 1963, *70*, 481–500.
Fortier, K. Police culture: Its effect on sound police-community relations. *The Police Chief*, 1972, *39*(2), 33–35.
Goffman, E. *Asylums*. Garden City, N.Y.: Anchor Books, 1961.
Goldstein, H. *Police corruption*. Washington, D.C.: Police Foundation, 1975.
Gough, H. G. A leadership index on the California Psychological Inventory. *Journal of Counseling Psychology*, 1969, *16*, 283–289.
Gough, H. G., & Peterson, D. R. The identification and measurement of predispositional factors in crime and delinquency. *Journal of Consulting Psychology*, 1952, *16*, 207–212.
Hartshorne, H., & May, M. A. *Studies in the nature of character: Studies in deceit* (Vol. 1); *Studies in self-control* (Vol. 2); *Studies in the organization of character* (Vol. 3). New York: Macmillan, 1928–1930.
Hogan, R. Development of an empathy scale. *Journal of Consulting and Clinical Psychology*, 1969, *33*, 307–316.
Hogan, R. A dimension of moral judgment. *Journal of Consulting and Clinical Psychology*, 1970, *35*, 205–212.
Hogan, R. Moral conduct and moral character: A psychological perspective. *Psychological Bulletin*, 1973, *79*, 217–232.
Hogan, R., & Dickstein, E. A measure of moral values. *Journal of Consulting and Clinical Psychology*, 1972, *39*, 210–214.
Klein, A., & Shealy, A. Dependency, rebelliousness in the adolescent drug abuser. In J. Singh & H. Lal (Eds.), *Drug addiction: New aspects of analytical and clinical toxicology* (Vol. IV). Miami: Symposia Specialists, 1974, pp. 273–276.
Kohlberg, L. Development of moral character and ideology. In M. L. Hoffman & L. W. Hoffman (Eds.), *Review of child development research* (Vol. 1). New York: Sage Foundation, 1964, pp. 383–431.

Lefkowitz, J. Psychological attributes of policemen: A review of research and opinion. *Journal of Social Issues*, 1975, *31*, 3–26.

Maller, J. B. Personality tests. In J. McV. Hunt (Ed.), *Personality and the behavior disorders*. New York: Ronald Press, 1944.

Mann, P. *Psychological consultation with the police department*. Springfield, Ill.: Charles C Thomas, 1973.

Matarazzo, J. D., Allen, B. V., Saslow, G., & Wiens, A. N. Characteristics of successful policemen and firemen applicants. *Journal of Applied Psychology*, 1964, *48*, 123–133.

Mills, R. B. Simulated stress in police recruit selection. *Journal of Police Science and Administration*, 1976, *4*, 179–186.

Mischel, W. *Personality and assessment*. New York: John Wiley & Sons, 1968.

Myers, I. B. *The Myers-Briggs Type Indicator Manual*. Princeton, N.J.: Educational Testing Service, 1973.

Niederhoffer, A. *Behind the shield: The police in urban society*. New York: Anchor Books, 1967.

Piaget, J. *The moral judgment of the child*. Glencoe, Ill.: Free Press, 1948. (Originally published, 1932.)

Sanford, N. The approach of the authoritarian personality. In J. McCary (Ed.), *Psychology of personality*. New York: Evergreen Books (Grove Press), 1959.

Shealy, A. E. Police integrity: The role of psychological screening of applicants. *Criminal Justice Center Monograph Number 4*. New York: John Jay Press, 1977.

REFERENCE NOTES

1. Heckman, R. W., Grover, D. M., Dunnette, M. D., & Johnson, P. D. *Development of psychiatric standards for police selection*. (PB-215 534). National Technical Information Service, Washington, D.C., 1972.

2. Bahn, C. *Police socialization and the psychosocial costs of police corruption*. Paper presented at the Second National Anti-Corruption Workshop, San Francisco, April 1976.

3. Fishman, J. *Measuring police corruption: An analysis of the project methodology*. Paper presented at the Second National Anti-Corruption Workshop, San Francisco, April 1976.

4. Swan, E. Police corruption: The rotten apple or the rotten barrel? In P. C. Green (Chair), *Psychology and law enforcement: Culture shock*. Symposium presented at the meeting of the Southeastern Psychological Association, New Orleans, March 1976.

5. Saunders, D. H. *Moderator variables in police selection*. Paper presented at the Working Conference on the Selection of Law Enforcement Officers, Quantico, Va., 1976.

6. Shealy, A. E., Deardorff, P., & Roberts, E. *Police corruption and measures of moral development*. Paper presented at the meeting of the American Psychological Association, Washington, D.C., September 1976.

7. Shealy, A. E., & Roberts, E. *Myers-Briggs Indicator types of police applicants.* Paper presented at the meeting of the Southeastern Psychological Association, New Orleans, March 1976.
8. Shealy, A. E. Psychological screening of police and predictive validity of personality tests. In M. Bard (Chair), *Police selection: Impact of administrative, professional, social, and legal considerations.* Symposium presented at the meeting of the American Psychological Association, Washington, D.C., September 1976.

13

THE ASSESSMENT CENTER METHOD IN THE SELECTION OF LAW ENFORCEMENT OFFICERS

Robert J. Filer
Department of Psychology, University of Richmond, Richmond, Virginia

All organizations, whether public or private, share common personnel problems. The most significant of these involve the identification of talent, the development of human resources within the organization, and compliance with various requirements that regulate the selection and promotion of personnel. Many government agencies and private companies have learned the hard way that effective performance at one level does not necessarily predict effective performance at a higher level. In addition, it is a truism that individual development does not occur in a vacuum. These organizations therefore are continually searching for more effective techniques for both entry-level and promotion or development selections.

Written tests, traditionally used for selection and promotion purposes in both government agencies and business enterprises, have been under constant attack during the last decade or so because of apparent adverse effects on minorities and significant questions about job relatedness. Numerous court decisions have denied the job relatedness of the tests used, and EEOC guidelines and other government regulations have insisted on pertinent validity. At the same time the importance of selection techniques for the prediction of job performance is not denied.

Partly because in some cases written tests have been difficult to evaluate and partly because in other cases they do not measure significant dimensions related to job performance, many organizations have increasingly found use for an alternative evaluation strategy that is particularly effective in identifying talent and development needs. Trends indicate the growing popularity of the assessment center method, with its "situational testing" for observing dimensions of behavior that are ordinarily difficult, if not impossible, to measure by other means. Court decisions further support the use of the assessment center technique as a fair method of making promotional decisions. For these reasons—fairness and accuracy—the assessment center has become an increasingly favored technique with industry and government organizations alike. Included in the latter category are the important groups of people responsible for safeguarding the community—law enforcement agencies.

WHAT IS AN ASSESSMENT CENTER?

An assessment center is a method that involves a multiple assessment strategy; it is not a place. Among the several possible evaluation techniques are various forms of job-related simulations, as well as interviews and psychological tests. Common job simulations include in-basket exercises, management tasks, group discussions, simulations of interviews with subordinates, fact-finding exercises, oral presentation exercises, and written communications exercises.

The essentials of the assessment center method are best described in the definition presented in the standards and in the ethical statement endorsed by the Third International Congress on the Assessment Center Method, held in Quebec, Canada, in May 1975. The following is a quote from this statement:

To be considered as an assessment center, the following minimal requirements must be met:

1. Multiple assessment techniques must be used. At least one of these techniques must be a simulation. A simulation is an exercise or technique designed to elicit behaviors related to dimensions of performance on the job by requiring the participant to respond behaviorally to situational stimuli. The stimuli present in a simulation parallel or resemble stimuli in the work situation. Examples of simulations include group exercises and fact-finding exercises.
2. Multiple assessors must be used. These assessors must receive training prior to participating in a center.
3. Judgments resulting in an outcome (i.e., recommendation for promotion, specific training or development), must be based on pooling information from assessors and techniques.
4. An overall evaluation of behavior must be made by the assessors at a separate time from observation of behavior.
5. Simulation exercises are used. These exercises are developed to tap a variety of predetermined behaviors and have been pretested prior to use to insure that the techniques provide reliable,

objective and relevant behavioral information for the organization in question.

6. The dimensions, attributes, characteristics or qualities evaluated by the assessment center are determined by an analysis of relevant job behaviors.

7. The techniques used in the assessment center are designed to provide information which is used in evaluating the dimensions, attributes or qualities previously determined.

In summary, the assessment center consists of a standardized evaluation of behavior based on multiple inputs. Multiple trained observers and techniques are used. Judgments about behavior are made, in part, from specially developed assessment simulations.

These judgments are pooled by the assessors at an evaluation meeting during which all relevant assessment data are reported and discussed and the assessors agree on the evaluation of the dimensions and any overall evaluation that is made.

Further on, the Congress's ethical statement emphasizes what kind of activities do not constitute an assessment center. These activities exemplify the opposite sides of an excessively limited approach to selection and promotion: either the use by multiple assessors of a single technique, such as simulation, test battery, or interview, or the use by a single assessor of multiple techniques. Clearly, a fundamental characteristic of the assessment center underscores the broad scope of information it yields for making objective decisions regarding potential employment or promotion.

THE HISTORY OF ASSESSMENT CENTERS

The first recognizable precursors of the current assessment center procedure can be traced to the selection of personnel during and before World War II. Multiple assessment procedures were first developed by German military psychologists. They believed that traditional methods of selection placed too much emphasis on specific abilities and traits and failed to take a holistic, or "total person," outlook regarding the individual being assessed. Hence, these psychologists chose to evaluate candidates' behavior in a complex situation. Similar philosophies and practices were followed by the Japanese during this time.

The Allies adopted the assessment center methodology at a somewhat latter date than the Axis powers. In 1942 the British army came to the conclusion that its traditional methods of selecting officers were producing too high a proportion of unsuccessful cadets during officer training. In response to this the British army formed the British War Officer Selection Boards, which, in addition to adopting many of the Germans' techniques and procedures, devised additional techniques that have become widespread in the postwar period. One example of these techniques is the leaderless group discussion exercise, to be discussed below.

In the United States situational assessment techniques were used for a much more limited purpose during World War II. The American Office of Strategic Services adopted the assessment center methodology in 1943 as a method of selecting intelligence agents. The OSS recorded the rationale and operation of its assessment procedures in considerable detail in the now classic book, *Assessment of Men* (1948). This documentation has provided a widely accessible foundation for further development in the field.

The first use of the assessment center in the private sector came about in 1956, in a research project known as the Management Progress Study, conducted by the American Telephone and Telegraph (AT&T) Company for the purpose of developing "career histories" of potential management personnel in order to determine the characteristics of successful managers and the changes in personality brought about by a managerial career. The most striking result of this study, which used assessment center techniques to measure dimensions of behavior considered necessary for success in AT&T management, was the effectiveness of the technique itself in predicting performance. At least 75% of those who later reached middle-management positions had been correctly identified by the assessment center, and 94% of those who did not advance beyond first-level management positions had also been identified correctly.

There has been a continuing trend toward the acceptance and adoption of the assessment center in American industry. Since the pioneer work of AT&T in the late 1950s and the 1960s, such industrial organizations as IBM, Ford, J. C. Penney, General Electric, Mead Johnson, Bank of America, Eastman Kodak, Ciba-Geigy, Hoffman LaRoche, Prudential, and various governmental agencies, including the IRS, the FBI, and the U.S. Department of Agriculture, have effectively used the method. The last several years have seen an explosion in the use of the assessment center, so that several hundred companies currently use some version of the technique, with the number of candidates evaluated estimated in the hundreds of thousands.

This increasing trend in business and government toward using assessment centers became reflected in law enforcement agencies. During the early 1960s situational testing was recognized as an important technique in the normal examination procedures for police work. Results of studies conducted by Chenoweth (1961) and Mills, McDevitt, and Tonkin (1966) showed that successful performance traits can be revealed through the use of situational tests. Mills (1969, 1972) presented a very favorable case for the multiple assessment methodology based on a philosophy similar to that underlying industrial assessment centers:

Our philosophy has been that a combination of approaches yields more information than a single approach, and that the careful diagnostic integration of several different types of information on each candidate by a team represents the most equitable and thorough evaluation possible. (1969, p. 238)

The foregoing history of research studies has traced the effectiveness of the assessment center as a method for predicting successful job performance in both business and government. This discussion will focus next on the operation of specific assessment centers in law enforcement agencies. The Richmond, Virginia Police Department provides an example of the use of the assessment center for promotional selection, while the Ft. Collins, Colorado Police Department sample illustrates entry-level police selection methods. Both uses of the assessment center, however, required extensive background activities prior to implementing assessment procedures on behalf of the candidates. Some additional research data on these background activities will be taken from the Kansas City Police Department. The activities to be completed prior to commencing the assessment center include the determination of dimensions to be assessed, the selection of appropriate instruments and exercises to assess the dimensions, and finally, the training of the assessment staff in the evaluation techniques and program operation.

DETERMINATION OF PERFORMANCE DIMENSIONS

Perhaps the most important task to be carried out in the initiation of an assessment center is the determination of the personality and ability dimensions that the assessment center is designed to measure. Assessors can be trained to observe many different aspects of behavior, but in order for the process to have validity and be acceptable under EEOC guidelines, they must know which traits are important. In order to do this, it is essential that the organization carry out a well-designed job analysis for the target position.

In the specific example of the Ft. Collins Police Department, this job analysis included a review of research literature, an examination of questionnaire data, group interviews with department members, conferences with experts in the police department, direct observation, and the "critical incidents" technique. In the Richmond Police Department initial interviews were conducted within both bureaus with officers representing various jobs to be analyzed. Time was also spent observing various members of the police department while they were on duty. Based on interview data and observation, a questionnaire was developed to be administered to all incumbents in the positions to be analyzed. In addition, representative incumbents for each position were individually interviewed in order to obtain additional insight into the duties and responsibilities of each position and to verify the information obtained on the questionnaires. An interview guide was developed to obtain consistency and objectivity in the interview.

The job analysis revealed four vital areas of function: management and supervision, commanding and investigating, training and development, and administration. In response to these requirements the following dimensions, critical for supervisory and managerial success, were developed for use in the assessment center for the position of police lieutenant:

leadership
planning and organization
use of delegation
logical thinking
management control
decisiveness
sensitivity
energy
stress tolerance
flexibility
communications effectiveness

THE SELECTION OF APPROPRIATE EXERCISES

Following the substantial information gained from the in-depth job analysis, exercises were designed to elicit the appropriate behaviors defined in the performance dimensions. All dimensions should be covered by a variety of exercises to ensure reliability and validity in the results. The city of Richmond assessment center included group exercises, one analysis, one in-basket exercise, and an interview simulation, the content of which was relevant to the duties of a police lieutenant.

Data from the Kansas City Police Department indicate that three exercises were developed and written by two sergeants, under the direction of the consultant: an in-basket exercise containing 30 problems, a career interview exercise, and a leaderless group exercise. Prior to the conclusion of his participation at the center, each candidate was asked to anonymously complete a questionnaire. All findings were positive, particularly the response to the question, "To what extent do you think the assessment center was job related for the rank of sergeant?"

to a very great extent—47
to a great extent—52
to some extent—4
to a slight extent—0
to a very slight degree—0

Two final important considerations must be taken into account for the background activities of the assessment center: (1) avoidance of unintentional biases that may tend to favor one group of applicants over another; (2) accounting for situational factors that may affect the validity of particular selection instruments when transferred to police departments serving smaller or larger communities.

TRAINING OF ASSESSORS

Reliability and validity of the testing exercises are further enhanced by the training of the assessors, which is the next step in the activities leading up to the assessment center. By observing a participant handling the problems and challenges of the higher level job simulated in the exercises, assessors are able to form a highly accurate composite picture of the candidate and to predict how he or she is likely to perform in the new position. Three important factors that contribute to assessor objectivity are listed below:

1. Assessors typically have no personal involvement with the participant.
2. Assessors are able to devote full attention to the task of assessing.
3. Assessors are trained in evaluation procedures.

In Richmond such training included the specific areas of observing and recording behavior, participating in the discussion leading to final evaluation, and writing the final evaluation report. Special attention was given to maintaining control and security over the exercise forms and the assessor's relationship with applicants.

The Kansas City Police Department chose captains from the department who had all served under sergeants, performed the duties of a sergeant, and directly supervised sergeants. Under the consultant's direction the captains received training that covered all phases of the assessment center process, including the discussion of the exact definitions of the dimensions. Further, each assessor observed and scored, through the use of video tapes and role playing, each exercise that would be used in the supervisory assessment center. A thorough critique, during which the assessors presented their findings to the group, followed each exercise. Each assessor received an assessor's manual, which included the exercises and examples of completed assessor reporting forms, and each rated two candidates.

This completes the preoperational phase of the assessment center process. Once care has been taken to ensure a thorough job analysis, exercises have been developed in accordance with the performance dimensions required by the specific department under consideration, and the assessors have been trained, the operation of the assessment center may commence. This operation will generally include in-baskets, tests, leaderless group discussions, role-playing games, case studies, written and oral presentations. For an overview of the complete assessment process, Figure 1 is self-explanatory.

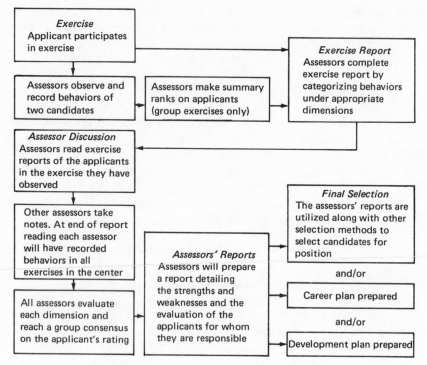

FIGURE 1   An assessment center flow chart.

USE OF ASSESSMENT CENTERS BY LAW ENFORCEMENT AGENCIES FOR PROMOTION (CITY OF RICHMOND)

The background for the use of the assessment center in the Richmond Police Department centered on the inability to promote throughout a period of approximately two years. Agreement was reached to use the assessment center method in the belief that it was a fair and thorough method for establishing promotional eligibility. Particularly significant in Richmond was the order of the U.S. District Court (1975) that stated,

Upon defendants' motion for approval of the form and format of the promotional tests and/or procedures to be used by the City of Richmond in making promotions to the positions of sergeant, lieutenant, captain and major in its Bureau of Police and upon careful consideration of the depositions, exhibits, and affidavits submitted in support of said motion, and upon consideration of the objections of plaintiffs-intervenors, it is hereby ORDERED that the defendants may proceed with the planned assessment centers and job knowledge tests as described in said deposition and affidavits in making promotions to the positions of sergeant, lieutenant, captain and major in the City of Richmond Bureau of Police. The Court in granting its approval approves the use of the assessment center technique and job knowledge tests as personnel selection techniques with each having the weight described in the deposition and affidavits described above. While the City may and should make reasonable modifications in its assessment centers without further approval of the Court in order to take advantage of improvements suggested by experience and developments in the field, the City is directed always to use valid, job related procedures and standards, with particular attention to the elimination of race as a factor in promotions.

Since approval under the federal court order, specific job-related tests and assessment center exercises have been used in Richmond for promotions at all advanced levels in the police department (see Table 1).

The following account of the Richmond Police Department assessment center applied to candidates who were evaluated for promotion to the position of police lieutenant. Figure 2 shows how the various exercises were located within the 2-day schedule to form a multiple pattern of assessment.

The first of two group exercises, the leaderless group discussion, involved

TABLE 1 Form and format for police officer promotional examinations

Position	Format	Assessment exercise[a]
Police major	2-day assessment center	Analysis Two group exercises In-basket Interview simulation Background interview
Police captain	2-day assessment center	Analysis Two group exercises In-basket Interview simulation
Police lieutenant	Job knowledge test, 2-day assessment center	Analysis Two group exercises In-basket Interview simulation
Police sergeant	Job knowledge test, 1-day assessment center	Analysis One group exercise In-basket Interview simulation

[a]The complexity of exercises varied with level of position. Specific job-oriented in-baskets were developed for police sergeant and police lieutenant positions.

First day	Participants	Assessors
8:30–9:00	Introduction to program	
9:00–9:30	Prepare group exercise I	Observe group exercise I
9:30–10:00	Participate in group exercise	
10:30–12:30	Complete in-basket exercise	Complete exercise reports
12:30–1:30		
1:30–4:00	Complete analysis exercise	Prepare 2 in-basket interviews
4:00–4:30	Complete participant report	Complete analysis exercise report

Second day	Participants		Assessors
	Group A	Group B	
8:30–9:00	Prepare interview simulation	Prepare interview simulation	
9:00–9:30	Interview simulation		Observe interview simulation A
9:30–10:30		Interview simulation	Observe interview simulation B
10:00–10:15			
10:15–10:45	Prepare confrontation exercise		Complete exercise reports
10:45–12:00	Confrontation exercise		Observe confrontation exercise
12:00–1:00			
1:00–2:00	In-basket interview	Prepare group exercise II	In-basket interview A
2:00–3:00	Prepare group exercise II	In-basket interview	In-basket interview B
3:00–3:15			
3:15–4:30	Group exercise II		Observe group exercise II
			Complete all exercise reports
Evening			Assessor discussion (break into 2 groups)

Third day		
		Assessor discussion (break into 2 groups)

Fourth day		
		Complete final evaluation report

FIGURE 2 Typical assessment center schedule.

the analysis of a problem by the group and the formulation of recommendations for its resolution. Participants were instructed to study the question individually for 45 minutes and then, as a group, discuss the issue among themselves and reach a consensus decision regarding the course of action to be advocated.

The police lieutenant in-basket exercise was designed to represent items that might cross a lieutenant's desk and require attention. The candidates were informed that they had assumed the duties of a police lieutenant and must deal with all the material that had accumulated since the departure of his or her predecessor. Several items were included in this exercise, ranging from the uncomplicated to the highly complex. Examples included items related to citizen complaints, training problems, violations of police ethics codes, equipment and procedure decisions, and a complaint from a patrol officer's wife objecting to the female partner her husband had been assigned. Items were constructed to furnish a great deal of information for assimilation and organization, with a number of interactions between the items. Candidates were instructed to go through the material, handle the problems whenever possible, and request additional information if necessary. The candidates were expected to perform some tasks themselves, delegate others to subordinates, and generally respond to the material as if they had actually been promoted to the position.

The third exercise used in the Richmond assessment center required individuals to participate in an analysis exercise. During this exercise candidates were given several pages of information regarding a particular question. They were expected to analyze and integrate this information and prepare reports with recommendations to their superior. A significant amount of time was employed to analyze the problem and form recommendations, after which the candidates gave a 5-minute oral presenation of their recommendations and their justifications. The presentation enabled the exercise to serve a double purpose: It provided an opportunity to evaluate the candidate's ability to analyze large bodies of information, logically, and his or her ability to make formal oral presentations.

The assessment center schedule further called for the use of the confrontation exercise. Two candidates interacted in a role-playing situation in which each candidate was given a body of background information on a controversial question and then assigned to the defense of one side or the other. The other candidate in each pair had been assigned the opposing side of the question and given the same information. After sufficient time to study the information and form their arguments, the two candidates were instructed to "have at each other" for a half-hour period, during which they attempted to convince each other of their respective positions. The exercise was constructed so that the candidates were able to defend either side without great difficulties occurring because of their beliefs regarding the question.

Another type of exercise, the interview simulation, permitted the candidate to function individually. Background material was provided on a problem situation concerning a patrol officer with a poor attitude. After examining the information at hand, the participant was directed to conduct a 15-minute interview with this patrol officer in order to attempt to rectify the problem. The patrol officer was played in this interview by a trained role-player who otherwise was not involved in the assessment center, either as a candidate or assessor.

Group exercise II, a variation of the group exercise described earlier, was conducted on the second day of the assessment center (see Figure 2). In this exercise individuals performed a particular function as a group in arriving at a decision regarding funds for distribution within a community under a grant. Each candidate was given information on a citizen worthy of receiving the grant. The attention of the candidates was directed to the dual nature of the exercise: to obtain as much of the grant as possible for the individual they represented and to help the group reach the most equitable possible distribution of the funds. Such an exercise can be expected to yield information about several of the dimensions vital to the police lieutenant position.

By now it is apparent that the specific dimensions of the city of Richmond's assessment center and the exercises designed to measure them closely resemble the desired management performance criteria within industrial settings. This resemblance resulted from reviewing the detailed job analysis, which indicated the importance of managerial and supervisory functions for police officer positions. In the following example of entry-level selection, there will be some modification of emphasis in the dimensions and exercises. However, the concepts of fairness and job relatedness will remain stable throughout the variation of details in the technique.

THE ASSESSMENT CENTER FOR ENTRY-LEVEL SELECTION (FT. COLLINS, COLORADO, POLICE DEPARTMENT)

Although assessment centers have primarily involved promotional situations and the determination of developmental needs, there is an interest and movement toward using the method at the entry level. In industry several organizations have found the method valuable in the selection of sales personnel at the entry level, and law enforcement agencies, such as the Ft. Collins, Colorado, and the Colorado State University police departments, have used the assessment center technique for the selection of police recruits for several years. Following prescreening by application review and ability testing, the one-day assessment center involved individual and panel reviews, group discussions and role-playing exercises.

The flexibility of the method allows for specific dimensions related to entry-level police work to be designed for the selection. These might include motivation for police work, self-confidence, emotional stability under stress, flexibility, mature relationship to authority, practical judgment, sensitivity, and social sense. Police officers, citizens, and psychologists may serve as assessors to evaluate interpersonal competencies, reactions to stress, and ability to improvise under unexpected circumstances. In the Colorado police departments candidates were observed in four situations: the individual psychological interview, the oral board interview, the leaderless group discussion, and situational testing. The last three activities are described in further detail below; the individual psychological interview was closely patterned on the oral board interview and therefore requires no specific explanation.

The Oral Board Interview

The oral board interview is a structured interview consisting of a series of *standard* questions asked of all applicants. The oral board itself is composed of a senior police officer, a psychologist, and a community representative. Board members ask the applicant questions and then independently evaluate the applicant on the appropriate dimensions. At the conclusion of the interview, the board members compare their ratings and arrive at a consensus for the overall evaluation. In general, questions asked of applicants have to do with their work and educational background, how their families and friends feel about their becoming police officers, and what they think they could contribute to the police department and community. In addition, candidates are asked to solve an ambiguous police problem. Approximately 1 hour is allowed for the administration and rating of each interview.

Leaderless Group Discussion

The leaderless group discussion exercise was added to the other activities after two years of experimentation. In this exercise six to eight applicants are brought into a room for a specified period of time to discuss a topic, such as the traits of a police officer, training needs, or the question of officers being armed. At the end of that time the group of applicants is asked to give the assessors its conclusions. Three assessors observe the applicants during the discussion and rate their performance on appropriate dimensions. A consensus rating was required of the assessors after they first made their independent ratings and discussed the applicant.

Situational Testing

In this exercise applicants are asked to assume that they are sworn officers and then to handle each of three simulated situations as they feel an officer would. In the Colorado assessment centers situations were developed with the following characteristics:

1. They were typical situations that an officer would encounter (as judged by current officers on the force) and in some cases were modeled after

actual incidents. Additional realism was achieved through the use of props.

2. The situations were purposefully stressful and ambiguous to force the applicants to perform under stress and to arrive at a decision even though there was not one correct solution.

The confederates in situational testing are given a story theme to follow so as to standardize as much as possible each of the situations. The confederates play an important function in this series of 3 situations; it is their responsibility to bring out as much behavior in the applicants as possible in the approximately 30 minutes scheduled for the exercise.

In the Ft. Collins and Colorado State University assessment centers the general procedure was for the applicant to be brought to the testing room and given a gun belt to wear. He or she was then briefly instructed in handcuffing and frisk procedure and was handed a card on which minimal instructions were typed. An example would be, "You are driving on patrol in the downtown area when you notice a young man (approximately 25 years of age) prying at a parking meter with a screwdriver. It is 4:45 p.m. Do your duty."

When the applicant had read and understood the card, he or she entered the room in which an irate citizen was kicking and prying at the parking meter. The "theme" that the confederate followed in this situation was that he had been looking for a parking place for 15 minutes and that, when he finally found one, his nickel jammed in the meter. The confederate was in a "big hurry," since he had to get into the hardware store for some plumbing supplies before it closed, as his basement was flooding. Once the applicant had completed one situation, he was handed instructions for the next until all three situations were completed.

Three assessors were used for this exercise: a psychologist, a staff police officer, and a citizen. The assessors observed each situation from behind a one-way mirror and made independent ratings at the conclusion of the exercise. The assessors then discussed each of the rating dimensions and were instructed, as was the oral board, to arrive at a consensus for their ratings.

CONCLUDING REMARKS

The primary objective of this chapter has been to demonstrate how fairness and job relatedness, two by-products of the assessment center, can improve the process of police selection and promotion. Traditional paper-and-pencil selection methods and other management identification techniques have been shown to be insufficient for an accurate appraisal of an applicant's qualifications. A number of important managerial abilities—such as planning and organizing, establishing priorities, leadership, relevant analytical skills, sensitivity to the needs of subordinates, management control, stress tolerance, and communications effectiveness—are very difficult to measure adequately with the use of written tests alone. Also, because of the job relevance and the procedures involved, assessment center results are generally readily accepted by individuals who object to traditional testing procedures. The following are some of the more significant advantages of the assessment center method.

1. The exercises used are simulations of on-the-job behaviors.
2. A large amount of information is generated by each participant in a relatively short time.
3. A variety of methods is used.
4. The exercises are constant for all participants.
5. There is a consensus among the assessors for each participant.
6. The observers typically have no personal involvement with the participants.
7. The observers are well trained in evaluation procedures.
8. The observers are able to devote full attention to the task of assessing.
9. Information obtained can be used effectively to develop personnel. Individuals are provided with specific behaviorally referenced indicators of strengths and weaknesses, and developmental programs can be planned in order to strengthen weaknesses so that an individual may be promotable in the future.
10. Assessors involved receive valuable training in behavioral observation techniques, and this training carries over to their regular performance.

The assessment center technique has not only gained considerable acceptance among examinees and management personnel involved as assessors but has also satisfied the legal requirements regarding fair employment and promotion practices. The implementation of the assessment center method in the Kansas City Police Department drew a highly favorable response in the subsequent evaluation of job relatedness. Captains who were involved in the program further acclaimed its utility as both a selection and developmental tool; a majority responded affirmatively to the question, "Would you send one of your subordinates to the assessment center?" The use of the assessment center in the Richmond Police Department was approved by the U.S. District Court for the Eastern District of Virginia.

The sample cases in this chapter have illustrated the responsiveness of the assessment center to the complexity and changing nature of police work by showing the involvement of police officers in the major phases of screening, the wide variety of exercises designed to assess applicants, and the use of multiple assessors who approach the candidates from different perspectives. A further consequence has been the increased effectiveness of those officers who participate in the selection activities as assessors.

However, because the assessment center method requires considerable human resources—typically 6 assessors for the evaluation of 12 candidates—there has been some concern about its practicality and cost. There are two approaches that might be studied and evaluated to remedy this problem.

In some geographical areas a consortium of police departments may be practical. Assessors from various jurisdictions could be trained and "traded" for scheduled evaluations of candidates. Such a consortium probably would be most effective where jurisdictions have minimal needs and reasonable geographical proximity.

It may be possible to develop a national assessment center mechanism under either private or public sponsorship. A national assessment center program would have frequently scheduled assessment centers at convenient locations. It may be feasible to develop evaluation methods using video tapes, which could be evaluated by a core of trained assessors. Perhaps the above approaches would mitigate the economic and time factors adversely affecting the implementation of assessment centers. In most cases the advantages of a defensible evaluation approach, the information obtained, and a superior, more stable record of personnel effectiveness over prolonged periods of time appear to outweigh the disadvantages.

As a final note, the three police assessment centers cited in this chapter seem to meet the specific requirements for law enforcement agencies, as stated in a recent court decision. Judge D. J. Lambros of the U.S. District Court, Northern District of Ohio, Eastern Division, in the case of *Royal Thomas Arnold et al.,* v. *John S. Ballard et al.,* expressed it this way:

> In assessing the written examinations and the other requirements imposed on applicants for the Akron Police Department, the complex and multifaceted role of police officers serving in major metropolitan area has been demonstrated. The tasks which are to be performed by these persons require the ability to perceive the situation being confronted and act immediately in a proper manner. The officers are in constant contact with the public and our immediate safety, for bad or good, is largely in their hands. There must be some criteria used to select those persons who will serve as police officers.
>
> However, public employers have a high duty to insure that the criteria used to select those persons are racially neutral. To allow all persons the full and complete opportunity to serve and represent their community must be the goal. . . .

SUMMARY

The personnel problems of identification of talent and development of human resources have prompted many public and private organizations to explore more effective techniques for both entry-level and promotion/development selections. In the last decade, it has become apparent that neither the traditional written test nor the personal interview can necessarily be relied on for accuracy in predicting job performance. Court decisions, in denying job relatedness of the traditional tests, have further challenged their fairness and required organizations to adjust personnel selection procedures to conform to EEOC guidelines.

The assessment center, a selection technique that has been gaining acceptance since World War II, has proved to be highly accurate in predicting job performance, and various court decisions have judged this technique to be a fair method of selection. This may be accounted for by the nature of the method, which includes a variety of exercises patterned after typical on-the-job situations. More than one exercise is used to test a candidate, and several trained assessors observe and evaluate his or her behavior according to various dimensions deemed essential for effective performance by an in-depth job analysis. Accordingly, the assessment center's validity as a selection tool is readily demonstrable and capable of satisfying legal requirements.

The work of law enforcement agencies is particularly complex and subject to constant modification. The degree of responsibility involved in safeguarding the community requires as accurate a method as possible for personnel selection. Management and interpersonal skills are prerequisite to ensure optimal functioning of police bureaus both within the department and externally, in their regular contacts with people. The assessment centers operated by the Kansas City Police Department, the Ft. Collins and Colorado State University police departments, and the Richmond Police Department have been responsive to these important needs. Specific dimensions, whether required for entry-level or promotional selection, for large or small police departments, were readily determined and appropriate assessment center exercises were designed from this information for evaluation by trained observers.

The characteristics of flexibility, job relatedness, and fairness make the assessment center technique a distinctly advantageous method of personnel selection and promotion for law enforcement agencies, as well as for other organizations. Yet some of the economic and time problems connected with its implementation have restricted its use. The problem for law enforcement agencies might be resolved by combining geographical areas in close proximity where jurisdictions have minimal needs and creating a pool of trained assessors to meet evaluation schedules for candidates. Another possibility would be a private or public national assessment center, where frequently scheduled assessment centers could be held at convenient locations. The advantages of a defensible evaluation approach, the information obtained, and a superior, more stable record of personnel effectiveness all recommend the assessment center as a valid tool in police selection and promotion and enliven our efforts to seek ways to overcome the "logistics" objections.

REFERENCES

Bray, D. W., Campbell, R. J., & Grant, D. L. *Formative years in business: A long-term AT&T study of managerial lives.* New York: Wiley-Interscience, 1974.

Bray, D. W., & Grant, D. L. The assessment center in the measurement of potential for business management. *Psychological Monographs,* 1966, *80* (17, Whole No. 625).

Bucalo, J. P., Jr. The assessment center—A more specified approach. *Human Resource Management,* Fall 1974, pp. 2–13.

Byham, W. C. Assessment center for spotting future managers. *Harvard Business Review,* 1970, *48,* 150–160.

Byham, W. C. The assessment center as an aid in management development. *Training and Development Journal,* 1971, *25,* 10–22.

Byham, W. C., & Wattengel, C. Assessment centers for supervisors and managers . . . An introduction and overview. *Public Personnel Management,* September–October 1974, pp. 352–364.

Chenoweth, J. H. Situational tests—A new attempt at assessing police candidates. *Journal of Criminal Law, Criminology, and Police Science,* 1961, *52,* 232–238.

Dunette, M. D. Multiple assessment procedures in identifying and developing managerial talent. In P. McReynolds (Ed.), *Advances in psychological assessment* (Vol. 2). Palo Alto, Calif.: Science and Behavior Books, 1971.

Filer, R. J. *Assessment centers in police selection.* Paper presented at Working Conference on the Selection of Law Enforcement Officers, FBI Academy, Quantico, Virginia, October 26–29, 1976.

Garforth, F. I. de la P. War office selection boards. *Occupational Psychology,* 1945, *19,* 97–108.

Gavin, J. F., & Hamilton, J. W. *Selecting police using assessment center methodology.* Colorado State University Report, 1974.

Glaser, R., Schwarz, P. A., & Flanagan, J. C. The contribution of the interview and situational performance procedures to the selection of supervisory personnel. *Journal of Applied Psychology,* 1958, *42,* 69–73.

Mills, R. B. Use of diagnostic small groups in police recruit selection and training. *Journal of Criminal Law, Criminology, and Police Science,* 1969, *60,* 238–241.

Mills, R. B. *New direction in police selection.* Paper presented at the symposium on the profile of the U.S. police officer, annual convention of the American Psychological Association, Honolulu, Hawaii, September 7, 1972.

Mills, R. B., McDevitt, R. J., & Tonkin, S. Situational tests in metropolitan police selection. *Journal of Criminal Law, Criminology, and Police Science,* 1966, *57,* 99–106.

Murray, H. A., & MacKinnon, D. W. Assessment of OSS personnel. *Journal of Consulting Psychology,* 1946, *10,* 76–80.

Office of Strategic Services Assessment Staff. *Assessment of men.* New York: Rinehart, 1948.

Third International Congress on Assessment Center Method. Standards and Ethical Considerations for Assessment Center Operations. Quebec, Canada, May 1975.

United States District Court, Eastern District of Virginia, Richmond Division. *The Richmond Black Police Officers Association, et al.*, v. *The City of Richmond, et al.* Civil Action No. 74-0267-R, September 22, 1975.

VanKirk, M. L. Selection of sergeants. *FBI Law Enforcement Bulletin,* March 1975, pp. 12-15.

14

SELECTION OF EFFECTIVE LAW ENFORCEMENT OFFICERS
The Florida Police Standards Research Project

Charles D. Spielberger, Harry C. Spaulding,
Margie T. Jolley, and John C. Ward
University of South Florida, Tampa, Florida

Recommended standards for the selection of police officers were outlined in the final report of the National Advisory Commission on Criminal Justice Standards and Goals, which was published in 1973. These standards specified that every police agency "employ a formal process for the selection of qualified police applicants. This process should include a written test of mental ability or aptitude, an oral interview, a physical examination, a psychological examination, and an in-depth background investigation" (pp. 337–341).

The procedures used in selecting police officers are the key to ensuring the employment of candidates who meet the standards recommended by the National Advisory Commission. Law enforcement administrators have long recognized this fact but have lacked effective selection tools. While most police agencies currently employ a variety of techniques and screening procedures for the selection of police officers, there is little objective evidence with regard to the reliability and validity of these methods. Haphazard applications of unvalidated assessment instruments have undoubtedly contributed to the selection of persons who are not qualified for police work.

The presence of even a few undesirable officers in a police agency has enormous social and financial implications. The excessive or injudicious use of force by an emotionally unstable officer can result in tragic consequences, and an officer who becomes involved in illegal activities causes an erosion of the

231

public's confidence in the agency. A major goal in police selection is screening out such "misfits" from positions in law enforcement.

Each new officer who terminates employment due to misconduct or incompetence costs the agency thousands of dollars. Most law enforcement agencies provide from 8 to 16 weeks of academy training for new recruits. In addition to the cost of this training, most departments pay academy cadets salaries even though the cadets are not providing any direct services to the community. The concern of police administrators with the high cost of ineffective selection procedures is summed up by Allan Rush (1963), assistant superintendent of the Kansas Highway Patrol, who stated, "The hiring of 'mistakes' with approximately $10,000 invested in recruiting, training, equipping and a minimum amount of experience, is a luxury we cannot afford . . ." (p. 18).

The situation in police selection is further complicated by difficulties encountered in the implementation of Equal Employment Opportunity (EEOC) guidelines. While the federal government recommends the use of psychological tests in police selection, recent decisions in state and federal courts have criticized standardized tests because of evidence that they discriminate against women and minority groups. Research on the selection of minority and female police officers is urgently needed to identify valid selection procedures that conform to the EEOC guidelines.

The Florida Police Standards Research Project (FPSRP) will be described in this chapter. The major goal of the FPSRP is to develop and validate a flexible battery of assessment procedures for use by law enforcement agencies on a statewide basis. First the historical factors that provided the impetus for the FPSRP will be reviewed, and the experimental design for this research and development project will be outlined. Next the selection of the predictor variables and criterion measures for the FPSRP will be discussed, and the subject population and data collection methods employed in the project will be described. In the final section of this chapter some preliminary findings of this ongoing longitudinal study will be reported.

DEVELOPMENT OF THE FPSRP

The jet streams of change that have generally influenced police selection techniques in the United States (see Furcon, chapter 1, this volume) have also been active in Florida. Human rights legislation, judicial and administrative decisions, and the increasing complexity of police work all contributed to a growing awareness among Florida law enforcement officials that police selection procedures needed to be improved. This recognition of a need for a more sophisticated approach to the selection of law enforcement officers stimulated the initiation of a statewide research effort that has involved an unusual degree of cooperation between university researchers and the law enforcement community.

In describing the context in which the FPSRP developed, several important recent events relating to the police profession in Florida should be noted. In 1967 the Florida legislature passed a new Police Standards Act, which was designed to improve law enforcement. The expressed intent of this act was stated as follows in the Florida Statutes (1967):

(1) It is the intent of the legislature to strengthen and upgrade law enforcement in Florida by attracting competent, highly qualified young people for professional careers in this field and to retain well qualified and experienced officers for the purpose of providing maximum protection and safety to the citizens of, and visitors to, this state.

(2) It is the further intent of the legislature to establish a minimum foundation program for law enforcement officers which will provide a state-wide minimum salary for all such officers, to provide a state monetary supplement to effectuate an upgrading of compensation for all law enforcement officers, and to upgrade the education and training standards of such officers. (p. IF-5)

The Florida Police Standards Board was formed to carry out the provisions of this legislation, and an early action of this board was to create the Bureau of Police Standards and Training.[1] One of the first achievements of this agency was the establishment of minimum recruit training standards. It is interesting to note that these standards were later selected as guidelines for national law enforcement standards by the International Association of Chiefs of Police (IACP). The Police Standards Board also took an early interest in assisting local agencies in the selection of well-qualified recruits.

In 1973 the Florida Association of Chiefs of Police requested technical assistance from the Florida Police Standards Board in developing psychological testing procedures for the selection of well-qualified candidates. In response to this request the board directed the staff of the Division of Police Standards and Training to determine the feasibility of developing a statewide program for the psychological screening of police applicants. As a first step, assistance was requested from the regents of the State University System of Florida, and the regents awarded a small grant to the University of South Florida to support surveys of the research literature on police selection.[2] In completing this feasibility study, a proposal for a more substantial research and development grant was submitted to the Law Enforcement Assistance Administration (LEAA).

An LEAA discretionary grant was awarded to the University of South Florida in April 1975 to initiate the FPSRP. This research and development

[1] The title of the Police Standards Board was subsequently changed to the Police Standards and Training Commission, and the Police Standards Bureau became the Division of Police Standards and Training.

[2] The research supported by the BOR grant was carried out under the direction of the senior author in collaboration with Dr. Mitchell Silverman.

project is now being carried out in close consultation and collaboration with the director and staff of the Florida Division of Police Standards and Training. The goals of the project are to construct and validate procedures for screening and selecting candidates for Florida law enforcement agencies.

The design of the FPSRP involves the administration of an experimental test battery to police recruits at the beginning of their academy training. On completion of the academy training program, grades and instructor ratings of performance and suitability for police work are obtained for each recruit. The officers are then followed through their probationary year, and job performance ratings are obtained from first-line supervisors at the end of this period. Similar ratings will also be obtained when the officers complete their first year in full patrol status. Statistical analysis of the data will determine how well test scores predict performance at the police academy and on the job during the probationary year and in patrol status.

The FPSRP has been conducted in four major phases. The first three phases have been completed, and the fourth is still in progress. Phase 1 was concerned with a critical evaluation of the current status of research on police selection measures. The instruments that are included in the test battery were selected and field tested in Phase 2. Selection and refinement of criterion measures also took place in this phase. In Phase 3 recruit classes were tested at selected police academies, and criterion data on academy and probationary period performance were subsequently obtained for these officers. Now, in Phase 4, additional subjects are being tested to permit cross-validation. Additional follow-up data are also being obtained on the original subjects.

The literature review conducted in Phase 1 of the FPSRP is briefly summarized in chapter 2 of this volume. The model for selection of law enforcement officers that provided the conceptual framework for this project is also described in that chapter. In the sections that follow in the present chapter the methods and procedures employed in Phase 2 of the FPSRP are discussed, along with the results that have been obtained to date in Phase 3.

PREDICTOR VARIABLES AND CRITERION MEASURES

The first step in Phase 2 of the FPSRP was the selection of predictor variables on the basis of the model described in chapter 2. This model identifies three major categories of predictor variables: (1) physical, biographical, and demographic variables; (2) psychological assessment; and (3) situational tests. It was initially intended that the predictor battery would include measures from each of these categories, but it soon became apparent that inclusion of situational testing, while desirable, would be extremely expensive and time-consuming. Accordingly, the final battery was made up of measures from the first two categories.

For the physical-biographical-demographic category, physical factors such as height and weight are usually measured directly, and biographical and demographic factors are generally obtained by means of questionnaire or information requested in application forms. The psychological assessment category is divided into three subcategories: (1) intellectual ability and aptitude; (2) values, attitudes, and interests; (3) personality and motivation. Psychological characteristics are generally measured by standardized tests, but some departments also utilize assessment interviews conducted by a psychologist or psychiatrist in the later stages of the selection process. The considerations leading to the selection of the specific biodata and psychological measures that were used in the FPSRP are discussed below.

Physical, Biographical, and Demographic Variables

Physical, biographical, and demographic variables (biodata) are widely used in police selection. Most law enforcement agencies inquire into a candidate's physical characteristics, personal background, level of education, and previous job experience. While the predictive validity of biodata has not been firmly established, it was considered essential to include representative biodata measures in the FPSRP test battery because of the widespread use of such measures in police selection.[3]

Fortunately, at the time that test instruments were being selected for the FPSRP, a validation study of biodata predictors of police performance was being completed in the Dade County, Florida, Public Safety Department (see Cascio & Real, chapter 7, this volume). From the 184-item questionnaire employed by the Dade County investigators, the 60 items that showed the best concurrent validity in their study were selected to comprise the "Personal History Questionnaire" that was used in the FPSRP Test Battery. The items in this questionnaire covered the entire range of biodata.

Intellectual Ability and Aptitude Variables

The intellectual ability/aptitude measure originally chosen for the FPSRP Test Battery was an instrument developed by the Educational Testing Service (ETS) for the IACP. The rationale for the construction of this test is described by Crosby, Rosenfeld, and Thornton in chapter 8 of this volume. Unfortunately, the ETS/IACP test was not completed in time for inclusion in the FPSRP Test Battery. Therefore, a replacement had to be found.

In searching for a substitute intellectual ability/aptitude measure, we discovered that the Nelson-Denny Reading Test (N-D) had been used for a

[3] For more information about the validity of biodata in predicting job performance, see chapters 2 and 7 of this volume.

number of years at Florida's largest police training academy.[4] The academy director and staff commented favorably on this test, and analyses of data from previous classes showed that N-D scores were good predictors of academy grades. These facts led us to include the N-D in the FPSRP Test Battery, and subsequent analyses have demonstrated that scores on the N-D are highly correlated with IQ scores on the California Test of Mental Maturity, a standard intelligence test.

The N-D is an objective test of reading skills and general intellectual ability. It was standardized in 1972 on large high school and college samples and has excellent test-retest reliability (Brown, Nelson, & Denny, 1973). There are subscales for measuring vocabulary and comprehension, and an additional score may be calculated by totaling these scores. The vocabulary and comprehension scores reflect important reading subskills, and the combined score provides a measure of overall reading ability. It is also possible to assess reading rate with the N-D, but there is relatively little evidence of the validity of this measure.

Values, Attitudes, and Interest Variables

In chapter 9 of this volume, Flint strongly recommends that interest measures be employed in the selection of law enforcement officers. On the basis of his research and practical experience in police selection, Flint notes that information about an individual's interests can often answer important questions about the applicant's motivation and potential enjoyment of police work and help to determine whether his or her interests are compatible with the needs of the department.

The Strong-Campbell Interest Inventory (SCII) (Campbell, 1974) is used to assess values, attitudes, and interests in the FPSRP. The SCII is an objective, self-report inventory consisting of 325 items, grouped into 7 parts. For the first 5 parts of the SCII the subject is asked to respond with "like," "indifferent," or "dislike" to interest items falling into the following categories: (a) occupation, (b) school subjects, (c) activities, (d) amusements, and (e) day-to-day contact with different types of people. The final 2 parts inquire about specific activity preferences and personal characteristics.

The following types of information are provided in the SCII computer-scored profile. These are (a) general occupational orientation (6 themes), (b) administrative indexes (used to detect test-taking response bias), (c) special scales (academic orientation, introversion-extraversion), (d) basic interests (23 scales), and (e) occupational interests (124 scales). The SCII scales are described in some detail by Flint (see chapter 9, this volume).

---

[4] We are grateful to Howard Rasmussen and Allen Shoaff of the Southeast Florida Criminal Justice Institute in Miami for recommending the Nelson-Denny Reading Test.

Personality and Motivation Variables

Measures of personality and motivation are widely employed to screen out applicants who are unsuitable for employment in law enforcement work (see Shealy, chapter 12, this volume). Four measures of personality and motivation were included in the FPSRP Test Battery. These are the California Psychological Inventory (CPI) (Gough, 1957), the State-Trait Anxiety Inventory (STAI) (Spielberger, Gorsuch, & Lushene, 1970), the "lie" scale of the Minnesota Multiphasic Personality Inventory (MMPI) (Dahlstrom, Welsh, & Dahlstrom, 1972), and an experimental measure of sociopathy called the SPY Scale (Spielberger, Kling, & O'Hagan, 1978).[5] Each of these instruments is discussed in more detail below.

An objective multidimensional personality test was considered essential for inclusion in the FPSRP Test Battery, to provide an efficient means of collecting information on a broad range of individual personality characteristics. On the basis of the review of the literature on police selection (see chapter 2, this volume), two tests appeared suitable for this purpose: the MMPI and the CPI. Both of these tests are empirically based and have been used successfully in previous police selection research. Since both require considerable time for administration, a choice had to be made between them. A pilot study conducted during Phase 2 of the FPSRP led to the selection of the CPI, primarily because a number of subjects objected to the wording of MMPI items. Furthermore, Gottesman (1975) has recently suggested that the MMPI is inappropriate for screening police applicants because the published norms for the MMPI are not representative for this population.

The CPI is a 480-item, true-false inventory that yields scores on 18 scales. Three of these scales measure test-taking attitudes, and the remaining 15 scales provide measures of personality dimensions, such as achievement-via-conformance, dominance, responsibility, and sociability.

The 15-item MMPI "lie" scale and an experimental sociopathy (SPY) scale developed from the MMPI were included in the FPSRP Test Battery. The "lie" scale was constructed to identify persons deliberately attempting to deny their faults in order to make a favorable impression. The SPY scale consists of 20 items empirically associated with sociopathic personality in prison inmates who displayed amoral and impulsive behavior without being constrained by anxiety or guilt.

As we have noted in chapter 2 of this volume, there is considerable recent evidence that the personality trait of anxiety is importantly involved in a police officer's adaptation to job-related stress. It has also been suggested that

---

[5] Rotter's (1966) Locus of Control Scale (I-E) was also included in the test battery. Since scores on this instrument did not relate to the success/failure criterion, the findings for the I-E scale are not reported.

differing levels of anxiety may affect the relationship between predictor and criterion variables in police selection validity research. The STAI was included in the FPSRP Test Battery to measure individual differences in anxiety. The STAI is a 40-item scale that measures anxiety proneness or "trait anxiety," as well as emotional reactions to stress or state anxiety—that is, how the subject feels "at the moment."

Selection of Criterion Measures for the FPSRP

The choice of criterion measures for the FPSRP was guided by the model for the selection of law enforcement officers described in chapter 2 of this volume. This model identifies three periods during which performance is usually evaluated in police selection research: (1) at the police academy, (2) during the probationary period, and (3) in patrol status after the probationary period. The FPSRP research design will eventually include performance measures from all three periods.

Two main considerations determined the selection of the specific criterion measures that were used in the FPSRP. First, we wished to choose criteria that were reliable, valid, and job related. Second, it was important to establish performance criteria that reflected the special requirements and concerns of the ultimate users of the FPSRP Test Battery, namely, Florida law enforcement agencies.

The literature review conducted in Phase 1 of the FPSRP provided information on the criterion measures that have been used with some success by other investigators in police selection research. In order to determine the factors that were considered important in performance evaluation by Florida law enforcement personnel, surveys were conducted in which the respondents were police chiefs and sheriffs, police officers in middle-management supervisory positions, first-line supervisors (sergeants and lieutenants), and police academy directors and instructors. A list of criterion measures was compiled from the published literature, and respondents were asked to indicate which, if any, of these measures were used at their agency. They were also asked to give their opinion of the usefulness of each procedure. Analysis of the survey responses revealed considerable agreement on the criteria that were considered most important in the evaluation of the performance of law enforcement officers. Moreover, agreement extended across supervisory levels and the size of the respondent's department.

In research on the prediction of performance at the police academy, grades are the most widely used criterion measures. While peer and supervisor ratings have also been employed in some studies, grades continue to be the primary criterion. In addition, successful completion of the training course versus failure (e.g., dismissal, resignation) is also used as a criterion measure. While it is generally assumed that academy performance is related to how well the graduate will perform on the job, this relationship has not been well established empirically.

On the basis of the literature review and the surveys of law enforcement personnel, 10 measures of performance at the police academy were selected as criterion measures for the FPSRP. Four of these were related to academic performance: (1) final average, (2) final test score, (3) interim test score, and (4) notebook score. These measures are currently used at all Florida police training academies and were readily available to project staff.

Four other academy criterion measures were based on personal traits that had been rated as "very useful" for the evaluation of academy trainees by more than 65% of the survey respondents. These traits were (1) general suitability for police work, (2) honesty and integrity, (3) quality of work, and (4) relations with others. Each academy trainee was rated on these traits by academy instructors using the Personal Appraisal and Evaluation Form (PAEF), a paired-comparison rating scale procedure developed by FPSRP staff. Two additional academy criterion measures were (1) successful completion of the recruit training course and (2) weapons firing scores.

For the probationary and patrol status periods the model for the selection of law enforcement officers described in chapter 2 lists five types of criterion assessments. These are (1) supervisor ratings, (2) peer ratings, (3) commendations/reprimands, (4) termination/resignation, and (5) promotions. The two criteria that were used in the validation of the FPSRP predictor variables were supervisor ratings of job performance and personal traits, and termination/resignation.

Supervisor ratings, which are more subjective than the termination/ resignation criterion, are generally used by most police agencies in the evaluation of job performance. The importance of supervisor ratings of performance during the probationary period is emphasized by Wilson and McLaren (1977). In their influential book on police administration, Wilson and McLaren state, "It becomes obvious that one of the great supervisory training needs in the police service is to convince first-line and middle-level supervisors that one of their major responsibilities is to separate borderline and unfit candidates who are able to get into the department despite the formal testing procedure and entrance requirements" (p. 270).

The survey responses of Florida law enforcement administrators were compared with behaviorally anchored police-rating scales in selecting a specific supervisor rating scale to be used for evaluating performance in the FPSRP. This comparison showed that the Landy-Farr rating scales, discussed in chapter 4 of this volume, encompassed most of the performance dimensions considered important by the survey respondents. The only important factor not covered by these scales was "integrity." Dunnette and Motowidlo (1976) had constructed a similar instrument, which included a rating of "integrity," and a modification of this scale was included, along with the Landy-Farr scales, in the final FPSRP job performance rating instrument.

A major goal of the FPSRP was to assist police agencies in screening out unfit or unsuitable candidates. The termination of an officer because of inadequate performance or inappropriate behavior is perhaps the clearest indication that mistakes were made in the selection process. In applying this criterion, careful distinction must be made between those officers who are discharged or whose resignation is requested and those who are performing satisfactorily but are physically disqualified or led to resign by personal reasons. Although the latter group may contain some individuals who lack sufficient motivation and interest in police work, there is no satisfactory way to distinguish these officers from officers who resign to accept better positions elsewhere.

In a police selection study described in chapter 2 of this volume, Levy (1971) grouped police officers into three categories: "currents," "failures," and "nonfailures." These categories were based on statements by each officer's department of the reason for termination and whether or not the terminated officer was considered worthy of being rehired. A similar classification was made in the FPSRP study. The department of each officer who terminated employment during the probationary period was asked to state whether the officer was considered worthy of being rehired. Terminated officers who were not considered rehirable and officers who failed at the academy comprised the "failure" group. Officers who were performing their duties satisfactorily and those who terminated during the probationary period but who were considered rehirable comprised the "success" group. In the analyses described in the following section, "failures" were contrasted with "successes" in an attempt to identify the characteristics of officers not suited for police work.

Subjects and Data Collection

The FPSRP tested successive classes of police recruits enrolled in basic law enforcement courses at seven Florida police academies. The Florida Division of Police Standards and Training assisted in the selection of these academies to ensure that representative samples of new recruits were tested. A major consideration in the choice of police academies for the study was the size and the type of law enforcement agency that assigned recruits to these training centers. To facilitate the generalizability of the results, the sample needed to include a wide cross section of large and small, rural and urban departments, as well as substantial numbers of women and minority officers.

The seven testing sites were Hillsborough Community College, Tampa; Lewis M. Lively Vocational Technical Institute, Tallahassee; Pinellas Police Academy, Clearwater; Southeast Florida Criminal Justice Institute, Miami; J. C. Stone Memorial Police Academy, Orlando; Tampa Police Academy, Tampa; and Withlacoochee Vocational Technical Center, Inverness. Table 1 shows the number of recruits tested at each of these academies.[6] A total of 317 recruits

[6] A sample of 35 Florida highway patrol recruits was also tested. Since the training

TABLE 1 Subject attrition at the police academies and during the first year of employment

	Caucasian males	Minority males	Females	Total
Total recruits tested at the training academies	208	56	53	317
Academy terminations[a]	5	. 1	6	12
Graduated from academy	203	55	47	305
Never hired by police agency	40	1	10	51
Retained after successful completion of probation	142	52	30	224
Terminations during probationary period	21	2	7	30
Considered rehirable by department[b]	5	1	3	9
Department would not rehire[a]	16	1	4	21
Total number of failures[a]	21	2	10	33
Total successful officers[b]	147	53	33	233

[a]Failures: academy terminations and officers terminated during the probation period who could not be rehired by their departments.

[b]Successful officers: officers who were retained after successfully completing the probationary period and officers terminated during the probationary period who were considered rehirable by their departments.

volunteered to participate in the study and signed consent forms that permitted project staff to obtain academy grades and other necessary performance information. The number of Caucasian males, minority males, and females, as well as the employment status of each subject in these groups, is also reported in Table 1.

The FPSRP Test Battery was administered at each training center, usually during a four-hour morning session on the second or third day of the course. The purpose of the project was explained to the recruit classes, and the subjects were assured that the test results would be kept strictly confidential and would be used only for research purposes. In order to determine minority status, the recruits were asked to identify themselves as black, Caucasian, or Hispanic. Black and Hispanic males were combined to comprise the minority males group ($N = 56$) because there were not enough subjects for separate analyses of these subgroups. Similarly, the relatively small number of females ($N = 53$) prevented further subdivision of this group.

and job requirements for these subjects were substantially different than for other entry-level law enforcement officers, the data analyses for the highway patrol officer are not presented in this chapter.

The employment status of each subject was closely monitored by project staff. As each academy class graduated, course grades for each officer were obtained from the official records of the Florida Division of Police Standards and Training. Within 2 weeks after graduation, project staff returned to the training academies to conduct rating sessions in which two or more instructors evaluated the academic performance and personal characteristics of each recruit.

Approximately 9 months after graduation from the police academy, information on the current employment status of each officer was obtained from the Florida Division of Police Standards and Training. The law enforcement agency where each officer was currently employed was contacted to determine whether the officer had completed the probationary period, and rating sessions were arranged in which first-line supervisors evaluated the officer's performance.

Prior to completing the rating scales, the supervisors were briefed on the goals and procedures of the FPSRP, the rating procedure was explained, and each supervisor was asked to evaluate only those officers under his direct supervision. Performance ratings for each officer were obtained from at least two supervisors. This process will be repeated when the officers complete their first full year in tenured patrol status.

PRELIMINARY FINDINGS IN THE FPSRP

Of the 317 recruits who were tested in the FPSRP, 224 successfully completed the probationary period, and 9 of the officers who terminated during probation were considered rehirable by their departments (see Table 1). These 233 officers were considered successes. A total of 33 officers who were terminated were considered failures; 12 officers were terminated at the training academy, and 21 officers were terminated during the probationary period and were not considered rehirable by their departments. The 51 officers who completed academy training but were never hired by a police agency were eliminated from further consideration.

In this section successes and failures will be compared to determine the predictive validity of each predictor measure for screening out failures. Discriminant function analyses to establish the best combination of test variables for predicting success or failure will also be reported. Additional analyses of the relationships between subjects' scores on each predictor variable and performance at the police academy and on the job have also been carried out, including multiple-regression analyses to determine the predictive validity of various combinations of predictors. The results of these more complex analyses will be reported elsewhere after cross-validation with a new sample in Phase 4 of the FPSRP.

The results of the success/failure comparisons will be presented in three sections. First the means and the predictive validity of the biodata items and the N-D will be presented. Next the results for the comparisons of successes and failures on the interest and personality measures will be reported. Finally the predictive validity of various combinations of predictor measures will be examined and evaluated.

Biodata and Ability Measures

The means and standard deviations for the six biodata items that significantly discriminated ($p < .05$) between successes and failures in either the Caucasian male or female groups are reported in Table 2, along with values for the t-tests of the differences between the means for these groups. Means and standard deviations for successes and failures in the minority male sample are also reported in Table 2, but t-tests were not computed because the number of failures in this group was too small to permit statistical analysis.

The Caucasian male success and failure groups were significantly different on 4 of the 60 biodata items. The successful officers were more likely than unsuccessful officers to report that they had participated in high school athletics, their families moved less frequently, they felt less need for job encouragement, and they placed higher value on achievement and the "ability to contribute something to society." Successful female officers differed from female failures on only two biodata items. The successful officers were more likely to report they were now or had previously been married, and that they were not particularly bothered by bragging co-workers.

The means and standard deviations of the four N-D subscales are presented in Table 3, along with t-tests of the differences between the means for successes and failures in the Caucasian male and the female groups. All the N-D subscales significantly discriminated between successes and failures for the Caucasian males, as can be noted in Table 3. Only the N-D comprehension scale significantly discriminated between female successes and failures, but differences between these groups in N-D total scores approached statistical significance ($p < .10$). Although t-tests could not be computed for the minority males, it can be noted in Table 3 that the successful minority males had substantially higher N-D scores than did the failures.

Interest and Personality Measures

Means and standard deviations for the SCII scales that discriminated between successes and failures in the Caucasian male and the female groups are reported in Table 4. The successful Caucasian male officers reported greater interest in business management and office practices than did the failures in this group. On the occupational scales the expressed interests of the successful male Caucasians were more like those of army officers (both male and female) than were the interests of the failures. In addition, differences

TABLE 2 Biographical inventory items that discriminated between successful and failed Caucasian male and female officers

	Caucasian males					Females					Minority males[a]			
	Successes (N = 147)		Failures (N = 21)		t^b	Successes (N = 33)		Failures (N = 10)		t^b	Successes (N = 53)		Failures (N = 2)	
	Mean	SD	Mean	SD		Mean	SD	Mean	SD		Mean	SD	Mean	SD
Athletic participation in high school	1.4	.5	1.2	.4	2.1**	1.2	.4	1.3	.5	1.2	1.5	.5	1.5	.7
Family moved less often	2.5	1.6	3.4	1.5	2.2**	2.2	1.4	2.0	1.5	<1	2.1	1.4	3.0	2.8
Less need for job encouragement	1.2	.4	1.4	.5	2.2**	1.1	.3	1.0	.0	<1	1.2	.4	1.0	.0
Important to achieve and make contribution	1.8	.4	1.5	.5	2.3**	1.3	.5	1.3	.5	<1	1.2	.4	1.0	.0
Married, widowed, separated, or divorced	1.6	.5	1.5	.5	1.1	1.5	.5	1.1	.3	2.1**	1.7	.5	1.5	.7
Not bothered by bragging co-workers	1.8	.4	1.8	.4	<1	1.8	.4	1.4	.5	2.4**	1.6	.5	1.5	.7

[a] t-tests were not calculated for the minority males because of the small size of the terminated group.
[b] t-test significance: * $p < .10$; ** $p < .05$.

TABLE 3 Nelson-Denny reading test scores for successful and failed Caucasian males, females, and minority males

	Caucasian males						Females						Minority males[a]			
	Successes (N = 147)		Failures (N = 21)		t^c		Successes (N = 33)		Failures (N = 10)		t		Successes (N = 53)		Failures[b] (N = 2)	
	Mean	SD	Mean	SD			Mean	SD	Mean	SD			Mean	SD	Mean	SD
Vocabulary	43.0	15.8	35.3	15.0	2.1**		44.1	12.8	32.0	19.4	1.8		28.8	12.6	11.5	2.1
Comprehension	29.7	13.9	25.1	8.7	2.1**		34.5	15.4	21.7	7.5	3.6**		26.6	11.9	19.0	9.9
Total (V + C)	72.7	25.4	60.4	17.3	2.8***		75.7	27.1	53.7	23.5	2.2*		51.6	20.0	30.5	12.0
Reading rate	256.4	114.6	210.0	46.7	3.3**		268.8	97.4	281.1	153.1	< 1		206.2	68.5	—	—

[a] t-tests were not calculated for the minority males because of the small size of the terminated group.
[b] These two subjects did not report reading rate scores.
[c] t-test significance: $* p < .10; ** p < .05.$

TABLE 4 SCII scales that discriminated between successful and failed Caucasian male and female officers

	Caucasian males						Females						Minority males[a]			
	Successes (N = 147)		Failures (N = 21)		t^b		Successes (N = 33)		Failures (N = 10)		t^b		Successes (N = 53)		Failures (N = 2)	
	Mean	SD	Mean	SD			Mean	SD	Mean	SD			Mean	SD	Mean	SD
General interests																
Conventional	50.9	9.0	47.0	8.2	1.8*		50.9	9.2	53.0	10.5	<1		53.0	10.9	54.0	2.8
Academic orientation	38.5	15.2	36.4	14.2	<1		45.2	12.3	34.6	15.2	2.1*		39.4	15.5	41.0	11.3
Military activities	64.2	10.4	59.6	12.0	1.8*		62.8	10.3	61.3	11.5	<1		68.2	8.2	69.0	9.9
Business management	51.2	9.5	46.8	8.0	2.0**		52.1	10.4	48.8	9.4	<1		55.8	9.3	56.0	5.7
Office practices	47.2	7.6	44.7	5.5	1.8***		50.2	10.5	55.9	10.5	<1		51.6	9.9	52.0	1.4
Occupational scales																
Police officer (male)[c]	48.4	10.8	45.0	10.4	<1		40.3	12.4	36.1	15.5	<1		50.4	10.4	48.0	9.9
Highway patrol (male)[c]	44.2	10.4	43.2	11.4	<1		31.1	11.6	29.7	8.3	<1		43.9	9.2	40.5	4.9
Army officer (female)	48.0	9.5	41.2	11.9	3.0**		38.8	7.6	35.3	8.6	1.2		47.3	9.4	39.0	7.1
Navy officer (male)	36.9	12.7	31.8	11.5	1.7*		30.1	12.4	23.0	17.1	1.4		38.7	13.6	38.0	5.7
Army officer (male)	36.7	10.9	31.0	11.7	2.1**		33.7	9.7	25.9	12.9	1.9		39.7	10.8	34.5	4.9

[a] t-tests were not calculated for minority males because of the small size of terminated group.
[b] t-test significance: * p < .10; ** p < .05.
[c] Although these scales failed to discriminate, they are included in this table because they are based on normative samples of police officers and highway patrol officers.

between the male Caucasian success and failure groups approached significance ·($p < .10$) on scales reflecting conventional attitudes, interest in military activities, and interests similar to those of navy officers.

The SCII showed little potential for discriminating between female officers who were classified as successes and failures. There were no significant differences on any scale. The only scale that even approached significance was academic orientation, on which successful females had higher scores.

It may be noted in Table 4 that there were no significant differences between successes and failures for either male Caucasians or females on the police officer or highway patrol officer scales. This was unexpected, since these scales were constructed on the basis of the responses of experienced and successful police officers. Examination of Table 4 shows that the Causcasian males and the minority males scored very near the SCII mean for police officers, indicating that their interests were similar to those of the officers in the scale construction sample.

The means and standard deviations for the personality measures that discriminated between successes and failures in the Caucasian male and the female groups are reported in Table 5. Successful Caucasian male officers scored significantly higher than did failures on the CPI dominance, capacity for status, sociability, achievement via conformance, and intellectual efficiency scales. The successful officers also tended to score higher on the CPI tolerance scale than did failures ($p < .10$).

Successful female officers were significantly higher than failures on scales that measured capacity for status, sense of well-being, responsibility, self-control, tolerance, good impression, achievement via independence, intellectual efficiency, and psychological-mindedness. The successful female officers also tended to score higher than unsuccessful officers on the CPI dominance, sociability, and communality (common sense) scales and lower in anxiety proneness, as measured by the STAI A-trait scale.

Discriminant Function Analyses

In the preceding analyses successes and failures were compared to determine the predictive validity of individual predictor measures. Although no single measure did well in discriminating between the groups, this was not unexpected. The rationale behind the employment of multiple measures in the FPSRP Test Battery was that the police officer's job is complex and multifaceted, and that a combination of predictors, including biodata and ability, interest, and personality measures, would be required to predict this complex criterion. In this section the predictive validity obtained for the best combination of FPSRP measures will be described.

Discriminant function analysis was employed in this study to evaluate the effectiveness of different combinations of measures in predicting success or failure. Mathematically, this technique consists of combining and weighting

TABLE 5 Personality measures that discriminated between successful and failed Caucasian male and female officers

	Caucasian males					Females					Minority males[a]			
	Successes (N = 147)		Failures (N = 21)			Successes (N = 33)		Failures (N = 10)			Successes (N = 53)		Failures (N = 2)	
	Mean	SD	Mean	SD	t^b	Mean	SD	Mean	SD	t^b	Mean	SD	Mean	SD
CPI														
Dominance	57.3	10.4	51.1	8.9	2.5**	58.9	11.5	51.7	9.7	1.7*	54.2	10.1	52.0	11.3
Capacity for status	48.1	9.6	43.1	10.2	2.2**	49.7	11.6	39.6	12.6	2.3**	47.3	7.3	47.5	2.1
Sociability	52.4	9.4	45.4	9.2	3.2**	54.5	11.2	46.9	14.1	1.8*	48.4	7.8	51.0	8.5
Sense of well-being	47.0	14.0	43.9	17.8	<1	51.0	8.5	32.4	13.0	4.1**	44.4	14.3	27.5	33.2
Responsibility	44.8	9.9	39.6	13.5	1.7	48.3	7.0	37.7	11.4	2.6**	43.8	9.7	40.0	8.5
Self-control	47.2	9.6	46.8	12.5	<1	49.8	10.2	40.2	12.6	2.4**	50.5	9.9	46.5	4.9
Tolerance	45.6	10.6	40.5	11.5	2.0*	50.1	10.4	30.0	7.0	5.4**	43.6	9.8	38.5	7.8
Good impression	48.8	11.0	47.2	9.8	<1	51.8	11.4	39.9	8.1	2.9**	54.1	11.3	49.0	1.4
Communality	49.8	15.4	47.2	17.6	<1	50.6	11.2	42.6	11.6	1.9*	42.2	17.6	26.5	26.1
Achievement via conformance	51.4	11.0	45.2	11.4	2.4**	53.5	9.0	41.4	16.8	3.3	51.1	10.4	47.0	15.6
Achievement via independence	48.2	9.9	45.8	11.5	1.0	53.8	11.2	39.9	7.6	3.5**	45.8	8.8	42.5	12.0
Intellectual efficiency	46.2	13.0	39.7	12.6	2.1**	51.3	8.8	34.6	10.3	4.5**	41.0	11.2	36.0	18.4
Psychological-mindedness	53.5	8.9	50.5	11.6	1.1	57.5	7.5	49.6	7.6	2.8**	52.4	8.6	41.0	7.1
STAI														
A-trait	32.5	7.4	31.4	9.5	<1	32.4	7.7	37.6	7.5	−1.8*	33.4	7.7	37.0	2.8

[a] t-tests were not calculated for minority males because of the small size of the terminated group.
[b] t-tests significance: * $p < .10$; ** $p < .05$.

248

the predictor variables into a "discriminant function" equation that best separates the two groups. Ideally, this procedure would result in a single dimension on which successes were clustered at one end and failures at the other. In real-life situations of course complete separation between criterion groups is rarely achieved and there is generally some degree of overlap between groups.

The best combination of variables for male Caucasians included items and scales from all three predictor categories. Four biodata items were included, together with the A-trait scale of the STAI, the sociability scale of the CPI, the total score from the N-D, and the army officer (*f*) scale of the SCII. The variables that entered the discriminant function for females included two biodata items, the STAI A-trait scale, four CPI scales (capacity for status, tolerance, intellectual efficiency, and psychological-mindness), and the army officer and nature scales of the SCII.

The results of the discriminant function analyses of the FPSRP are reported in Table 6. Among the Caucasian males, it can be seen, the discriminant function correctly identified 71% of the failures and 84% of the successes, while incorrectly identifying 29% of the failures and 16% of the successes. In the female group the discriminant function correctly identified 78% of the failures and incorrectly identified 22% of the failures as successes. Of the actual successes 100% were correctly identified. The efficiency of the two discriminant function equations, expressed as the overall proportion of correctly identified cases, was 82.5% for the male Caucasians and 95.2% for the females.

SUMMARY AND CONCLUSIONS

In this chapter we have described the first three phases of the FPSRP, a longitudinal predictive-validity study designed to develop and validate a flexible assessment battery for statewide use in the selection of law enforcement officers. Our goal has been to clarify and describe how such

TABLE 6 Percentage of successes and failures correctly and incorrectly predicted by the discriminant function analyses

	Correct prediction		Incorrect prediction		
	N	*%*	*N*	*%*	Total
Caucasian-male successes	122	84	23	16	145
Caucasian-male failures	15	71	6	29	21
Female successes	33	100	0	0	33
Female failures	7	78	2	22	9

projects are developed, to discuss important considerations that are involved in the selection of predictor variables and criterion measures, and to present some preliminary findings from the study.

The validity of the FPSRP predictor measures was examined in terms of the ability of these measures, taken singly and together, to discriminate between officers who were successes and failures. Successes were defined as officers performing satisfactorily at the end of a 1-year probationary period or previously employed officers considered as rehirable by their departments. Failures consisted of the recruits who failed at the police academy and officers who were discharged or who resigned and were not considered rehirable by their departments. These criteria were applied to the male Caucasian and female groups but could not be used for minority males because of the small number of failures.

Four biodata items discriminated between Caucasian male successes and failures. The successful officers were more likely to report (1) participation in high school athletics, (2) fewer family moves, (3) less need for job encouragement, and (4) higher values for achievement and societal contributions. Successful females differed from failures on only two biodata items. They were less likely to be single, and in addition, they more often reported that they were not bothered by bragging co-workers.

All four N-D scales significantly discriminated between successes and failures for Caucasian males, with the successful officers scoring higher on these scales. Successful Caucasian males also scored higher on the SCII army officer, business management, and office practices scales than did the failures. The N-D comprehension scale discriminated significantly between female successes and failures, but these groups did not differ on any of the SCII interest scales.

A number of personality variables significantly discriminated between successes and failures for both the Caucasian male and the female groups. The successful Caucasian males scored higher than did the failures on the CPI capacity for status, intellectual efficiency, sociability, dominance, and achievement via conformance scales. Successful females scored significantly higher on the following CPI scales: capacity for status, intellectual efficiency, sense of well-being, responsibility, self-control, tolerance, good impression, achievement via independence, and psychological-mindedness.

The choice of appropriate criterion measures is critical in police selection studies. Given the goal of screening out unfit or unsuitable officers, the success versus failure criterion employed in the FPSRP seems especially appropriate. Early identification of potential failures can reduce the human and financial costs generally associated with incorrect selection decisions. Combining variables from all three predictor categories in the discriminant function analyses correctly identified 82.5% of the male Caucasians and 95.2% of the females as either successes or failures.

The preliminary results of the FPSRP provide encouraging evidence of the predictive validity of demographic variables and psychological tests in police selection. However, final conclusions must await cross-validation of the present results with a large new sample. This is scheduled to take place in Phase 4 of the FPSRP, in which we also plan to follow the original subjects for up to three years. In examining the performance of these officers as they gain experience and become eligible for promotion, supervisors' ratings will be used in addition to the success/failure criterion.

REFERENCES

Brown, J. J., Nelson, M. J., & Denny, E. C. *Examiner's manual: The Nelson-Denny Reading Test*. Boston: Houghton Mifflin, 1973.

Campbell, D. P. *Manual for the Strong-Campbell Interest Inventory*. Stanford, Calif.: Stanford University Press, 1974.

Dahlstrom, W. G., Welsh, G. S., & Dahlstrom, L. E. *An MMPI Handbook* (Vol. 1). Minneapolis: University of Minnesota Press, 1972.

Dunnette, M. D., & Motowidlo, S. J. *Police selection and career assessment*. National Institute of Law Enforcement and Criminal Justice, Law Enforcement Assistance Administration, U.S. Department of Justice, Grant No. 73-N1-99-0018-G and N1-99-0001-G. November, 1976.

Florida Statutes, Chapter 23. Part IV, June 21, 1967.

Gottesman, J. *The utility of the MMPI in assessing the personality patterns of urban police applicants*. Hoboken, N.J.: Stevens Institute of Technology, 1975.

Gough, H. C. *Manual, California Psychological Inventory*. Palo Alto, Calif.: Consulting Psychologists Press, 1957.

Levy, R. J. *Investigation of a method for identification of the high-risk police applicant*. Berkeley, Calif.: Institute for Local Self Government, 1971.

National Advisory Commission on Criminal Justice Standards and Goals. *Task force on police*. Washington, D.C.: U.S. Government Printing Office, 1973.

Rotter, J. B. Generalized expectancies for internal versus external control of reinforcement. *Psychological Monographs, 1966, 80*(1, Whole No. 609).

Rush, A. C. Better police personnel selection. *The Police Chief, 1963, 30*, 18-26.

Spielberger, C. D., Gorsuch, R. L., & Lushene, R. E. *Test manual for the State-Trait Anxiety Inventory (STAI)*. Palo Alto, Calif.: Consulting Psychologists Press, 1970.

Spielberger, C. D., Kling, J. K., & O'Hagan, S. E. Dimensions of psychopathic personality: Anxiety and sociopathy. In R. Hare and D. Schalling (Eds.), *Psychopathy and behavior*. New York: Wiley, 1978.

Wilson, D. W., & McLaren, R. C. *Police administration*. New York: McGraw-Hill, 1977.

V

FAIR EMPLOYMENT PRACTICES AND CIVIL RIGHTS COMPLIANCE IN POLICE SELECTION

15

IMPACT OF CIVIL RIGHTS LEGISLATION AND COURT ACTIONS ON PERSONNEL PROCEDURES AND PRACTICES

Melany E. Baehr
Industrial Relations Center, The University of Chicago, Chicago, Illinois

INTRODUCTION

The Civil Rights Act of 1964, with its Title VII aimed at establishing nondiscriminatory employment practices, was the start of a still continuing sequence of challenge and change for the practitioner in the personnel area. During the past decade new legislation has expanded the coverage of the act, new interpretations and rulings have clarified its application, and new standards and guidelines for the selection and promotion of employees have been established. All these developments have had a profound impact on personnel procedures and practice. The specific area of impact to be dealt with here is the validation of selection and promotion procedures.

Current refinements and rigors in the validation process represent the cumulative effects of more than 10 years of interaction between the applied practices of personnel specialists and the mandates of legislators and judges. Laws and rulings dictate how the specialist should proceed, and the specialist's research findings are in turn incorporated into later laws and rulings. This is a desirable, constructive pattern of exchange and renewal. It has served to coordinate the best thinking of personnel psychologists and governmental bodies in a reciprocal effort. Nondiscriminatory selection and promotion are still more goals than fact, but what should be done and what can be done are coming closer together.

The body of this chapter consists of three main sections. The first one attempts to trace the major trends in legislation dealing with equal opportunity employment and the concurrent development of enforcement agencies and published guidelines. This brief summary provides the background against which vital changes in personnel procedures and practice have taken place. The second section considers some of the results and implications of selection test validation studies conducted under the Equal Employment Opportunity Commission (EEOC) *Guidelines* regulations (EEOC, 1966, 1970). These studies illustrate some of the technological innovations introduced into selection test validation procedures by one applied institute in its attempts—marked by both successes and frustration—to conform to *Guidelines* requirements. In the final section, the discussion will turn to the requirements of the new "Federal Executive Agency Guidelines on Employee Selection Procedures," issued by the Departments of Justice and Labor and the U.S. Civil Service Commission (November 23, 1976), with suggestions for future accepted test usage in light of the present regulatory situation.

MAJOR TRENDS IN LEGISLATION OVER THE PAST DECADE

A survey of the past decade reveals three basic trends in legislation and its enforcement, which directly affect the efforts of the personnel profession in the area of validation. The first of these is the increasing coverage of the law, reaching to more and more institutions and employees. Second is the extension of technical requirements for the validation process to include all procedures involved in selection, placement, and promotion. The third trend is toward far more stringent and detailed requirements for validating tests or test batteries. However despite the clear direction of these trends, the next decade opens in conditions of confusion and even conflict, as will be noted at the end of this section.

Increasing Number of Institutions and Employees Covered by Legislation

The scope and application of fair employment legislation have broadened steadily. In the beginning the 1964 Civil Rights Act as a whole prohibited discrimination against a wide range of population subgroups in a variety of contexts. Title VII of this act was directed to the employment context. It became effective on July 2, 1965, as the Equal Employment Opportunity Act. Its provisions forbade employers, labor unions, and employment agencies to discriminate on the basis of race, color, religion, sex, or national origin, except as specified in Section 703(e), that is, except in instances where religion, sex, or national origin could be demonstrated to be bona fide occupational qualifications.

Title VII also assigned responsibility for administering its provisions by establishing the EEOC. This advisory body was appointed by the president and began its operation shortly after the act was passed. In August 1966 it published the first *Guidelines on Employment Testing Procedures,* designed as a manual for personnel psychologists in their efforts to apply and conform to the directives of Title VII. Feedback on these efforts led to revisions, and the new *Guidelines on Employee Selection Procedures* was published in 1970.

In like manner, Title VII itself did not remain static. Executive Order 11246, September 24, 1965, amended by Executive Order 11375, October 13, 1967, extended the provisions of the title to federal government agencies and their contractors and also specified responsibility for enforcement. Much of this responsibility fell on the secretary of labor. Accordingly, in September 1968 then-Secretary Wirtz issued the "Order of Secretary of Labor on Employment Tests by Contractors Subject to Provisions of Executive Order 11246" (U.S. Department of Labor). This "order" was similar in general purpose to the *Guidelines,* since it was designed to help the agencies and contractors covered by the executive order in their efforts to abide by its provisions. Further details and refinements were added in April 1971 by the Office of Federal Contract Compliance (OFCC), Department of Labor, in the form of a new block of text in chapter 60 of the order. This block was titled "Employee Testing and Other Selection Procedures" (OFCC). It is generally referred to as the OFCC order or OFCC regulations. This order itself was further amended in January 1974 (OFCC).

Neither Title VII nor Executive Orders 11246 and 11375 applied to state or local governmental bodies. These had been covered partially through the fair employment acts or laws of individual states.

However, in line with the emerging pattern of broader and broader coverage, a new Equal Employment Opportunity Act was passed in March 1972 (in essence, Title VII of the Civil Rights Act with 1972 amendments). This new act specifically extended federal fair employment practices to all state and local governments as well as to public and private educational institutions. It also extended the authority and jurisdiction of the EEOC. In the 1964 act, the activities of this commission were limited to conference, conciliation, and persuasion. The 1972 act empowered the EEOC to bring action or suits in a U.S. district court. Thus, widening coverage by the law has been accompanied by widening authority for enforcement. The need for this authority is underscored by the fact that, at the time of this writing, fair employment legislation reaches essentially all institutions and positions in the United States. About the only exceptions are employers with fewer than 15 employees, elected or appointed officials and their advisers, and sensitive security positions.

Extension of Technical Requirements for Validation to Cover All Procedures in the Selection Process

Extended coverage of persons has been matched by extended coverage of process. The use and validation of psychological tests was the central issue in both the 1966 and 1970 *Guidelines*. However, the 1970 publication broadens the definition of *test* to include a wide range of employment standards and procedures, such as the use of personal background information, medical and physical requirements, ratings of observed behavior, and face-to-face interviews of all kinds.

A host of court decisions attest to the fact that these typical elements in employment decisions are taken seriously. The requirement of a high school diploma for lower level jobs was one of the issues in the well-known case of *Griggs* v. *Duke Power Company* (1968). On the professional level, the requirement of an M.A. degree or a passing score on the Graduate Record Examination for teachers was challenged in a case brought under the auspices of the National Association for the Advancement of Colored People (NAACP) against Starkville Separate School District in Mississippi (*Armstead* v. *Starkville*, 1971). The use of background information—particularly arrest and conviction records—was one basis for complaint in a case against the Minneapolis Fire Department (*Carter* v. *Gallagher*, 1971). More recently physical and medical standards have come under attack. A number of these deal with the application of height requirements—developed for positions traditionally held by males of northern European background—to females and to males of generally smaller statured ethnic groups, such as those of Hispanic descent (for example, *Officers for Justice*, 1975).

The broadened definition of *test* has led to challenges for both employers and personnel psychologists. Indeed, the very meaning of *validation* is difficult to establish in these next contexts.

Increasing Rigor in Validation Requirements for Psychological Tests Themselves

The difficulty just mentioned is enhanced by a clear trend to increasing rigor in validation requirements for psychological tests themselves. This trend is very evident from a comparison of the 1966 and 1970 EEOC *Guidelines*. The earlier publication dealt with broad professional standards. These included the need for qualified personnel to perform both test administration and test interpretation, the extent to which normative populations must represent all applicant subgroups, and the technical soundness of tests used. Soundness was judged by a set of standards issued (and revised at a later date) jointly by the American Psychological Association, the American Educational Research Association, and the National Council on Measurement in Education (*Standards*, 1966, 1974). With respect to test validity the 1966 *Guidelines* encouraged the use of job-related ability tests and recommended that tests be judged in relation to whatever abstract or concrete attribute they were designed to measure.

In contrast to these generalized professional requirements, the 1970 *Guidelines* requires validation to show that a test accurately measures a skill, knowledge, aptitude, or characteristic relevant to performance. A further important point emerges. It has been widely demonstrated (Ash, 1966; Baehr, Furcon, & Froemel, 1969; Dugan, 1966; Kirkpatrick, Ewen, Barrett, & Katzell, 1968; Krug, 1966; Lopez, 1966) that the mean scores on tests of general ability, intelligence, and academic aptitude are usually lower for blacks than for whites. These differences are regarded as a result of social and cultural deprivation. Therefore the 1970 *Guidelines* insist on separate validations for different ethnic groups, including a graphic representation of the relationship between test score(s) and performance for each group.

These new *Guidelines* requirements were only the beginning of an ongoing and accelerating effort to achieve more and more comprehensive standards for the validation of psychological tests. A relevant example is the matter of defining the conditions under which validation results for a particular occupation in a particular organization may be transferred to another similar occupational unit within that organization or, more broadly, to a similar occupation in another company in the same industry. The circumstances under which such transfers are permissible are defined in both the 1970 EEOC *Guidelines* and the 1971 OFCC order. Need for a ruling here is increasingly important because of the emerging practice of industry-wide validation studies in the private sector and national studies across departments in the public sector.

As with the other trends in equal employment legislation, the increasing stringency of requirements for test validation has been accompanied by legal action and court decisions across the country. An illustrative and significant recent opinion was handed down by the Supreme Court in the case of *Albemarle Paper Company* v. *Moody* (1975). Here the court declared, "Measured against the Guidelines, Albemarle's validation study is materially defective in several respects . . ." (p. 406).

The Confused and Ambiguous Guidelines

The past decade has thus been marked by very clear trends in legislation, which have been largely upheld in court action. The principles enunciated in the 1970 EEOC *Guidelines* and the OFCC order of 1971 have enjoyed an ever widening acceptance by the states, such as Maryland, on July 11, 1972; Michigan, on September 29, 1972; Oklahoma, on June 16, 1973; Missouri, in October 1973; and Kentucky, on November 8, 1974 (Current developments, 1976). Increasing numbers of governmental agencies have also endorsed the principles of the *Guidelines* or given them clear support. These agencies include the Office of Revenue Sharing, November 1975; the LEAA on December 3, 1975; and the Justice Department, in a brief filed with the Seventh Circuit Court of Appeals in Chicago in the spring of 1976 (Current developments, 1976). All this acceptance of the EEOC *Guidelines* came to an apparent halt with the publication, already referred to, of the "Federal

Executive Agency Guidelines on Employee Selection Procedures" on November 23, 1976, by the Departments of Justice and Labor and the U.S. Civil Service Commission (CSC) despite the objections and final abstention of the EEOC.

A short history of events leading up to this publication starts with the establishment of the Equal Employment Opportunity Coordinating Council (EEOCC) by the 1972 Equal Employment Opportunity Act. Council membership included representation by the Departments of Justice and Labor, the CSC, the Commission on Civil Rights, and the EEOC. Their task was to coordinate the validation activities of a number of major government departments, and one of their first charges was the development of the *Uniform Guidelines on Employee Selection Procedures.* This charge was seen as highly important, since the CSC and the EEOC have overlapping responsibilities and yet the inconsistencies in their published standards for validating tests have led to the incongruous imposition of more rigorous standards on private employers than on the federal government itself.

The EEOC participated in development of the two first drafts of the *Uniform Guidelines*, which were published for review and comment in July 1973 and August 1974. However, after an internal review of the third draft (EEOC, 1975), the EEOC decided not to approve this particular *Guidelines* and proceeded to prepare their own draft for consideration by the EEOCC. After a meeting in which this EEOC draft was discussed, the Departments of Labor and Justice and the CSC decided that their differences with the EEOC were irreconcilable and that further discussion would not be productive. The EEOCC then published what are now known as the *Federal Executive Agency (FEA) Guidelines.* EEOC, to underline its own dissenting position, promptly republished its 1970 *Guidelines* without change one day later, on November 24, 1976 ("Guidelines," 1976).

The *FEA Guidelines* have, in general, been attacked by civil rights and women's groups and hailed by the business community. All this, however, leaves the practitioner in the confusing situation of having two sets of guidelines under which to operate. It is possible that new legislation now proposed will give the EEOC broad enforcement powers and jurisdiction over all major civil rights laws and regulations. Meanwhile, it seems that the practitioner and theoretician alike may best be served at the present time by an analysis of the principal differences between two sets of guidelines coupled with some suggestions for future accepted procedures for test usage. These suggestions are based on the results of selection test validations conducted by the IRC under the EEOC *Guidelines.* The following section summarizes some key findings from these studies and points out the implication of these findings for specific steps in the validation process.

RESULTS AND IMPLICATIONS OF SELECTION TEST VALIDATIONS CONDUCTED UNDER EEOC GUIDELINES

An article headlined "Failing System—Job Tests Are Dropped by Many Companies Due to Antibias Drive" (Lancaster, 1975) has received considerable attention from both test users and advocates of test validation. The article points out that the major reasons for companies' dropping or sharply curtailing their use of tests are the time, expense, and difficulty involved in validating tests according to EEOC requirements. Newspaper headlines and leads are often dramatically stated and do not always accurately reflect the full content of the article. In this particular instance the text concludes with some strong testimonials from companies using validated tests. These companies felt that the validated tests were doing their intended job of improving the utilization of the work force and that validation costs are largely offset by savings stemming from reduced training failures.

In our experience test usage by member companies and clients decreased sharply soon after passage of the 1964 Civil Rights Act. Generally, the organizations that stopped using tests were those that had resisted proposals for test validations. Then, over time, all other procedures in the selection process became subject to validation, with legal action increasingly directed at the use of personal background data in employment interviews. As these trends have taken place, the use of tests has once again been on the ascendancy. Our general impression is that the overall use of tests may indeed still be reduced but that, where tests are used, their usage is on a sounder and more professional basis. Such usage would be the hoped-for outcome of legislation.

The material in the rest of this section describes some of our failures, frustrations, and successes in our efforts to implement validation studies in accordance with the 1970 *Guidelines*. Each of these studies raised problems and challenges, which will be summarized in relation to the steps in the validation process where they appeared to have most relevance.

Psychological Assessment of Patrol Officer Qualifications in Relation to Field Performance (Chicago Police Department)

This study (Baehr et al., 1969) was a concurrent criterion-related validation—and a "key" one from the standpoint of its research implications. It was also the first large, federally funded study undertaken by the IRC in the public sector. Its research implications involve at least two important aspects of the validation process.

Differential validity

The first phase of this study was conducted in 1967, at which time the *Guidelines* did not require separate validations by race. Furthermore, because of preselection of the subjects, we did not expect to find either predictor or criterion differences between the white and the black incumbent patrol officers. These incumbents had already been screened by the CSC, had passed a background investigation, had graduated from the training academy, and had held their jobs for at least 1 year. Since our testing and appraisal schedules called for two "waves" of activity at different times, we simply drew two representative patrol officer samples, in which members of the racial subgroups were included in approximately the same proportions as existed in the Chicago Police Department. However, as a precaution, we did separate multiple regressions of predictors against criterion measures for the white and the black subgroups in each sample, in addition to the regression for the total group.

For the total group, we obtained a satisfactorily high and statistically significant primary validity coefficient. However, there was a statistically significant further increase in this coefficient when it was calculated separately for the white and the black subgroups. This finding prompted a comparison of results for the subgroups on both the predictor and the criterion measures. We discovered that white patrol officers scored significantly higher than did black patrol officers on most of the predictors, especially on the measures of personal background, mental ability, and special aptitude. However, there was no evidence of corresponding differences on the measures of performance.

We had stumbled on the classic situation of parallel regression lines for racial subgroups, which would later be covered in the 1970 *Guidelines*. There was a significant relationship between test results and performance for each racial subgroup, but the graphic "fit" between the measures was different in the two subgroups. We developed a relatively simple empirical procedure (Baehr, Saunders, Froemel, & Furcon, 1971) to investigate this fit. The validities and cross-validities were calculated separately for each subgroup and for the total group, using, in succession, prediction equations derived from each of these groups. This exercise again demonstrated the desirability of using the race-specific equations.

The question then arose as to the procedure for implementing these equations for practical purposes of selection. A test score in itself has little meaning except as it relates to some quality or construct. In this instance we were concerned with the test score as a possible measure or predictor of on-the-job performance. The police department, in turn, was concerned with the probable future performance of its newly hired officers. Thus the logical procedure seemed to be to set a selection cut-off point in terms of a particular level of predicted performance rather than in terms of a particular test score. Use of the race-specific equations would, under the existing conditions of a systematic depression of test scores for minority group applicants without a corresponding difference in performance, result in lower test scores being acceptable for hiring minority group members.

It seemed that our future practice in validation studies was set. Race-specific validations produced higher validity coefficients, were relatively easy to handle, and seemed certain to lead to the hiring of a larger proportion of minority-group members. However, later studies showed that our early enthusiasm was not wholly justified. The classical situation with race-specific regression lines, genuinely parallel but with significantly different intercepts, did not arise often, and the relationships between predictors and criteria manifested themselves in strange and unexpected ways.

Differential test response

The results of this police study raised significant questions as to why there were test differences by race in this highly selected sample of patrol officers and why these differences appeared where they did. A first general hypothesis was that the lower test scores for the black subgroup were a result of poorer facility in handling the English language. However, our results did not support this hypothesis. Observed differences between the racial subgroups were often as great—and sometimes even greater—on the nonverbal tests as on the verbal. On analysis, it became apparent that there was a fairly strong and quite interesting adverse relationship between the significance of the difference between racial group mean predictor scores and the time limit for the test. The shorter this time limit the lower the test scores for minority group members tended to be. This finding suggests that the use of loosely timed or untimed tests would be one method for reducing adverse impact.

Performance appraisal

Over the years the Industrial Relations Center (IRC) has developed a standard approach to performance appraisal for purposes of test validation. Combinations of three types of measures are used—the organization's own performance appraisals, "objective" indexes of critical work behavior obtained from organization records, and a specially implemented supervisory assessment of performance, most often using the paired-comparison technique (Baehr, 1968; Thurstone, 1927). A follow-up longitudinal study (Furcon, Froemel, Franczak, & Baehr, 1971) in the Chicago Police Department afforded an opportunity to investigate the stability of these different types of measures, derived yearly over a 3-year period.

The results indicated that subjective supervisory assessments based on the paired-comparison technique showed a satisfactorily high stability (approaching $r = .6$) for racial groups individually and for the total group. This was higher than for any of the five objective measures studied. Of these, three showed 3-year stabilities that were so low as to be inappropriate for use as criteria in a predictive study, and another was rather dubious. The most stable objective index was the arrest record.

Improvement of Selection and Utilization Procedures for Personnel in the Supermarket Industry (Supermarket Institute)

This research project (Baehr & Burns, 1972), initiated in 1969, was the IRC's first large national study designed to validate selection test batteries for particular occupations across different companies and geographic locations within the same industry. Specifically, we sought to validate a selection test battery for each of four key occupations in the supermarket industry—store manager, department head, cashier/checker, and clerk—with samples drawn from 21 companies.

The study addressed itself to the *Guidelines* provision that an organization may use validation results obtained elsewhere in the same industry only when it can be demonstrated that these results are derived from comparable jobs (i.e., jobs with basically the same task elements) and that there are no major differences in job contexts or sample composition which might significantly affect validity. To this end, IRC project staff and an advisory board of supermarket personnel developed a three-way analysis-of-variance design for each of the four occupational groups, as shown in Figure 1. Essential variables of sales volume, geographic region, organizational structure, race, part-time or full-time employment, and merchandise specialization were assigned as they seemed relevant. While the result was a "clean" theoretical design, in practice it was very difficult to implement completely because of the widely scattered geographic locations and the need to rely on volunteer subjects. After funds and tempers had been overdrawn on both sides, we decided to proceed with the analysis of available data even though some of the cells in the matrices were underrepresented. The project results discussed below amply justify the *Guidelines* requirement of empirical investigation of the contextual variables of the job and of the composition of the employee samples.

In the store manager validation, differences in geographic location and sales volume had no significant effects. (The latter finding came as a considerable surprise to industry personnel.) However, it appeared that more stringent selection standards might have to be set for store managers from decentralized—as opposed to corporate—organizational structures.

In the cashier and clerk validations, preanalyses indicated a need for separate validations for each racial group (white, black, and Spanish-surnamed) and for part-time and full-time employees. This would have meant 12 separate validations in all. Furthermore, although at present cashiers are predominantly female and the clerks predominantly male, there is an increasing tendency for members of both sexes to do both jobs. That males and females respond differently in some psychological test areas is highlighted by the fact that for

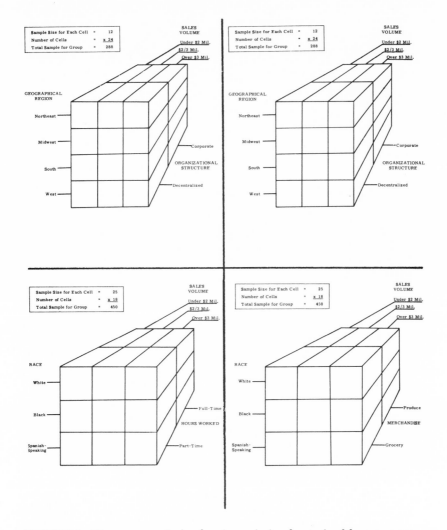

FIGURE 1 Three-way analysis of variance design for each of four occupational groups in the supermarket industry.

many years a number of tests have had different norms for these two groups. Since females are a legally protected group, a final sectioning of our clerk and cashier populations by sex would have created a need for 24 separate validations to establish legally acceptable selection procedures for these two entry-level positions in the supermarket industry. Limits to time and funds prevented us from making the attempt to carry the study this far.

These experiences certainly support *Guidelines* requirements for empirical investigation of differences in employee populations and operating conditions on the job. At the same time, however, they raise serious questions concerning the feasibility of the differential validity approach in criterion-related studies of occupations with racially and sexually mixed employee populations operating in differently structured work contexts and work weeks.

Regressing predictors against performance measures in those validations that we did undertake in this study produced a bewildering variety of relationships among the resulting regression lines. In some instances these lines were either colinear or parallel, both of which results could be handled fairly easily to produce equitable selection procedures. More often, however, the lines intersected and, in one case at least, the regression line actually had a negative slope. This particular situation resulted from the fact that part-time cashiers scored significantly higher than full-time ones on the majority of the predictors but, as a group, were rated lower on the performance measures. In the context of the study, we could not pursue the question of whether the lower performance ratings reflected bias on the part of full-time supervisors against part-timers (who are a sizable proportion of the work force in some supermarkets).

These findings serve as a warning that unthinking or mechanical use of separate race or other group-specific prediction equations does not automatically lead to equitable selection. Indeed, in the case of intersecting regression lines, employee subgroups would be differently and disparately handled above and below the point of intersection. In summary, these results clearly indicate the need for improved technology and definition in handling validation analyses and, in a wider context, the need for a vigorous pursuit of simplified validation procedures that will still provide equitable selection.

A National Study to Validate a Selection Test Battery for Bus Operators (Department of Transportation)

The national study to validate a selection test battery for bus operators (Baehr, 1977), carried out at five separate geographic locations, was funded by the Urban Mass Transportation Administration of the United States Department of Transportation. It dealt with a single occupation—that of the urban bus operator. Both the concurrent and predictive validation models were implemented across locations for three racial groups (white, black, and Spanish-surnamed) both singly and in combination. The major findings of this study are summarized below.

1. The concurrent and predictive models yielded essentially similar results.
2. It was possible to utilize a single race-common prediction equation.
3. Use of this race-common prediction equation produced little or no adverse impact on any of the racial groups.
4. The demonstrated validity and cross-validity of the final prediction equation were far in excess of *Guidelines* requirements.

Some of the procedures and technical innovations that helped in achieving these rather satisfactory results are described here briefly under the step in the validation procedure for which they are relevant.

Occupational analysis

From the beginning of this study, we had to foresee and plan the procedures that would be involved in implementing the final validated test battery on the national scale for which it was to be designed. The central problem here was that the battery would be used by geographically scattered transportation companies that had not participated in the validation itself. We would need some relatively simple but reliable means for comparing the requirements of the job in nonparticipating companies with the requirements in the authorities on which the validation had actually been done. Thus the occupational analysis would have to perform a further function, in addition to those usually required in a criterion-related validation.

With this procedural need in mind, we developed a standardized and quantified instrument for defining the relative importance of the various skills and attributes required for successful performance as a bus operator. This instrument can be used on an individual basis by either supervisors or incumbents without professional or clerical supervision. Results are presented in the form of "requirements" profiles. These stabilize after relatively few supervisory assessments, and we have also obtained good data from assessments made by incumbents. This procedure has now been refined and applied with good effect in three different police patrol officer studies, which are described in chapter 3 of this volume.

Performance appraisal: Elimination of racial bias in supervisory performance ratings

The subjective performance measures used in this study were supervisory ratings made by means of the paired-comparison (PC) technique. The supervisors (66 white and 2 black) provided ratings on various members of the racially mixed sample of operators. An initial comparison of total performance indexes across the three racial groups revealed a complicated set of relationships among the objective performance criterion of tenure, the race of the operator, and the subjective supervisory performance ratings.

Working from this initial comparison, we observed that both the black and the Spanish-surnamed operators, as groups, received lower PC ratings than did white operators, as a group. We also noted that operators from the minority groups had significantly lower job tenure than did operators from the white group. These observations prompted a statistical examination of the joint effects of race and of tenure on the PC rating. This examination led eventually to the use in the statistical-analysis stage of the study of four PC-derived performance measures—the raw PC rating and this rating corrected successively for tenure alone, for racial bias alone, and for both tenure and racial bias. The procedures for doing this and the results achieved are detailed elsewhere (Saunders, Baehr, & Froemel, 1977).

In summary, the major findings derived from use of the four PC-derived measures were as follows:

1. The vast majority of assessing supervisors, including both the blacks, showed no racial bias. However, a few supervisors were extremely biased, and their bias would have seriously affected the validation results had appropriate corrections not been applied to the ratings.
2. The corrections could be applied in such a way that all the supervisory assessments and all four variants of the PC rating could be used in the study without any loss of cases.
3. Correcting the PC rating only for racial bias eliminated the differences across the racial groups, while correcting it only for tenure did not.
4. PC corrected only for racial bias was the best predicted of the four PC measures and was selected as the major performance criterion for the study.

Test development: Traditional test scores versus self-report

The trial test battery used in this study consisted of 11 measurement instruments, including traditional psychological tests of mental abilities, aptitudes, and behavior, as well as some specially constructed, scorable, self-report forms. Three instruments survived validation, and they were all self-report forms covering, respectively, the applicant's background, perceived skills and behavior attributes, and emotional health status. These self-report forms not only demonstrated the greatest validity among the 11 instruments in both the concurrent and predictive validation models but, in addition, showed least adverse impact on minority group applicants. The latter finding is in sharp contrast to the typical behavior of scores from traditional tests of the same constructs.

Differential validity

This was the IRC's first study on an entry-level, racially mixed applicant group in which use of a single, race-common regression line produced both highest cross-validities and lowest adverse impact. Another "first" for us was the procedure for plotting the test scores. Traditionally, test scores are plotted directly against the performance measure. In this study, they were plotted against the *probability of (minimally) successful performance* for each of the three racial groups and the total group, using both the race-common and the race-specific equations. The rationale and detailed procedure for doing this are described elsewhere (Baehr, 1977).

In the practical application of this procedure to the bus-operator study, we presented the ogive plots on probability graph paper so that they appeared as straight lines. Thus presented, the lines for the race-specific equations had varying slopes, reflecting the varying magnitudes of the validity coefficients, which, in turn, stemmed largely from differences in sample sizes. Use of the race-common equation resulted in essential colinearity of lines for the three racial groups and for the total group.

Note that this procedure precludes the possibility of parallel lines. Since all lines must pass through the point of 50% probability of successful performance, they must be either colinear or intersecting. Therefore, regardless of which equation is chosen for final use, there will always be one predicted criterion score that corresponds to a 50% probability of successful performance and can be interpreted in the same way for all applicants.

As an aid to final selection of a prediction equation, we used both the race-common and the race-specific equations to generate predicted criterion scores for all subjects. We then calculated the potential rejection rates (as percentages) for each racial group at two adjacent cut-off performance levels. The results clearly indicated that use of the race-common equation substantially reduces adverse impact for the Spanish-surnamed group and does not unduly penalize the white or black group.

The validation studies described in this section were conducted with a sincere effort to conform to 1970 *Guidelines* requirements. However, this effort did not prevent us—as it should not prevent any conscientious researcher—from critically examining the effects of these requirements or from attempting refinements and innovations in the hope that these might better implement the spirit of the law. With this hope in mind, we now offer—for serious consideration—some suggestions that may achieve accepted or even required usage in the future.

REQUIREMENTS OF THE FEA AND EEOC GUIDELINES, WITH SUGGESTIONS FOR FUTURE ACCEPTED TEST USAGE

Cooperative versus Local Validation Studies

While the EEOC *Guidelines* make provision for multiunit, or cooperative studies, the *FEA Guidelines* actively encourage them. This would seem to be an advance despite the fact that cooperative studies have their own particular hazards and generally increase the complexity of the validation process. It certainly seems more realistic to validate a selection procedure for the patrol officer's position by geographic region or by size and type of department than for each police department in the country to conduct its own validation. However, the cooperative procedure must include adequate safeguards to ensure that job conditions and employee populations are sufficiently similar to warrant generalization of validation results.

The great specificity of criterion-related validity has long been known, is attested to in the APA *Standards* (1966, 1974), and was amply illustrated in our own supermarket study, where we could not even generalize from full-time to long-term part-time employees of the same race doing identical jobs in the same organization. While this study may be an extreme example, it is a dramatic demonstration of the necessity for a thorough investigation of the comparability of work contexts and employee populations both among cooperating organizations and between them and nonparticipants. Yet the *FEA Guidelines* give only the general requirements that a cooperative study meet validation standards, that a job analysis show that the job has substantially the same duties at different locations, and that the study include an investigation of test fairness. However, if that last condition is not satisfied, the borrowing user may utilize results until studies conducted elsewhere show test unfairness or until it is feasible to conduct an internal study. (Such an internal study will not be required on fewer than 30 cases.)

In short, encouragement of cooperative studies is an advance. However, the looseness with which the requirements for their implementation are stated leaves many loopholes for test misuse.

Criterion Validation versus Equal Acceptance of Criterion, Content, and Construct Validation

The *FEA Guidelines*' equal acceptance (60-3.12) of the three classical validation procedures described in the psychological literature is considered an advance. Instead of focusing research on one type of validation, this attitude opens new fields of validation research. Yet once more the advance is seriously reduced by loose wording of directions and safeguards for the implementation of the various validation procedures.

This weakness is particularly apparent in the treatment of construct validity, which, although generally regarded as the most complex of the three procedures, is given least space in the *FEA Guidelines*. The most serious deficiency is the minimal level of requirements for "anchoring," or showing that performance on the selection procedure is validly related to performance of critical job duties. We are told [60-3.12(d)(3)], "Normally, sufficient empirical research evidence would take the form of one or more criterion-related validity studies meeting the requirements of 60-3.12(b)." The implication that a demonstration of external performance-criterion validity is not essential is strengthened by the suggestion to refer also to the second sentence of 60-3.12, which states, "Nothing in these guidelines is intended to preclude the development and use of other professionally acceptable tecnhiques with respect to validation of selection procedures."

In addition, there is little of the emphasis on investigation of test fairness insisted on in the procedures for performance-criterion validation. This issue is mentioned only in the section dealing with the documentation of validity evidence [60-3.13(e)(1)(v)], which states, "*Where* [italics added] any of the studies included an investigation of test fairness, the results of this investigation should be provided (ESSENTIAL)." It is also interesting that, in documenting research evidence for construct validity, it is not necessary to report means and standard deviations of predictor scores for relevant racial, ethnic, and sex subgroups, as is required for both performance-criterion and content validation.

The issue of demonstrating the relationship between the construct measured and job performance has already surfaced in the courts, as in the case of *Douglas et al.* v. *Hampton* (1975) in connection with the Federal Service Entrance Examination. Here the CSC made claims to "rational validity" and also made its bias against criterion validation very evident.

We are faced with an equal acceptance of construct validation combined with loose statements as to its requirements. This combination will place a heavy burden on any court judge and will also create avenues for test abuse.

Traditional versus New Performance-related Validation Techniques

As we have seen above, the *FEA Guidelines* do encourage the development of other "professionally acceptable" techniques and indeed, by virtue of a lack of any further comment, leave the field wide open. It would seem likely that such techniques would minimally require some form of "anchoring," as in construct validation.

A fact that may not have been sufficiently considered is that, when it is feasible to implement a classical performance-criterion validation, all conditions will probably also be met for implementing simplified or approximated performance-related validation techniques. The IRC is presently planning studies in which three successively simplified validation techniques, described elsewhere (Baehr, n.d.), will be implemented concurrently with a classical performance-criterion validation. The results of this last will serve as the criterion for judging the validity of the other techniques. If the outcome is satisfactory, the new techniques could thereafter be used in situations where classical performance-criterion validation is not feasible.

Such an approach is, I believe, more in keeping with the requirements of validity generalization, more demonstrably job related, and therefore more desirable than complex and often only loosely anchored construct validity studies.

Differential Validity and Test Fairness

As treated in the *FEA Guidelines*, the issue of test fairness has already been touched on in this section. Nowhere is it associated with the differential validity insisted on in the EEOC *Guidelines.*

In practice, differential validity is one procedure for dealing with the test fairness issue. In some instances, as in our Chicago patrol officer study, specific validations by race proved to be a straightforward and equitable way of dealing with the fact that differences between the racial groups on the predictors did not reflect corresponding differences in performance. This is the case, however, only when there are optimal statistical conditions of parallel regression lines for the different groups with significant differences between their intercepts. By contrast, this straightforward approach alone was simply not feasible in the supermarket study, where we were dealing with employees differing in both race and sex and working in differently structured contexts for differing numbers of hours—all of which resulted in a need for proliferating separate validations. In the bus operator study, undertaken later, we developed procedures for using a race-common regression line, which resulted in valid selection with minimal, if any, adverse impact.

The *FEA Guidelines* do clear the way for use of new models of test fairness but certainly do not "guide" with respect to either their selection or their implementation. To my knowledge, there are at least three well-documented theories of fair selection that have been advocated by well-known researchers and that have essentially incompatible principals of operation. No reference is made to these or to the conditions of operation under which each could appropriately be applied.

We are merely told that test fairness studies are not feasible unless there are at least 30 persons in each group and the groups are comparable. What should be done with adequate groups is unclear. Consulting the source for the reference made to the *Standards* (1974) does not help matters. A short statement in this publication saying that it is essential to avoid bias in test selections or even the *appearance* of discriminatory practice is followed by a long "comment," as follows:

> Comment: This is a difficult standard to apply. Sources of item or test bias are neither well understood nor easily avoided. The very definition of bias is open to question. The competent test user will accept the obligation to keep abreast of developments in the literature and, at the very least, to demonstrate a sensitivity to the problem and to the feelings of examinees. (p. 60)

While this may be a good academic stance, it in no way reassures the practitioner who must implement validation studies.

Evaluation of Adverse Impact for the Total Selection Process versus Its Evaluation for Each Step of the Process

The *FEA Guidelines* differ sharply from the EEOC ones in stating that, if the total selection process for a job has no adverse impact, then the individual steps in this process need not be evaluated separately for such impact [60-3.4(b)]. Now both *Guidelines* require validation only when there is evidence of adverse impact. Thus, it seems that this FEA provision will allow a situation where the effects of an early selection-process step, that has unknown or even no validity and severe adverse impact can be balanced out by the effects of a later step with unknown validity and "reverse adverse impact." The net result would be a total selection procedure with no adverse impact and thus no need for validation. Such a procedure hardly seems in keeping with the spirit of civil rights legislation.

Equal Opportunity versus Merit Employment

I was of course pleased to find in the *FEA Guidelines* a statement (60-3.1) that "all users are encouraged to use selection procedures that are valid, especially users operating under merit principles." However, I believe that more than "encouragement" is required. Use of selection procedures of unknown validity may indeed reduce to random selection. Given similar or unlimited population pools for all racial groups, a random procedure will result in an equal selection of candidates for all race and sex subgroups. While in the narrow sense of the definition, this may be regarded as equal opportunity employment, it can in no way be regarded as consistent with the principles of merit employment, since it will also select equally from the qualified and the unqualified. I do not believe that, in the long run, such a procedure would serve the interests of equal opportunity employment, either. Rather a random procedure would take its toll in human frustration and failure and in the undermining of American institutions. It seems to me essential that validity be required of all selection and promotion procedures regardless of whether they result in adverse impact.

During a four-year-long history of tortuous development and uncertain acceptance, the *FEA Guidelines* appeared in three draft versions as the EEOCC's *Uniform Guidelines*. In these draft versions the material was subjected to a variety of criticism from interested parties. These included the federal CSC, the EEOC, and the APA. This last organization produced a third draft of its own principles for test validation (APA, 1975). The most severe criticism was leveled by the NAACP's Legal Defense Fund. In fact, the most persistent criticism has come from civil rights groups, which maintain that the new *Guidelines* take a softer stand—particularly in the areas of performance-criterion and differential validity—and retreat from the rigorous standards required by the EEOC *Guidelines* and enforced in court decisions. However, the new *Guidelines* have their adherents, as well, since they were finally issued by the Departments of Justice and Labor and the CSC and are now also endorsed by members of the APA Division of Industrial and Organizational Psychology.

In my view, a major reason for the conflicting and sometimes changing attitudes touched on above lies in the fact that the very strength of the *FEA Guidelines* is at the same time their weakness. They courageously open wide avenues of research into the many complex issues encountered in the validation process. They burst out of procedures that might have become too narrowly focused and inflexibly defined if the EEOC *Guidelines* had remained unchallenged. However, they do *not* provide adequate safeguards to ensure that the freedom and opportunities they offer will be used ethically and professionally to advance the cause of civil rights. The test user or researcher is left to make critical decisions about validation processes, such as the type of validation to be employed, the number of cases that will be suitable to the circumstances, the method for investigating test fairness, and the procedure for anchoring construct validation. Loopholes certainly exist for those who have a mind to find them, and these loopholes could open the way to inadequate validation and test abuse. It is to be hoped that these loopholes will be closed one way or another before they are used to the detriment of the practitioner and the psychological profession.

SUMMARY

The first section of this chapter traces the major trends in legislation dealing with equal opportunity employment and the concurrent development of enforcement agencies and published guidelines that took place in the decade following the Civil Rights Act of 1964. A first significant trend is seen as an increasing legal coverage, reaching to more and more employees and institutions. The second is an extension of the technical requirements for test validation to include all procedures—formal and informal, scored and unscored—involved in selection, placement, and promotion. The final major trend is the increasing stringency of the requirements for validating tests or test batteries.

It is against this background that the personnel specialist must operate. Therefore, the second section describes some of the experiences and findings of one applied institute in its attempts at both conformity and innovation in following the requirements of the 1970 EEOC *Guidelines*. The results of some of its key validation studies are summarized with reference to the basic steps in the validation process from which these results emerged. Points covered include methods of dealing with applicants from different race and sex subgroups and the increasingly important issue of the transportability or generalization of validation results.

Now, in the second decade of civil rights enforcement, the practitioner is in the confusing position of having to operate under two rather different sets of requirements, as represented by the 1970 EEOC *Guidelines* and the 1976 *FEA Guidelines*. The final section of this chapter analyzes some of the salient differences between these two sets of requirements and offers some suggestions for future accepted validation procedures and test usage.

REFERENCES

Albermarle Paper Company v. *Moody.* U.S. Supreme Court (No. 74-389), June 25, 1975.

American Psychological Association, Division 14 (Industrial and Organizational Psychology), Executive Committee. *Principles for the validation and use of personnel selection procedures* (third draft). April 1, 1975.

Armstead v. *Starkville Separate School District.* U.S. District Court, Northern District of Mississippi, Eastern Division (No. EC-70-51-S), April 8, 1971.

Ash, P. Race, employment test, and equal opportunity. *Industrial Management, 1966, 8,* No. 3, 8–12.

Baehr, M. E. *The appraisal of job performance.* Occasional paper No. 27-R1. Chicago: University of Chicago, Industrial Relations Center, 1968.

Baehr, M. E. *National validation of a selection test battery for male transit bus operators: Final report.* Springfield, Va.: National Technical Information Service, 1977.

Baehr, M. E. *Outline of a study of alternatives to the classical performance-based selection test validation for entry-level positions in the transportation industry.* Project to be undertaken by the University of Chicago, Industrial Relations Center, in cooperation with participating transit authorities, n.d.

Baehr, M. E., & Burns, F. M. *The improvement of selection and utilization procedures for personnel in the supermarket industry.* Chicago: University of Chicago, Industrial Relations Center, 1972.

Baehr, M. E., Furcon, J. E., & Froemel, E. C. *Psychological assessment of patrolman qualifications in relation to field performance.* Washington, D.C.: U.S. Government Printing Office, 1969.

Baehr, M. E., Saunders, D. R., Froemel, E. C., & Furcon, J. E. Prediction of performance for black and for white patrolmen. *Professional Psychology, 1971, 2,* 46–57.

Carter v. *Gallagher,* U.S. District Court, District of Minnesota, Fourth Division (No. 4-70-Civ. 399), March 9, 1971.

Current developments. Labor, Justice, and Civil Service will issue new testing guidelines. *Daily Labor Report,* November 19, 1976, No. 225, A-12.

Douglas et al. v. *Hampton.* U.S. Court of Appeals, District of Columbia Circuit (No. 72-1376), February 27, 1975.

Dugan, R. D. Current problems in test performance of job applicants: II. *Personnel Psychology, 1966, 19,* 18–24.

Equal Employment Opportunity Commission. *Guidelines on employment testing procedures.* Washington, D.C.: August 24, 1966.

Equal Employment Opportunity Commission. *Guidelines on employee selection procedures.* Washington, D.C.: July 31, 1970.

Equal Employment Opportunity Coordinating Council. *Uniform guidelines on employee selection procedures* (final committee draft). Washington, D.C.: June 11, 1975.

Federal executive agency guidelines on employee selection procedures. *Federal Register,* November 23, 1976, *41,* 51752–59.

Furcon, J. E., Froemel, E. C., Franczak, R. G., & Baehr, M. E. *A longitudinal study of psychological test predictors and assessments of patrolman field performance.* Chicago: University of Chicago, Industrial Relations Center, 1971.

Griggs v. *Duke Power Company.* U.S. District Court for the Middle District of North Carolina, Greensboro Division (No. C-210-G-66), September 30, 1968.

"Guidelines on employee selection procedures." *Daily Labor Report,* November 24, 1976, No. 228, A-5, E-1.

Kirkpatrick, J. J., Ewen, R. B., Barrett, R. S., & Katzell, R. A. *Testing and fair employment: Fairness and validity of personnel tests for different ethnic groups.* New York: New York University Press, 1968.

Krug, R. E. Some suggested approaches for test development and measurement. *Personnel Psychology,* 1966, *19*, 24–35.

Lancaster, H. Failing system—Job tests are dropped by many companies due to antibias drive. *Wall Street Journal,* September 3, 1975, pp. 1, 19.

Lopez, F. M., Jr. Current problems in test performance of job applicants: I. *Personnel Psychology,* 1966, *19*, 10–18.

Officers for Justice v. *Civil Service Commission of City and County of San Francisco.* U.S. District Court, Northern District of California (No. C-73-0657 RFP), May 2, 1975.

Saunders, D. R., Baehr, M. E., & Froemel, E. C. Identification of, and correction for, effects of racial bias and job tenure on supervisory ratings of bus-operator performance. *Psychological Reports,* 1977, *40*, 859–865.

Standards for educational and psychological tests and manuals. Prepared by a joint committee of the American Psychological Association, the American Educational Research Association, and the National Council on Measurement in Education (Cochairpersons, John W. French and William B. Michael). Washington, D.C.: 1966.

Standards for educational and psychological tests. Prepared by a joint committee of the American Psychological Association, the American Educational Research Association, and the National Council on Measurement in Education (Chair, Frederick B. Davis). Washington, D.C.: 1974.

Thurstone, L. L. The method of paired comparisons for social values. *Journal of Abnormal and Social Psychology,* 1927, *21*, 384–400.

U.S. Department of Labor, Office of Federal Contract Compliance. Part 60-3-Employee testing and other selection procedures (amendment to Executive Order 11246). *Federal Register,* April 21, 1971, *35*, No. 77, 7532–35.

U.S. Department of Labor, Office of Federal Contract Compliance. Amendment to OFCC Order on Employee Testing Procedures. *Daily Labor Report,* January 18, 1974, No. 13, D-2.

U.S. Department of Labor, Office of Secretary. Order of secretary of labor on employment tests by contractors subject to provisions of Executive Order 11246. *Daily Labor Report,* September 24, 1968, No. 186, E1-E-4.

16

SOME IMPLICATIONS OF EQUAL EMPLOYMENT OPPORTUNITY PROCEDURES
A Practitioner's Point of View

Gene Fox
Industrial Relations Center, The University of Chicago, Chicago, Illinois

More than 200 years ago our nation established itself as a commonwealth founded on principles of freedom, equality, and justice. For millions of Americans, however, the ideal languishes in the abstract. Minority subgroups, as defined by several and diverse population characteristics, have been systematically excluded from the opportunity to participate equally in the material benefits of housing, education, and employment. As the record shows, progress toward full enjoyment of the inalienable rights has been agonizingly slow.

Constitutional guarantees notwithstanding, systematic attack on institutionalized discrimination awaited enactment of the Civil Rights Act (1964). In its entirety the act proscribed a wide range of discriminatory practices, which effectively disenfranchised members of various minority subgroups. Title VII of the act, specifically calculated to eliminate discrimination in employment, was reflected in the language of the Equal Employment Opportunity Act, which became the law of the land on July 2, 1965. With certain exclusions, this act forbade employment practices that discriminated on the basis of race, color, religion, sex, or national origin.

Responsibility for administering the provisions of Title VII was assigned to the newly created Equal Employment Opportunity Commission (EEOC). Under the provisions of the 1964 act, however, the EEOC was not granted powers of enforcement. Although constrained to an advisory role, this commission sought to provide both direction and momentum for implementation of the act. Direction was issued in the form of guidelines (1966, 1970) that sought to clarify provisions of the law for personnel administrators and selection specialists. Pressure to conform was brought to bear on employers through the investigation of complaints and subsequent efforts to achieve negotiated settlements where allegations of discriminatory personnel practices were sustained.

At some risk of understatement, it might be observed that employers did not eagerly embrace the imperatives of the new law (although in fairness, there have been notable exceptions). Voluntary movement toward compliance was the exception and not the rule. As a result, unprecedented numbers of aggrieved individuals and classes in the private sectors carried their cases to the courts for satisfaction. Much of the litigation was trivial in the sense that it served only to resolve endemic disputes and hence exerted but marginal influence on the general course of fair employment practice. On the other hand, the application of the law was substantially strengthened and redirected from time to time by trend-setting cases such as *Griggs* v. *Duke Power Company* (1968).

Passage of the Equal Employment Opportunity Act (1972) was one of the most significant events in the history of fair employment practice. Under provisions of the new law, the EEOC was assigned enforcement power, which enabled it to initiate action against employers in Federal District Court. Of far-reaching consequence was an extension of scope, which brought previously exempt private employers and all agencies of state and local government under the jurisdiction of the act. The result was an immediate upsurge of litigation in the public sector. Around a multiplicity of equal employment opportunity issues, the legal actions continue unabated. Nowhere, it is safe to assert, have the issues been contested with greater vigor than we have observed in the law enforcement area.

Given the magnitude of the problem of providing full opportunity for minority employment in policing, it is difficult to assess the extent of progress at any given moment in time. It is likely that current documentation underestimates progress owing to the lag effects in the accumulation and compilation of data. If a continuance of trend can be assumed, substantial progress, at least in relative terms, can be claimed. Comparing census tract reports (1960, 1970), for example, shows that the percentage of blacks employed in police and detective work advanced during the decade of the 1960s from 3.7% to 6.5% of the total number employed in those occupational categories. It is anticipated that the 1980 census report will reflect a more substantial rate of change, barring any reversal of trend, which might conceivably occur as a result of unfavorable economic conditions. These modest gains provide no grounds for complacency, however, since the problem remains acute in its overall dimension. At this point few, if any, major urban police agencies have achieved acceptable levels of race and sex representation in the work force. A problem of considerable magnitude remains and there is no prospect that labor peace will return to policing until such time as a satisfactory redress has been achieved.

Significant social reform rarely occurs, we believe, in the absence of governmental intervention supported by a substantial substrata of public sentiment. If the premise is correct, it seems unlikely that equity principles in employment, whether private or public, would have enjoyed support beyond lip service in the absence of compulsion. We therefore find no quarrel with the intent and purpose of Title VII. It seems unmistakably clear that the spirit of the law reflects the public interest, and a reasoned enforcement of its provisions is therefore amply justified.

Admittedly, the implementation of Title VII has generated uncomfortable levels of frustration and tension. As Baehr points out (chapter 15, this book), the practitioner seeking to fashion workable and professionally sound programs of improvement within the framework of the law, is caught up in a bewildering complexity of competing needs, ambiguous and often conflicting policy directives, and an increasingly indigestible record of contradictory court interpretations. Thus it is small wonder that the mosaic of applied solutions appears to reflect the artistic license of some obscure patchwork design.

The reality of local autonomy and the prevailing emphasis on locally validated procedures has understandably impeded efforts to establish uniformity in applied remedies. A model solution, invariant in detail and equally applicable in all settings, is obviously unattainable and indeed inappropriate, in deference to contextual variability. It would be gratifying if we could observe that successive solutions, although evolved in the relative isolation of diverse settings, systematically contributed to an integrated body of knowledge, thus enhancing the prospect of industry-wide standardization. Regrettably, there is little evidence of this happening.

Undoubtedly, several years must pass before an adequate assessment of current equal employment opportunity practices can be made. We believe there are at least reasonable grounds for apprehension that some of the applied solutions of today ·will appear in retrospect to have been more cosmetic than curative. However, as Flint points out (chapter 9, this volume), the personnel problems of today demand solution. Decisions cannot be deferred pending "the ultimate regression equation."

It is not the purpose of this chapter to discuss the technological considerations that guide us to decisions in the selection and promotion of police personnel. In this volume and elsewhere, as referenced by the contributing authors, these issues have been ably discussed. In contrast, the reader is here asked to reflect on some little-discussed questions that arise in connection with "applied remedies," as they currently evolve in practice. Attention is specifically directed to the implications, present and future, of current implementation strategies. As practitioners,[1] we share a heavy burden

---

[1] The writer's perspective is shaped by his role as an external consultant. In these

of decision. It is our collective responsibility to ensure that the solution of today does not present problems of greater dimensions tomorrow.

THE TIME BIND

The concept of "deliberate speed," as enunciated in *Brown* v. *Board of Education* (1954) is an integral part of remedial programs—and particularly so when the program is initiated under jurisdiction of the court. Unfortunately for those who must implement the program, the element of speed is given greater deference than that of deliberation.

In the typical scenario, a case for de facto discrimination is established and the defendant agency finds itself under immediate compulsion to institute a court-fashioned remedy. The details of the remedy, whether or not specified, will vary from case to case. At least, the agency will be required to modify its selection procedures so as to incorporate professionally developed screening instruments. The objective is to redress inequities and to achieve a condition in which sex and racial representation within the department reflects proportionately their numbers in the general population. The modified procedure must ensure, to the degree possible, that members of protected classes survive the screening procedure at rates approximately equal to the survival rate of the dominant (usually white male) majority.

In some instances further hiring or promotion may be enjoined pending evidence that the new procedures meet the requirements of the court. The remedy may further stipulate hiring goals and in some cases monetary or other forms of reparation. Invariably time is of the essence.

Rarely will an agency have the technical resources needed to implement programs of the required scope, and these resources must be found externally. In usual practice a request for proposal is circulated to prospective resources as an initiating step. Not infrequently, the language of the request is nonspecific, conveying insufficient information related to the scope of the work and the organizational climate within which it must be performed. The request may also, and frequently does, stipulate difficult conditions in the form of budget limitations and deadlines for the tendering of the proposal and accomplishment of the work.

To respond or not to respond, this is the external consultant's dilemma. An affirmative decision means entering a competitive situation where the parameters of the involvement are at many points undefined. There is insufficient time for discovery and planning detail; the consultant must commit himself or herself, hoping that the unspecified and the unknown can be successfully negotiated in a postaward period. If an award is granted, the

---

pages, however, the term *practitioner* applies inclusively to police administrators, merit board officers, government officials, jurists—to all those who, by virtue of their roles as planners and decision makers, affect the course of fair employment practice.

consultant must then move into a strange and often hostile work environment, contractually committed to resolve a problem situation of unknown dimensions. A less auspicious circumstance cannot easily be envisioned.

The successful implementation of a remedial program hinges on both quality and acceptance issues. The consultant may evolve procedures that are technologically impeccable and also sound in terms of legal defensibility. The probability of a successful outcome will be minimal, however, if the proposed program fails to engage the client system in a fully cooperative effort.

Resistance is a factor that may be anticipated to impede progress in any change process. The tendency to resist is understandably aggravated by fear when the process seeks to effect fundamental changes in conditions of employment. It is imperative therefore to seek solutions that simultaneously meet quality and acceptance criteria. To achieve acceptance and reliable support, we believe that those affected must be involved in the planning and decision-making process. Here the constraints of time are severely limiting. At best, productive working relationships develop slowly, and team building may be particularly difficult in an organization where the change effort is preceded by litigation.

In a very different sense, the element of time may seriously prejudice the outcome of a remedial program. A court may, for example, set deadlines for achieving proportional representation of minorities within the agency. Frequently the goal is expressed in terms of a percentage of the total work force to be achieved by some specified future date. The principle cannot be faulted, and these prerogatives clearly reside with the court. Unfortunately, the specified remedies sometimes appear to ignore the reality. In terms of numbers, it should be fairly simple to distinguish between the attainable and the unattainable. Historical data provide a reasonable basis for estimating normal attrition. By adjusting these data to account for predictable retirements with some allowance for job market fluctuation, it should be possible to estimate with reasonable accuracy the agency's hiring potential within the short (3-5 year) run. In many cases it is apparent that goals are established without regard for the reality of normal hiring practice and the degree of relief that this has the capacity to provide. Thus the agency may from the outset find itself charged with an impossible task.

Not uncommonly, the court declines to provide the specifics of remedy and may, on findings of fact, charge plaintiff and defendant with the responsibility for negotiating an acceptable working agreement. This agreement, when achieved, becomes the basis for a consent decree, which is approved and subsequently monitored by the court. In negotiating the terms of a consent decree, the plaintiff may be expected to press for conditions that maximize his or her advantage. Here again, time may be a key element, since clearly the plaintiff's interest is best served by an early resolution. The defendant, on the other hand, must avoid agreements that cannot be met and therefore must accurately assess the agency's position with regard to numbers, percentages, or dates that are clearly unreasonable in terms of the agency's capacity to perform.

Whether stipulated by the court or approved by the court as the expression of negotiated consent, terms that strain practical limits poorly serve the interest of all parties. The plaintiff's reaction to unmet expectations is somewhat predictable. His or her obvious recourse is a following petition to the court for satisfaction. The disposition of the court is more difficult to predict, and the agency in default has no assurance that evidence of a good faith effort will provide immunity from further penalty.

THE MINIMUM QUALIFICATION STANDARD

Traditionally, personnel administrators have been afflicted with the "chairman of the board syndrome." This has meant in practice that the candidates for entry-level positions, whether public or private, have been required to demonstrate qualifications far in excess of those minimally necessary for successful performance on the entry-level job. The extravagance of excessive requirements varies widely, reflecting in part the diverse philosophies of employing organizations but, more important, the vagaries of the labor market. In a tight market, where available jobs outnumber suitable applicants, the standards are customarily relaxed to some predetermined level—a level calculated to effect acceptable compromise between the urgency of staffing needs and perceptions of the "ideal candidate" for employment. If, on the other hand, labor is plentiful, hiring decisions are most likely to reflect ideal standards; as a result, overqualification will generally characterize hirees for the job in question, whereas applicants whose qualifications merely match the job requirement will be excluded from employment opportunity.

There is considerable evidence to suggest that overqualification, at any given responsibility level, mitigates against the likelihood of optimum performance on the job in question. The element of challenge, that is, the opportunity to fully utilize personal capacities, is frequently cited as an important source of job satisfaction. The principle of job matching appears, therefore, to be sound. There is no advantage to the employer in hiring overqualified applicants; in fact, there are grounds to anticipate that this practice may result in perfunctory performance, low morale, and probably short tenure. Relaxing the rigor of selection standards, on the other hand, expands the pool of qualified applicants to include members of disadvantaged groups not otherwise eligible for employment. If the theory holds, the adequately but not overly qualified, by virtue of working at or near their potential, can be expected to perform better on the entry-level job.

We believe that a judicially modified selection standard is not incompatible with maintaining or upgrading performance standards. While the elimination of excessive entry requirements may provide a solution to the immediate problem, the career expectations of newly sworn officers must surely contribute to a different—and perhaps more difficult—future problem. Predictably, this problem arises when the tenure requirement for promotion has been met. There are probably few job incumbents who resign themselves to a static career line, with no prospect of advancement. For the career officer, advancement is synonymous with the attainment of higher rank. Inability to successfully engage in the competitive promotional process will in most cases be perceived as an unjust deprivation. Should it be the case that cohorts of minority officers are disproportionately excluded from promotional opportunity, the goal of proportional representation is put in jeopardy and the equity of the promotional process becomes vulnerable to legal challenge.

There are no simple answers to this dilemma. It is obvious that the quality of education has deteriorated and may be continuing to do so. While this apparently affects members of minority groups most acutely, the Caucasian majority is not unaffected. Barring a reversal of current trends, it seems reasonable to anticipate that increasing numbers of applicants will arrive at the job market poorly qualified in terms of basic educational preparation. The most glaring deficiency is probably the inability to communicate. The problem does not occur in isolation. On the contrary, it is so widespread and compelling that college curricula frequently are found to include remedial courses in spelling, sentence construction, and writing skills.

This unfortunate characteristic of applicant populations has implications for the entire process of personnel administration. In test development, for example, innovations must be found in order to provide for an adequate assessment of basic abilities without undue reliance on verbal response. It is no longer reasonable, if indeed it ever was, to assume that poor performance on tests of verbal facility signifies an enduring incapacity for training, development, and useful service.

The probationary period provides an extended opportunity not only to monitor the probationer's behavior but to further the remedial program. A systematic coaching process in the context of the job experience may indeed be the most effective means of providing needed support during a critical developmental period. Observation of performance obviously provides a reliable basis for the prediction of success potential. Despite all efforts on the part of the agency, some candidates will fail to measure up. In this event there should be no hesitation to invoke the provisionary terms of the hiring agreement to prevent the unqualified candidate from acquiring permanent status.

The need for professional development does not end with the probationary period; nor do we feel that the agency's responsibility ends here. In the complexity of today's society most occupations require continual upgrading of the work force, and the quest for leadership impels employers to provide opportunities for continuing education. It is gratifying to see that many police agencies stress the value of academic accomplishment, reinforcing their value system by fully or partially reimbursed tuition plans. Police personnel are taking advantage of these opportunities at an ever increasing rate, and the patrol officer with a master's degree is no longer extraordinary. It must be assumed that higher education in police service accomplishes the desirable goal of upgrading the caliber of the work force. It is uncertain, however, that academic course work infallibly produces superior leaders or that the ability to compete in the promotional process is significantly improved in the college classroom. Specifically designed in-service training programs might be more effective in this regard and would be recommended as a supplement to formal instruction.

ECONOMIC CONSTRAINTS

The allocation of resources has always been an important concern of the police administrator. Typically, practical considerations compromise the ideal, and few agencies have at any time known the luxury of unlimited funding. The principle of priority-based management is therefore a familiar aspect of public service administration. It is unfortunately true, however, that the delivery of service is constrained by financial considerations now as never before. For many agencies the problem is of crisis dimensions. This is particularly true in the urban setting.

The surface characteristics of the dilemma are all too apparent. The demand for service is rapidly and persistently increasing. Crime is on the upswing, and there is a ground swell of public sentiment for "law and order." Moreover, new and different sets of needs are perceived by the citizenry as society becomes more complex; consequently, there are burgeoning demands for social services, and the police and other public agencies are compelled to respond.

As the provision of service is expanded, one would naturally expect a proportionate increase in operating costs. Additional service might, for example, imply a need for additional personnel—an immediate and calculable element of cost projection. Although significant, personnel costs may be likened to the tip of the iceberg. The phenomenon of cost escalation is a product of multiple factors, many of which are not subject to administrative control. The changing technology is a case in point. Equipping the modern police department requires unprecedented capital expenditures. Double-digit inflation obviously complicates the problem.

The delivery cost of public service will doubtless continue to escalate. This trend unfortunately has no counterpart in the availability of public funding. On the contrary, austerity programs in governmental agencies are more representative of the rule than of the exception in today's runaway economy. Most seriously affected are municipal governments. Here the problem of rising costs is often compounded by an erosion of the tax base, resulting from production losses, unemployment, and out-migration.

What, we must ask, are the implications of a severely constricted economy for commitments on behalf of equal employment opportunity principles? To anticipate that personnel programs will remain unaffected is naive. Perhaps, then, a better way to pose the question would be: "In what respect and to what extent will fair employment practices be affected?"

The "position freeze," or "stop-hire" edict, is a nearly universal response in budget reduction situations. In many cases capital expenditures cannot be deferred. Variable costs may be reduced somewhat through operational control, but the potential savings will often be minimal. General overhead costs are reasonably fixed. Thus, the agency head who must implement a budget reduction program has but one viable means—to cut the personnel budget. It is only in this area that substantial and immediate cost reduction can be achieved. The strategy varies with the situation. First cuts ordinarily affect any new position allotments that may have been authorized in support of departmental growth. In addition, a gradual reduction in force may be instituted by not filling vacancies that occur as a function of normal attrition. The extreme situation may necessitate an immediate and perhaps substantial reduction in force, in which case a layoff program must be implemented. In any case, incremental representation of minorities in the work force is effectively curtailed. On the assumption that high-tenure employees are predominantly male Caucasians, some limited adjustment might be expected to occur over time as a function of retirement. The degree of relief provided by this mechanism will vary from agency to agency, depending on the present composition of the work force. Generally, however, the prospect of relief by way of normal retirement is minimal.

It has been suggested that a planned early retirement schedule might be instituted in furtherance of affirmative action goals. Again, the rationale is to separate substantial numbers of male whites, who largely comprise the high-tenure employee population, thereby opening the way for new hirees, among whom minority groups would be represented. In principle, such a plan might have merit, but the feasibility of implementation would require careful study.

The obvious approach would be to adjust eligibility criteria for retirement and to solicit voluntary cooperation. If the plan implied no diminution of benefits, a favorable reaction on the part of eligibles might reasonably be anticipated. Given the meaning of work in our society, however, a favorable reaction would not be ensured. Job relationships provide many sources of satisfaction beyond the guarantee of an adequate maintenance income, and the prospect of an early career termination may not have widespread appeal. The success of a voluntary program would therefore be somewhat difficult to predict.

A compulsory program might be considered as an alternative in the event that a voluntary program proved unsuccessful. Inherent in such a plan, however, are problems that would need investigation, and no untested assumptions should be entertained concerning the feasibility of implementation. At the very least, a difficult and perhaps lengthy negotiation might be anticipated in arriving at a procedure that would equitably serve the interests of the parties. Coming immediately to mind as possible problem areas are legal and contractual issues related to retirement provisions. There would also be economic questions in connection with pension funds, which are normally held in trust and administered under strict provisions of law. Under most plans the pay-out schedule is actuarially determined. An unusual burden of disbursement associated with mass retirement might therefore tax a plan beyond its capacity, unless supplementary funding were made available.

There appears to be no unassailably viable mechanism for establishing proportional representation of minority employees where a static, no-hire situation exists. Under layoff conditions the situation becomes even more serious. The "last in–first out" principle almost invariably governs the layoff procedure, and minority employees are usually last in and thus first affected. This situation cancells the positive effect of affirmative action hiring. In times of economic crisis the prospect, at best, is a preservation of the status quo.

THE VAGARIOUS SYSTEM

In too many cases the affirmative action program gets under way only after litigation, which may be protracted and hard fought. The shock waves of the legal encounter understandably persist long after the court has rendered its decision. In consequence, fundamental changes must be wrought in a working climate of frustration, suspicion, and hostility. The immediate, and perhaps most difficult, task facing the external consultant in this situation is to determine who is, in reality, the client. The scope of the targeted problem is rarely all-encompassing. In the municipal situation, for example, it is most likely that the locus of the problem lies in a particular department or agency where allegations of past discriminatory practice have been sustained. Let us assume that this agency is the police department and, further, that the agency is mandated to implement a remedial program in recruiting, selection, or promotion.

Given this information, it might appear frivolous—or naive—to raise questions concerning the client's identity. As described, the particulars of the situation would seem clearly to place the police department in the client role. To proceed on that assumption, however, might prove to be a tactical error of unanticipated consequence. It is more realistic to assume that power relationships, rather than the site of the problem, define the client's identity. From this frame of reference it seems most reasonable to ask, "Who is the client we must serve? Is it the police department? The merit board? The city manager? The mayor? The city commission? The community? Or is it all of these?

In a true sense, the community is the client, and it is the will of the community, as expressed by their chosen representatives, that ultimately determines the character of public service. It would seem therefore that incorporating community preferences into the program planning, insofar as this is technically feasible, might be adopted as an optimum strategy. Unfortunately, however, the community speaks with many—and often discordant—voices. It has been said that a good consultant delivers what the client wants, whereas a superb consultant delivers what the client needs. In this situation it is far easier to determine what the client needs than to achieve an understanding of preferences. Therefore, neither those managing the process from within the system nor the external consultants should anticipate a consensus and undivided support from the community at large.

The community may be divided into many factions along lines of special interest. Applicant populations, for example, may include several well-defined minority groups, each competing independently for available jobs, along with the majority groups. Frequently union interests are represented. There may be two or more labor organizations in competition, each strongly supporting individual and sometimes adversary positions. In addition, there are the views of city management, of police administration, and perhaps of a civil service bureau to be reconciled on planning and policy issues. Therefore the problem of building and maintaining relationships may far outweigh the problems involved in the design of sound and appropriate technical procedures.

Frequently the fair employment program deals only with the issues of recruiting and selection entry-level personnel, as may have been directed in a legal proceeding. This leaves untreated the issue of minority representation in supervision. It would be a rare instance in which minorities were adequately represented in the supervisory ranks and underrepresented at the first level of responsibility. In organizations with a history of discrimination, the pattern is in fact one of increasingly disproportionate representation at the higher levels of rank structure.

Professionally qualified leadership is vital to the effectiveness of a police organization. We believe that minority personnel should contribute to this leadership and, moreover, that their inclusion in the ranks of supervision significantly enhances the effectiveness of a biracial or multiracial agency. Since agencies typically promote from within, the selection and development of supervisory personnel should command consideration at least equal to that given the selection and training of recruits.

Although innovations are appearing in many agencies, archaic promotional procedures remain so widespread as to represent the mode. Intelligence tests and content-based, objectively scored written examinations are still the front-runners in terms of popular usage. In most instances these are tests of convenience only, completely indefensible in terms of validity evidence. While tests of this nature may measure some aspects of intelligence, they are notably deficient in the capacity to assess a broad range of attributes that are known to be predictive of executive and managerial success.

Various technologies are available for effective promotional screening.

Most promising, perhaps, are the assessment center procedures, which rely heavily on job simulation. The assessment center, although gaining in popularity, is often criticized on the grounds of cost. The per-case outlay of the assessment center admittedly exceeds that of the written test, but in view of the responsibility entrusted to the police supervisor, it may be somewhat incongruous to place undue emphasis on cost criteria.

The promotional process should be equitable, and it should ensure that those selected for advancement are indeed best qualified. Whether or not the procedure is shown to have adverse racial impact, good personnel practice would require that empirical evidence of validity be established and maintained.

Improvement in one aspect of personnel administration may point up inconsistencies or deficiencies in other areas. This frequently is true in the context of the validation study. The procedures we use to award promotions can be no more reliable than the criterion measure that we apply in assessing job performance. In many agencies the procedures now in use are of 1920 vintage, and their ineffectiveness is generally acknowledged. The search for a stable and meaningful criterion for validation purposes may therefore provide the impetus for revamping performance appraisal procedures on an organization-wide basis. Where this happens, it is a gratifying example of the "ripple" effects that invariably occur in a constructive change process.

Seemingly, there is an unfortunate reluctance on the part of employing organizations to voluntarily implement affirmative action programs and, even under the imminence of compulsion, to fully address the employment issue. If we take the municipality as an example, it is not uncommon to find that de facto discrimination exists in all departments and at all levels within the system. Although the system-wide class action suit is not unknown, it is more often the case that an action successfully carries against a single department, such as police or fire. This normally results in a remedial course of action directed at the specific area of complaint. Too often—and this confounds understanding—other parts of the system are ignored. As a result destructive tensions and frustrations build and the prospect of further costly litigation is virtually ensured. We believe that the piecemeal approach is self-defeating. There are economies of scale and substance in an integrated, system-wide approach to fair employment issues.

CONCLUSION

Title VII legislation set the stage for a significant program of social reform. The concept of equal employment opportunity is firmly grounded in law, and there is some evidence of achievement. Putting the concept into practice, however, has been difficult, costly, and painful—for applicant groups, for employer groups, and for the public at large. We predict that the situation will continue to be problematic.

The process will not be finished until such a time as equity principles prevail in all matters affecting opportunities for a productive work life. An immense task remains. Ultimate solutions may not be attainable in our time, but we cannot risk the consequence of procrastination. Good will, wisdom, and perseverance will accelerate our progress.

REFERENCES

Brown v. *Board of Education.* U.S. Supreme Court (No. 347 U.S. 483), May 17, 1954.

Civil Rights Act of 1964. Public law 88-352, 78 Stat. 241, July 2, 1964.

Equal Employment Opportunity Act. Public law 92-261, 86 Stat. 103, March 24, 1972.

Equal Employment Opportunity Commission. *Guidelines on employment testing procedures.* Washington, D.C.: August 24, 1966.

Equal Employment Opportunity Commission. *Guidelines on employment selection procedures.* Washington, D.C.: July 31, 1970.

Griggs v. *Duke Power Company.* U.S. District Court for the Middle District of North Carolina, Greensboro Division (No. C-210 G-66), September 30, 1968.

U.S. Bureau of the Census. *Census of population: Subject reports. PC (2)-7A. Occupational characteristics.* Washington, D.C.: U.S. Government Printing Office, 1960.

U.S. Bureau of the Census. *Census of population: Subject reports. PC (2)-7A. Occupational characteristics.* Washington, D.C.: U.S. Government Printing Office, 1970.

APPENDIX
Proceedings of the National Working Conference on the Selection of Law Enforcement Officers

The National Working Conference on the Selection of Law Enforcement Officers was held at the FBI National Academy in Quantico, Virginia, on October 26-29, 1976. This conference was sponsored by the FBI and the Law Enforcement Assistance Administration (LEAA). Clerical support for planning and conducting the conference was provided by the Florida Police Standards Research Project (FPSRP).

The general purpose of the working conference was to provide a forum for the exchange of information among researchers and law enforcement officials concerned with police selection. The conference had four major goals: (1) to evaluate the present state of knowledge on police selection, (2) to identify methodological and practical problems in research on police selection, (3) to consider special problems that are encountered in the development of valid assessment procedures for the selection of female and minority group candidates, and (4) to facilitate the communication of research findings among behavioral scientists and police administrators currently involved in research on the selection of law enforcement officers.

The speakers at the working conference were leading researchers in the field of police selection, behavioral scientists, police officials, and legal experts who were knowledgable about fair employment practices and civil rights compliance issues. The invited participants included representatives of the sponsoring agencies, researchers in the field of police selection, and officials associated with major national agencies concerned with police selection issues. A common denominator among those attending the working conference was a vital interest in the selection of effective law enforcement officers. Rosters of the conference speakers and invited participants are included in this appendix.

The conference was organized and planned by a committee that consisted of representatives of the sponsoring agencies. The members of the planning committee were Ronald D. Branch, LEAA Office of Civil Rights Compliance; Sidney Epstein, National Institute of Law Enforcement and Criminal Justice; Donald Fish, Florida Police Standards and Training Commission; John W. Pfaff, FBI National Academy staff; J. Price Foster, LEAA Office of Criminal Justice Education and Training; Charles F. Rinkevich, regional administrator, LEAA Atlanta office; and Charles D. Spielberger, FPSRP, who chaired the planning committee. Lawrence Monroe, FBI National Academy staff, and Harry Spaulding, FPSRP, were responsible for local conference arrangements.

The planning committee was responsible for developing the conference agenda, identifying the researchers and law enforcement officials invited to present papers, and developing the policy and procedures for inviting participants to attend the conference. These responsibilities were carried out in consultation with the sponsoring organizations and other agencies and the officials concerned with the selection of law enforcement officers.

The 3-day working conference was organized into five sessions. The general format for the conference was designed to stimulate open discussion and the exchange of information and ideas among the researchers and participants. Individual sessions consisted of authoritative formal presentations, question-and-answer periods, and panel discussions. The first four sessions focused on current concepts, research methodology and empirical findings pertaining to job analysis, performance appraisal, and the selection of law enforcement officers. In the final session, issues relating to fair employment practices and civil rights compliance were considered. The major topics covered during each session are listed below, and the complete program for the conference is included in this appendix.

Session 1. General problems in the selection of law enforcement officers
Session 2. Evaluating the performance of law enforcement officers
Session 3. Biographical aptitude, and interest factors in police selection
Session 4. The use of personality tests in police selection
Session 5. Fair employment practices and civil rights compliance issues in police selection

The *Proceedings* of the working conference on police selection provides summaries of all the papers that were presented at the conference (Spielberger & Spaulding, 1977; see chapter 2 References).

AGENDA FOR THE NATIONAL WORKING CONFERENCE

WEDNESDAY, OCTOBER 27, 1976

Session 1: General Problems in the Selection of Law Enforcement Officers, C. D. Spielberger, Chair

8:30	C. D. Spielberger—A model for the selection of law enforcement officers
9:00	Discussion
9:15	John E. Furcon—General overview of police selection research
9:45	Discussion
10:15	Melany E. Baehr—Occupational analysis in police selection research
10:45	Discussion
11:00	Robert Yates—Job analysis of the FBI special agent position
11:30	Discussion

Session 2: Evaluating the Performance of Law Enforcement Officers, Sid Epstein, Chair

2:00	Terry Eisenberg—Performance evaluation: The criterion problem in police selection
2:30	Discussion
2:45	James L. Farr—Evaluation of police officer performance: The development of peer and supervisory rating scales
3:15	Discussion
3:45	Joseph Fabricatore—Performance evaluation at the police academy
4:15	Discussion
4:30	Michael D. Roberts—Performance evaluation of police officers in the field during the probationary period
5:00	Discussion

THURSDAY, OCTOBER 28, 1976

Session 3: Biographical Aptitude, and Interest Factors in Police Selection, Donald Fish, Chair

8:30	Wayne Cascio—Biographical predictors of police performance
9:00	Discussion
9:15	Andrew Crosby—The multijurisdictional police officer examination
9:45	Discussion
10:15	Robert T. Flint—The use of the Strong-Campbell Interest Inventory in police selection

10:45   Discussion
11:00   Samuel D. Sherrid—Changes in police values
11:30   Discussion

Session 4: The Use of Personality Tests in Police Selection, Larry Monroe, Chair

2:00   Norman D. Henderson—Validity coefficients under voluntary and actual test conditions
2:30   Discussion
2:45   Allen E. Shealy—Use of the MMPI and the Myer-Briggs type indicators in police selection: Selection from a homogeneous population of applicants
3:15   Discussion
3:45   Robert J. Filer—Assessment centers in police selection
4:15   Discussion
4:30   D. H. Saunders—Moderator variables in police selection
5:00   Discussion
8:00   L. W. Taylor—Banquet speaker

FRIDAY, OCTOBER 29, 1976

Session 5: Fair Employment Practices and Civil Rights Compliance Issues in Police Selection, Ronald Branch, Chair

8:30   David Rose—From the legal point of view
9:00   Discussion
9:15   Richard Caretti—From the police administrators' point of view
9:45   Discussion
10:15   General discussion

ROSTER OF SPEAKERS AND PARTICIPANTS

Conference Planning Committee

Ronald D. Branch, Esq., Office of Civil Rights Compliance, Law Enforcement Assistance Administration, U.S. Department of Justice, Washington, D.C. 20531

Sid Epstein, PhD, social scientist, Crime Prevention Division, National Institute of Law Enforcement and Criminal Justice, Washington, D.C. 20531

Donald Fish, director, Division of Standards and Training, Police Standards and Training Commission, Tallahassee, Florida 32302

J. Price Foster, PhD., director, Office of Criminal Justice Education and Training, Law Enforcement Assistance Administration, U.S. Department of Justice, Washington, D.C. 20531

John W. Pfaff, unit chief, behavioral science, FBI National Training Academy, Quantico, Virginia 22135

Charles F. Rinkevich, regional administrator, Law Enforcement Assistance Administration, Atlanta, Georgia 30308

C. D. Spielberger, PhD, professor and director, doctoral program in clinical and community psychology, Department of Psychology, University of South Florida, Tampa, Florida 33620

Conference Speakers

Melany E. Baehr, PhD, Industrial Relations Center, University of Chicago, Chicago, Illinois 60637

Richard J. Caretti, inspector, commanding officer, records, placement, and counseling, Detroit Police Department, Detroit, Michigan 48202

Wayne F. Cascio, PhD, associate professor of psychology and management, School of Business and Organization Sciences, Florida International University, Miami, Florida 33199

Andrew C. Crosby, PhD, International Association of Chiefs of Police, Gaithersburg, Maryland 20760

Terry Eisenberg, PhD, San Jose Police Department, San Jose, California 95110

Joseph M. Fabricatore, PhD, clinical psychologist, Personnel Department, City of Los Angeles, Los Angeles, California 90012

James L. Farr, PhD, Department of Psychology, Pennsylvania State University, University Park, Pennsylvania 16801

Robert J. Filer, PhD, professor of psychology, University of Richmond, and president, Psychological Consultants, Inc., Richmond, Virginia 23230

Robert T. Flint, PhD, associate professor psychology, University of Minnesota, Minneapolis, Minnesota 55455

Eugene Fox, PhD, director of field activities, Law Enforcement Human Resources Division, Industrial Relations Center, University of Chicago, Chicago Illinois 60637

John E. Furcon, PhD, director, Law Enforcement Manpower Research Project, Industrial Relations Center, University of Chicago, Chicago, Illinois 60637

Norman D. Henderson, PhD, professor of psychology, Oberlin College, Oberlin, Ohio 44074

Michael D. Roberts, PhD, San Jose Police Department, San Jose, California 95110

David Rose, Civil Rights Division, U.S. Department of Justice, Washington, D.C. 20530

D. R. Saunders, PhD, senior psychologist, Mathtech, Inc., Princeton, New Jersey 08540

Allen E. Shealy, PhD, associate professor, Department of Psychiatry, University of Alabama, Birmingham, Alabama 35233

Samuel D. Sherrid, PhD, director of graduate studies in criminal justice, New York Institute of Technology, Old Westbury, New York 15568

Robert Yates, Federal Bureau of Investigation, FBI National Training Academy, Quantico, Virginia 22135

Invited Participants

Dale Beerbower, manpower development specialist, Atlanta Regional Office, Law Enforcement Assistance Administration, Atlanta, Georgia 30308

Thomas R. Collingwood, PhD, staff psychologist, City of Dallas Police Department, Youth Services Program, Dallas, Texas 75101

Ken Cooke, assistant chief, Administrative Division, Georgia State Peace Officer Standards and Training Council, Decatur, Georgia 30032

George Datesman, chief, Planning and Analysis Division, Office of Criminal Justice Education and Training, Law Enforcement Assistance Administration, U.S. Department of Justice, Washington, D.C. 20531

Charles Davoli, director, Division of State Planning, Bureau of Criminal Justice Planning and Assistance, Tallahassee, Florida 32304

Kenneth R. Joseph, PhD, academic chief, United States Department of Justice, FBI National Training Academy, Quantico, Virginia 22135

Jerry Letwin, Equal Employment Opportunity Commission, Washington, D.C. 20037

Ferris Lucas, executive secretary, National Sheriffs Association, Washington, D.C. 20036

John J. Lucey, law enforcement specialist, Enforcement Division, Office of Regional Operations, Law Enforcement Assistance Administration, Washington, D.C. 20531

Mike Marks, Brighton, Massachusetts

John Matthews, PhD, assistant professor, Institute of Contemporary Corrections, Sam Houston State University, Huntsville, Texas 77340

D. Daniel McLellan, PhD, JD, East Lansing, Michigan 48223

Avrum Mendelsohn, PhD, staff psychologist, Bureau of Testing Services, Hillside, Illinois 60662

Larry Monroe, Federal Bureau of Investigation, FBI National Training Academy, Quantico, Virginia 22135

Glenn R. Murphy, director, Research Division, International Association of Chiefs of Police, Gaithersburg, Maryland 20760

Ralph Olmos, Minnesota Peace Officer Training Board, St. Paul, Minnesota 55104

Joel Pate, Division of Standards and Training, Police Standards and Training Commission, Tallahassee, Florida 32302

Howard M. Rasmussen, director, Southeast Florida Institute of Criminal Justice, Miami, Florida 33167

James Reese, director, personnel and training, Miami Police Department, Miami, Florida 33152

Herbert C. Rice, Esq., Silver Spring, Maryland 20901

John Rogers, PhD, director, Criminal Justice Program, College of Multidisciplinary Studies, University of Texas, San Antonio, Texas 78285

Jim Scharf, PhD, Research Division, Equal Employment Opportunity Commission, Washington, D.C. 20037

James H. Shaw, PhD, department psychologist, King County Department of Public Safety, Seattle, Washington 98104

Tom Shedlick, Esq., director, Office of Civil Rights Compliance, Law Enforcement Assistance Administration, U.S. Department of Justice, Washington, D.C. 20531

Harry C. Spaulding, coordinator, Florida Police Standards Research Project, Department of Psychology, University of South Florida, Tampa, Florida 33620

Richard Staufenberger, PhD, Police Foundation, Washington, D.C. 20006

Cindy Sulton, Police Foundation, Washington, D.C. 20006

Lewis W. Taylor, special assistant to the administrator, Law Enforcement Assistance Administration, U.S. Department of Justice, Washington, D.C. 20531

Fred J. Toler, executive director, Texas Commission on Law Enforcement Officers Standards and Education, Austin, Texas 78701

John Ward, Florida Police Standards Research Project, Department of Psychology, University of South Florida, Tampa Florida 33620

Leon Wesrogan, personnel research psychologist, Personnel Research and Development Center, U.S. Civil Service Commission, Washington, D.C. 20415

AUTHOR INDEX

Abbatiello, A., 15, 18, 24
Alexander, R. A., 181, 192, 195
Allen, B. V., 13, 15, 16, 27, 204, 209
Archuleta, A. O., 13, 24
Arther, R. O., 17, 24
Arvey, R. D., 63, 75
Ash, P., 259, 275
Asher, J. J., 134, 140
Azen, S. P., 14, 15, 18, 19, 24, 28, 79, 85, 180, 194

Badalamente, R. V., 20, 24
Baehr, M. E., 4, 10, 11, 14, 19, 24, 33, 37, 59, 60, 87, 88, 92, 96, 107, 109, 110, 111, 147, 153, 156, 165, 180, 181, 192, 194, 195, 259, 261, 262, 263, 264, 266, 268, 271, 275, 276, 279
Bahn, C., 198, 199, 200, 209
Bailey, R. L., 17, 26
Balascoe, L., 181, 192, 195
Balch, R. W., 16, 24
Bannon, J. D., 167, 176
Banton, M., 167, 174
Bard, M., 210
Barnabas, B., 15, 16, 24
Barnette, W. L., Jr., 160, 165
Barrett, G. V., 181, 192, 195
Barrett, R. S., 259, 276
Barron, F., 201, 208
Bass, A. R., 192, 195
Beckum, L. C., 17, 28
Beech, R. P., 15, 28, 171, 176
Bennett, R. R., 15, 24

Bent, D. H., 103, 111
Berger, W. G., 170
Blanz, F., 109, 110
Blum, R. H., 15, 16, 17, 19, 20, 21, 24, 180, 195
Blumberg, A. S., 174
Bock, R. D., 109, 110
Bolster, B. I., 130, 140
Bond, N. A., Jr., 165
Boothe, S., 79, 85
Borgen, F. H., 157, 160, 165
Boyer, J. K., 11, 24
Bracey, D. H., 198, 208
Bray, D. W., 228
Briar, S., 168, 175
Brown, B., 17, 28
Brown, J. J., 236, 251
Bucalo, J. P., Jr., 228
Buel, W., 134
Burns, F. M., 87, 264, 275
Burton, R. V., 199, 208
Byham, W. C., 228
Byrd, D. A., 13, 25

Campbell, D. P., 157, 158, 159, 160, 161, 165, 236, 251
Campbell, J. P., 63, 75
Campbell, R. J., 228
Cascio, W. F., 14, 21, 119, 120, 140
Chaiken, J., 14, 15, 20, 25, 134, 140
Chenoweth, J. H., 17, 25, 83, 85, 214, 228
Chesler, M., 175
Chiaramonte, R. M., 18, 25
Christensen, P. R., 165

Chwast, J., 168, 174
Cliff, N., 110
Cochrane, R., 170, 175
Cohen, B., 14, 15, 20, 25, 134, 140
Colarelli, N. J., 15, 16, 20, 25, 79, 85
Cole, N. S., 192, 195
Cronbach, L. J., 155, 164, 165
Crosby, A., 23
Cross, A. C., 14, 25
Cruse, D., 12, 16, 25

Dahlstrom, L. E., 237, 251
Dahlstrom, W. G., 237, 251
D'Arcy, P. F., 17, 25
Deardorff, P., 201, 209
Decotiis, T. A., 106, 111
Dempsey, C. A., 13, 25
Denny, E. C., 236, 251
Dickstein, E., 201, 208
Dillman, E. G., 17, 25
DuBois, P. H., 15, 18, 25, 181, 195
Dudycha, G. J., 19, 25
Dugan, R. D., 259, 275
Dunnette, M. D., 3, 9, 10, 12, 17, 19, 25,
    63, 73, 75, 92, 111, 168, 175, 197,
    209, 228, 239

Earle, H. H., 14, 18, 24
Eastes, S., 157, 165
Einhorn, H. J., 192, 195
Eisenberg, T., 3, 10, 12, 13, 16, 18, 20, 25,
    26, 77, 85, 156, 165, 167, 168, 175
Ekstrom, R. B., 149, 153
Ewen, R. B., 259, 276

Fabricatore, J. M., 14, 18, 19, 24, 25, 28,
    79, 85
Farber, M. G., 168, 175
Farr, J. L., 12, 19, 26, 61, 63, 67, 74, 75,
    121, 136, 140
Feather, N. T., 170, 175
Fenster, C. A., 16, 25
Filer, R. J., 18, 23, 228
Finnigan, J. C., 117, 118, 119, 140
Fishman, J., 198, 209
Flanagan, J. C., 228
Flint, R. T., 16, 23, 159, 165, 236, 279
Forbes, J. B., 181, 192, 195
Fortier, K., 198, 208
Fosen, R. H., 168, 175

Fox, G., 11
Franczak, R. G., 33, 60, 88, 92, 96, 111,
    181, 195, 263, 275
Freytag, W. R., 63, 67, 69, 75, 121, 141
Friedland, D., 181, 195
Froemel, E. C., 7, 10, 14, 19, 24, 33, 59,
    60, 88, 92, 96, 107, 109, 110, 111,
    147, 153, 165, 180, 181, 192, 194,
    195, 259, 261, 262, 263, 268, 275,
    276
Fry, L., 16, 27
Furcon, J. E., 6, 9, 10, 14, 19, 24, 33, 59,
    60, 87, 88, 90, 92, 96, 106, 107, 110,
    111, 147, 153, 156, 165, 180, 181,
    192, 194, 195, 259, 261, 262, 263,
    275

Gallati, R. R. J., 16, 25
Garforth, F. I. de la P., 82, 85, 228
Garver, T., 181, 192, 195
Gavin, J. F., 17, 25, 83, 85
George, C. E., 20, 24
Ghiselli, E. E., 109, 110, 111
Glaser, R., 228
Glickman, A. S., 168, 175
Goffman, E., 199, 208
Goggin, W. L., 15, 19, 24
Goldstein, H., 197, 198, 208
Goldstein, L. S., 13, 14, 26
Gordon, G. C., 15, 26
Gorsuch, R. L., 237, 251
Gottesman, J., 3, 10, 16, 23, 26, 237,
    251
Gough, H. G., 201, 208, 237, 251
Grant, D. L., 228
Green, P. C., 209
Greenstein, T., 15, 24
Griggs, E., 11, 24
Grover, D. M., 3, 9, 10, 92, 111, 197, 209
Guilford, J. P., 157, 165
Guion, R. M., 62, 73, 75, 106, 111
Guller, I. B., 15, 26

Haley, K. N., 17, 29
Halling, B. E., 13, 26
Halterlein, P. J., 20, 24
Hamilton, J. W., 17, 25, 83, 85
Hammond, K. R., 14, 25
Hankey, R. O., 18, 27, 167, 175
Hare, R., 251
Harper, G. T., 160, 165

Hartshorne, H., 199, 208
Heckman, R. W., 3, 9, 10, 92, 111, 197, 209
Hellervik, L. W., 63, 75
Henderson, M., 179
Heneman, H. G., III, 106, 111
Hess, L. R., 15, 26, 181, 195
Heywood, H. L., 18, 27
Hoffman, L. W., 208
Hoffman, M. L., 208
Hogan, R., 16, 26, 79, 85, 180, 200, 201, 202, 205, 207, 208
Holland, J. L., 156, 157, 158, 162, 165
Homant, R., 170, 175
Hoobler, R. I., 13, 24, 26
Hooke, J. F., 15, 16, 19, 26
Hotelling, H., 109, 111
Hull, C. H., 103, 111
Hunt, J. McV., 209
Hunter, J. E., 182, 195
Hurrell, J. J., 16, 26

Jackson, T. T., 20, 24
Jenkins, J. G., 103, 111
Jewell, K., 13, 29
Johansson, C. B., 157, 159, 165
Johnson, P. D., 3, 9, 10, 92, 111, 197, 209
Jones, E. M., 18, 27

Kates, S. L., 13, 15, 16, 26
Katzell, R. A., 259, 276
Kelly, R. M., 168, 175
Kendall, L. M., 62, 63, 75
Kennedy, P. K., 18, 27
Kent, D. A., 3, 10, 12, 16, 17, 18, 20, 25, 26, 77, 85, 156, 165, 167, 175
Kirkpatrick, J. J., 259, 276
Klein, A., 207, 208
Kley, J., 13, 29
Kling, J. K., 237, 251
Knudten, R. D., 168, 175
Kohlberg, L., 199, 200, 204, 208
Kole, D. M., 15, 26
Kollender, W. B., 13, 26
Krauss, H. H., 15, 16, 19, 26
Kroes, W. H., 16, 26
Krug, R. E., 259, 276
Krus, D. J., 110
Kurtines, W., 79, 85

Lal, H., 208
Lambros, D. J., 226

Lancaster, H., 261, 276
Landy, F. J., 12, 19, 26, 61, 62, 63, 67, 74, 75, 121, 136, 140, 141
Learned, K. E., 26
Lefkowitz, J., 3, 10, 199, 209
Levy, R. J., 14, 20, 26, 240, 251
Liddle, L. R., 18, 27
Locke, B., 15, 16, 25, 28
Lopez, F. M., Jr., 259, 276
Lushene, R. E., 237, 251

MacKinnon, D. W., 228
Maller, J. B., 200, 209
Mandel, K., 180, 195
Mann, P., 198, 209
Margolis, B. L., 16, 26
Marks, M., 179
Marsh, S. H., 13, 15, 16, 27, 180, 195
Martin, E. M., 15, 27
Matarazzo, J. D., 13, 15, 16, 27, 204, 209
May, M. A., 199, 208
McAllister, J. A., 14, 20, 27
McCall, J. N., 160, 165
McCary, J., 209
McCormick, E. J., 48, 60
McCreedy, K. R., 19, 27
McDevitt, R. J., 17, 27, 83, 85, 181, 195, 214, 228
McGhee, G. L., 13, 27
McLaren, R. C., 239, 251
McNamara, J. H., 167, 174, 175
McNamara, R., 15, 27
McQueeney, J. A., 13, 24, 26
McReynolds, P., 228
Mecham, R. C., 48, 60
Merrill, M. A., 15, 27
Meyer, J. C., 16, 27
Miller, J., 16, 27
Miller, M. G., 15, 28, 170, 172, 173, 175
Mills, R. B., 17, 27, 83, 85, 181, 195, 197, 209, 214, 228
Mischel, W., 209
Montgomery, H. R., 14, 15, 18, 19, 24, 180, 194
Moore, S. A., 20, 24
Morman, R. R., 18, 27
Motowidlo, S. J., 12, 17, 19, 25, 168, 175, 239
Mullineaux, J. E., 15, 18, 27, 181, 195
Murphy, J. J., 16, 27
Murphy, P., 197
Murray, H. A., 82, 228

Murray, J. M., 168, 175
Myers, I. B., 205, 209

Nelson, M. J., 236, 251
Nevin, J., 13, 29
Nichols, R., 14, 15, 29
Nicholson, T. G., 118, 141
Nie, N. H., 103, 111
Niederhoffer, A., 15, 27, 167, 174, 175, 198, 209
Nolting, O. F., 13, 27
Nowicki, S., 16, 28

O'Connor, E., 181, 192, 195
O'Connor, G. W., 13, 28
Oglesby, T. W., 16, 28
O'Hagan, S. E., 237, 251
Osborne, G. D., 13, 14, 28

Parker, L. C., 16, 28
Penner, L., 170, 175
Peterson, D. R., 201, 208
Peterson, R. A., 157, 165
Piaget, J., 199, 200, 209
Piliavan, I., 168, 175
Pounian, C. A., 15, 28
Prelutsky, B., 13, 28

Rabow, J., 175
Rankin, J. H., 16, 28, 167, 175
Rasmussen, H., 236
Real, L. J., 14, 21, 119, 140
Reinke, R. W., 13, 25
Reiser, M., 16, 28
Rio, R., 20, 24
Roberts, E., 201, 205, 209, 210
Roberts, M. D., 19, 28
Rokeach, M., 15, 28, 169, 170, 172, 174, 175
Rosenfeld, M., 9, 10, 23
Roth, M. C., 16, 28
Rotter, J. B., 237, 251
Rubin, J., 12, 16, 25
Rush, A. C., 15, 16, 28, 232, 251

Saal, F. E., 63, 67, 75, 121, 141
Sanford, N., 204, 209
Saslow, G., 13, 15, 16, 27, 204, 209

Saunders, D. R., 14, 17, 19, 24, 28, 109, 110, 111, 209, 262, 268, 275, 276
Schalling, D., 251
Schmidt, F. L., 182, 195
Schwab, D. P., 106, 111
Schwarz, P. A., 228
Shavelson, R. J., 17, 28
Shealy, A. E., 16, 18, 23, 28, 199, 201, 205, 207, 208, 209, 210
Sherrid, S. D., 15, 16, 28, 168, 170, 171, 175, 176
Shoaf, A., 236
Shotland, R. L., 170, 176
Siegel, M., 15, 16, 20, 25
Siegel, S. M., 79, 85
Silverman, M., 233
Simoneit, M., 82, 85
Singh, J., 208
Siskind, G., 155, 165
Skolnick, J. H., 168, 176
Smith, A. B., 15, 28
Smith, P. C., 62, 63, 75
Snibbe, H. M., 14, 15, 18, 19, 24, 28, 79, 85, 180, 194
Snibbe, J. R., 14, 28
Snyder, J., 15, 28, 170, 172, 175
Sparling, C. L., 15, 29
Spaulding, H. C., 13, 25, 28, 29
Spaulding, V. V., 15, 29
Spencer, G., 13, 14, 15, 29
Spielberger, C. D., 13, 25, 28, 29, 237, 251
Springbett, B. M., 130, 140, 141
Stahl, O. G., 175
Stamford, B. A., 13, 29
Staufenberger, R. A., 175
Steinbrenner, K., 103
Stephens, E. C., 17, 29
Sterling, J. W., 160, 165
Sterne, D. M., 15, 29
Stouffer, S. A., 169, 170, 174, 176
Sutton, M. A., 165
Swan, E., 198, 209
Swank, C. J., 17, 29
Symonds, M., 16, 29

Terman, L. M., 13, 15, 29
Territo, L., 17, 29
Thomas, D., 13, 29
Thornton, R. F., 9, 10, 23
Thurstone, L. L., 13, 15, 29, 263
Tift, L. L., 15, 29

Tolbert, C. C., 13, 29
Tonkin, S., 17, 27, 83, 85, 181, 195, 214, 228
Trojanowicz, R. C., 118, 141
Trumbo, D. A., 62, 75

Urry, V. W., 182, 195

VanKirk, M. L., 229

Walker, W. F., 15, 28
Wall, C. R., 12, 16, 17, 25, 26
Watson, R. I., 181, 195
Watson, R. K., 15, 18, 25
Wattengel, C., 228

Webster, E. C., 130, 141
Weiner, N. L., 15, 29
Welsh, G. S., 237, 251
Westley, W. A., 167, 176
Whitmore, E., 15, 19, 24
Wiens, A. N., 13, 15, 16, 27, 204, 269
Wilb, G. M., 167, 176
Wilson, D. W., 239, 251
Wilson, J. Q., 167, 176
Winter, J. A., 175
Wolfe, J. B., 16, 29

Yates, R. A., 13, 29

Zacker, J. W., 15, 29

SUBJECT INDEX

Ability measures, FPSRP, 243
Administrative actions, and jet streams of change, 4
Administrative uses of personnel evaluation data, 70
Administrator, selection challenges, 7
Agriculture Department, 214
Albemarle Paper Co. v. *Moody,* 4, 259, 275
Allen v. *City of Los Angeles,* 79, 85
American Bar Association, and educational standards, 117
American Education Research Association, 258
American Psychological Association, 258, 270, 273, 275
American Telephone and Telegraph Co. (AT&T), Management Progress Study, 214
Analysis exercise, assessment center, 221
Anxiety, and selection, 16–17
Aptitude measures, previous research on, 180–181
Armed services record, discussed in selection interview, 127
Armstead v. *Starkville Separate School District,* 258, 275
Army Alpha Test, 8
Army General Classification Test, 8
Arrest records, in background investigation, 133
Assessment center:
  advantages, 225
  defined, 212–213
  determination of performance dimensions, 215–216

Assessment center (*Cont.*):
  and entry-level selection, 222–224
  exercises, selection of, 216–217
  flow chart, 218
  history, 213–215
  in selection, 17–18, 84
  training of assessors, 217
  use of promotion, 218–222
Assessment of Men, 214
Assessors, training of, 217
Association memberships, in background investigation, 134
Attitudes:
  FPSRP variables, 236
  and selection, 168
Authoritarianism, and moral judgment, 204
Autonomy, and moral judgment, 201, 204

Background investigation, in selection, 130–134
Baltimore Police Department, 118–119
Bank of America, 214
Basic Interest Scales, SCII, 157, 163
Behavior, relationship with tests and ratings in ideal vs. actual conditions, 192–194
Behavioral styles, and education, 118
Behavior Anchored Scales (BAS):
  adapting to particular police department, 74
  and applicant ratings, 121
  cooperative research efforts in, 74–75

Behavior Anchored Scales (BAS) (*Cont.*):
  development for patrol officers, 62–67
  factor analysis, 68–69
  field testing, 67–69
  implementation of evaluation system,
    69–74
  vs. other performance measures, 69
  psychometric properties of, 67–68
Bias, systematic, and differential validation,
  189–192
Biodata, FPSRP, 235, 243
Biographical variables:
  FPSRP, 235
  as predictors of performance, 134–140
  in selection, 13–14
Blacks:
  differential validation and systematic
    bias, 190–191, 192
  personality scale ratings, 185
Brightness Scale, 185
British War Officer Selection Boards, 82,
  213–214
Brown v. *Board of Education*, 280, 289
Bureau of Police Standards and Training,
  233
Bureau of the Census, 289
Business use of assessment centers, 214
Bus operators:
  selection test battery validation study,
    266–269
  and transportability of test battery, 35–
    40

California F-scale, 204
California Psychological Inventory (CPI),
  16, 23, 180, 237, 247, 249, 250
California Test of Mental Maturity, 181,
  236
Carter v. *Gallagher*, 258, 275
Cattell Culture Fair Test, 185
Central tendency, and Behavior Anchored
  Scales, 68
Character references, and background inves-
  tigation, 133–134
Chicago Police Department, 33
  psychological assessment of patrol
    officer qualifications and per-
    formance, and EEOC guidelines,
    261–264
Ciba–Geigy, 214
Civil Rights Act (1964), 4, 255, 274, 277
Civil Rights Act (1972), 257, 278

Civil Service Commission, 260, 271, 273
Cleveland Police Department, 183, 190
Cleveland Police Validation Project, 183–
  184
Clinical psychologist, selection challenges,
  5–6
Club memberships, in background investi-
  gation, 134
Cognitive abilities, in test for applicants,
  149
Colorado State University Police Department, 222
Communication, nonverbal, in selection
  interview, 129
Community, and equal opportunity, 286–
  288
Concurrent validation:
  and corruption study, 203
  validity of studies, 182–183
Concurrent validity, 12
Confrontation exercise, assessment center,
  221
Consortium study, transportability in, 35–
  40
Construct validation, equal acceptance with
  criterion and content validation,
  270–271
Content validation, equal acceptance with
  criterion and construct validation,
  270–271
Control:
  locus of, and moral development, 204
  of selection interview, 128
Counseling, and performance evaluation
  data, 71
Corruption:
  empirical study, 201–203
  and measurement of moral judgment,
    200–201
  and moral development, 199–200
  screening of high-risk applicants, 204–
    207
  and selection, 197–199
Counseling, personnel evaluation data in, 70
Credit, in background investigation, 133
Criterion measures:
  Florida Police Standards Research
    Project, 238–240
  in forecasting road patrol officer per-
    formance, 136–137
Criterion validation vs. equal acceptance
  with content and construct validation, 270–271

Dade County, Florida, Public Safety Department, 119, 121, 134-138
Data collection, FPSRP, 240-242
Davis v. Washington, 4
Demographic variables:
    FPSRP, 235
    in selection, 14-15
Department of Labor, 276
Department of Transportation (DOT), 34, 266
    selection test battery validation study, bus operators, 266-269
Differential Aptitude Tests, 185
Differential test response, in psychological assessment of qualifications and performance, 263
Differential validation, and internal validity of validation procedures, 189-194
Differential validity:
    bus operator selection test battery validation study, 268-269
    in psychological assessment of qualifications and performance, 262-263
    and test fairness, 271-272
Discriminant function analyses, FPSRP, 247-249
Documents, confidential and required, in background investigation, 131
Douglas et al. v. Hampton, 271, 275
Driving record, in background investigation, 132

Eastman Kodak Co., 214
Economic restraints, and equal opportunity, 284-286
Education:
    in background investigation, 132
    discussed in selection interview, 127
    and minimum qualification standard, 283
    standards, 117-120
Educational Testing Service, 9, 235
Educator, selection challenges, 6-7
Edwards Personal Preference Schedule (EPPS), 180-181, 190-191, 204
Empathy, and moral judgment, 201
Employees, covered by fair employment legislation, 256-257
Employment history, in background investigation, 132-133
Enterprising type, 158-159

Equal employment opportunity:
    economic restraints, 284-286
    vs. merit employment, 273-274
    and minimum qualification standard, 282-284
    and time bind, 280-282
    vagarious system, 286-288
Equal Employment Opportunity Act (1965), 256, 277
Equal Employment Opportunity Commission, 11, 256, 275, 277, 289
    Guidelines on Employee Testing Procedures, 232, 256, 257, 258, 259-260, 269, 271, 273, 274, 289
    selection test validations, 261-269
Equal Employment Opportunity Coordinating Council, 4, 260, 273, 275
ESTJ type, 205
Ethics, of conscience vs. responsibility, and moral judgment, 201, 205
ETS/IACP test, 235
Evaluation:
    negative-feedback loop model, 83
    preemployment, 77-80
    of training, 80-84
Executive Order 11246, 257
Executive Order 11357, 257
Exercises, selection, assessment center, 216-217
External validity:
    of police validation studies, 182-183
    of validation procedures, 185-189
Eysenck Personality Inventory (EPI), 16

Factor analysis of performance measures, 68-69, 88, 103-107
Family history and neighborhood check, in background investigation, 131-132
Federal Bureau of Investigation, 214
"Federal Executive Agency Guidelines on Employee Selection Procedures," 256, 259-260
Federal Executive Agency (FEA) Guidelines, EEOC, 260, 269, 270, 271, 273, 274
Federal Service Entrance Examination, 271
Feedback, and performance evaluation data, 71-73
Field testing, of Behavior Anchored Scales, 67-69

Field training officers, and performance
    evaluation, 19
Financial status, in background investiga-
    tion, 133
Florida Association of Chiefs of Police, 233
Florida Division of Police Standards and
    Training, 233, 234, 240, 242
Florida Police Standards Board, 233
Florida Police Standards Research Project
    (FPSRP):
    criterion measures, 238–240
    development of, 232–234
    discriminant function analyses, 247–249
    predictor variables, 234–238
    preliminary findings, 242–247
    subjects and data collection, 240–242
Flow chart, assessment center, 218
Ford Motor Co., 214
Forecasting:
    road patrol officer performance, 135
    and selection, 115
Fort Collins Police Department, 215
    assessment center for entry-level selec-
        tion, 222–224
FPSRP Test Battery, 235, 236, 237, 238,
    241, 247

General Electric Co., 214
Goals and objectives, personal, discussed in
    selection interview, 128
Government, use of assessment centers, 214
Griggs v. Duke Power Co., 4, 258, 276, 278
Guilford–Martin Temperament Inventory,
    180

Health and medical information, in back-
    ground investigation, 133
Hoffman–LaRoche, 214
Hypotheses, forming in selection interview,
    130

IBM Corp., 214
Improbity Scale, 198
In-basket exercise, assessment center, 221
Institutions covered by fair employment
    legislation, 256–257
Instruments, in value survey, 169–170
Intellectual ability, FPSRP variables, 235
Intellectual ability and selection, 15
Intelligence, and performance, 120

Interests:
    FPSRP variables, 236, 243–247
    outside, discussed in selection interview,
        128
    of police officers, 158–159
Interest tests, use of, 156–157
Internal Revenue Service, 214
Internal validity:
    of police validation studies, 182–183
    of validation procedures, 189–194
International Association of Chiefs of
    Police (IACP), 9, 12, 23, 143, 233,
        235
International Personnel Management Asso-
    ciation, 9, 143
Interview:
    extended, 82
    and personal history, in background in-
        vestigation, 131
    simulation, assessment center, 221–222
    (see also Selection interview)
I-O psychologist, selection challenges, 6

J-coefficient, 4
Job analysis:
    development of procedures, 33–34
    transportability from one organization
        to another, 38–46
    transportability of nonparticipant in
        consortium study, 35–38
Job description:
    implications for use of different instru-
        ments, 54–59
    quantitative, comparison of, 46–54
Job Functions Inventory for Police Officers
    (JFI), 34, 53, 54, 57, 58
Job performance (see Performance)
Job Performance Description Scales (JPDS),
    92–93, 103, 106
Judicial decisions, and jet streams of change,
    4

Kansas City Police Department, 215, 216,
    217, 225

Landy–Farr rating scales, 239
Law enforcement, and jet streams of
    change, 5
Law Enforcement Assistance Administra-
    tion, 12

Leaderless discussion group, assessment center, 219, 221, 223
Legislation:
fair employment, institutions and employees covered by, 256–257
and jet streams of change, 4
Likes and dislikes, open-ended questions on, 126
Locus of control, and moral development, 204
Locus of Control Scale, 237
Los Angeles Police Department, training evaluation in, 81–83

Management Progress Study, AT&T, 214
Mead Johnson, 214
Measurement of moral judgment, 200–201
Medical information and health, in background investigation, 133
Memberships, clubs and organizations, in background investigations, 134
Merit employment, vs. equal opportunity, 273–274
Military service, in background investigation, 132
Minneapolis Police Department, 159, 160
Minnesota Multiphasic Personality Inventory (MMPI), 16, 23, 180, 205, 206, 207, 237
Model, selection, 21–23
Moderator variable, 4
Moral development, 199–200
Moral judgment:
and corruption, 204–205
measurement of, 199–200
screening process, 205–207
Moral knowledge and moral judgment, 200
Motivation:
during testing, 183
FPSRP variables, 237–238
and performance, 120
Multimedia Instruction for Law Enforcement (MILE), 81–82
Multiple-hurdle approach to selection, 115–117
Multivariate analysis of variance (ANOVA), 35–37, 40, 44, 47, 50, 52, 57
Myers–Briggs Type Indicator, 205

National Advisory Commission on Civil Disorders, and educational standards, 117

National Advisory Commission on Criminal Justice Standards and Goals, 231
National Association for the Advancement of Colored People (NAACP), 258
Legal Defense Fund, 273
National Council on Measurement in Education, 258
Negatives, digging for, in selection interview, 128–129
Neighborhood check and family history, in background investigation, 131–132
Nelson–Denny Reading Test, 235–236, 243, 245, 250
New York City Police Department, 134
Nonparticipant in consortium study, transportability of, 35–38
Nonverbal communication, in selection interview, 129
Note taking, in selection interview, 129

Occupational analysis, bus operator selection test battery validation study, 267
Office of Federal Contract Compliance (OFCC), 257, 259
Office of Revenue Sharing, 259
Office of Strategic Services, 82, 84, 214, 228
Officers for Justice v. *Civil Service Commission of City and County of San Francisco*, 258, 276
Open-ended questions, in selection interview, 126–127
Oral board review, assessment center, 223
"Order of Secretary of Labor on Employment Tests by Contractors Subject to Provisions of Executive Order 11246," 257
Organization memberships, in background investigation, 134

Paired comparison (PC):
forced-choice, in corruption study, 202
performance appraisal rating, 88, 89, 103, 106
Patrol officers
behavior anchored scales for, 62–67
dimensions of job, 148

Patrol officers (*Cont.*):
  psychological assessment of qualifications and performance, 261-264
  road, forecasting performance of, 135
Peer ratings:
  and aptitude measures, 185-186
  BAS system data in, 70-71
  correlation with personality factors, 190-191
  in corruption study, 202-203
  and personality scales, 185
  (*See also* Behavior Anchored Scales)
Penney (J. C.) Co., 214
Performance:
  biographical predictors of, 134-140
  computer-generated profile, 71-72
  definitions and dimensions, 64
  determination of dimensions, 215-216
  and education, 118-120
  patterns of, 107-108
  and personality, 186-189
  and personality and aptitude scales, 180-181
  and qualifications, psychological assessment of, 261-264
  of road patrol officer, forecasting, 135
  and selection, 12
  selection research criteria, 18-20
  (*See also* Performance measures)
Performance appraisal:
  and elimination of racial bias in supervisory ratings, 267-268
  and psychological assessment, 263-264
Performance measures:
  correlation across years, 89-90, 93-97
  factor analysis of, 68-69, 88, 103-107
  objective, 108
  research on, 109-110
  research variables, 91-92
  subjective, 109
  and tenure, 97-103, 107-108
Personal Appraisal and Evaluation Form (PAEF), 239
Personal history and interview, in background investigation, 131
Personality:
  FPSRP variables, 237-238
  and performance, 186-189
  and selection, 16
Personality measures:
  FPSRP, 243-247

Personality measures (*Cont.*):
  as predictors of performance, 187-189
  previous research on, 180-181
Personnel research:
  personnel evaluation data in, 70-73
  and selection, 7
Physical variables:
  FPSRP, 235
  in selection, 13
Planning for selection interview, 125-126
Police academy, and performance evaluation, 18-19
Police department, adapting Behavior Anchored Scales to, 74
The Police Chief, 117
Police Foundation, 12, 134
  Task Force on Education and Training, 117
Police Officer Occupational Scale, SCII, 159-160
Police Standards Act (Florida, 1967), 233
Polygraphs, and selection, 17
Position Analysis Questionnaire (PAQ), 48, 53, 55-56
Posttest, in values survey, 172, 173
Predictive validation studies, validity of, 182-183
Predictive validity, 12
Predictor variables:
  Florida Police Standards Research Project, 234-238
  in forecasting road patrol officer performance, 136
  in selection, 13-15
Preemployment evaluation, 77-80
Preparation, for selection interview, 124-125
President's Commission on Law Enforcement and Administration of Justice, 11, 12, 29, 251
  and educational standards, 117
Pretest, in values survey, 170-171, 173
Promotion, assessment center use for, 218-222
Prudential Insurance Co., 214
Psychological assessment:
  of qualifications and performance, 261-264
  in selection, 15-17
Psychological tests, validation requirements, 258-259
Psychology:
  and jet streams of change, 4-5

Psychology (*Cont.*):
    in screening and evaluation, 79-80
Psychology-Law Society, 4
Psychometric properties, Behavior
    Anchored Scales, 67-68
Psychometric psychologist, selection chal-
    lenges, 6

Qualifications:
    minimum standard, and equal oppor-
        tunity, 282-284
    and performance, psychological assess-
        ment, 261-264
Quantitative job descriptions, comparison
    of, 46-54
Questions, open-ended, in selection inter-
    view, 126-127

Race, differential validity of test by, 151-
    152
Race differences, in SCII, 160-161
Racial bias, elimination in performance
    appraisal, 267-268
Raters, performance evaluation, training
    of, 73-74
Rating:
    Behavior Anchored Scales distributions,
        68
    relationship with behavior and tests in
        ideal vs. actual conditions, 192-
        194
    (*See also* Peer ratings; Supervisory
        ratings)
Rating halo, Behavior Anchored Scales, 68
Realistic type, 158
Reasons for leaving, open-ended questions
    on, 126-127
Research:
    differential validation, and personality
        and performance correlations,
        190-192
    on performance measures, 109-110
    on personality and aptitude measures,
        180-181
    on selection, performance criteria in,
        18-20
Restriction of range:
    and differential validity, 192
    and predictive power of tests, 186-187
    and predictive validity, 182

Richmond Police Department, 215
    use of assessment center for promotion,
        218-222
Road patrol officer, forecasting performance
    of, 135
Rokeach Terminal Value Survey, 169
Rorschach Inkblots Test, and selection,
    16, 23
*Royal Thomas Arnold et al. v. John S.
    Ballard et al.*, 226

Santa Clara County Sheriff's Office, 147,
    153
Screening of high-risk candidates, 204-207
Screen-out/select-in distinction in preem-
    ployment evaluation, 77-78
Selection:
    application of test, 152-153
    approaches to, 145-146
    assessment center in, 17-18, 84
    background investigation, 130-134
    and corruption, 197-199
    critical roles in, 5-7
    design of test for, 146-147
    entry-level, and assessment center,
        222-224
    evaluation of adverse impact, 272-
        273
    extended interview in, 82
    extension of validation requirements,
        257-258
    and forecasting, 115
    future perspectives, 9-10
    issues in, 8
    jet streams of change in, 4-5
    minimum qualification standards and
        equal opportunity, 282-284
    model for, 21-23
    multiple-hurdle approach to, 115-117
    need for written test for, 143-145
    negative feedback loop model, 83
    performance criteria in research on,
        18-20
    positive signs, 9
    predictor variables, 13-15
    psychological assessment in, 15-17
    and situational tests, 17-18
    Strong-Campbell Interest Inventory in,
        161-164
    test battery validation study, bus opera-
        tors, 266-269
    test development procedure, 147-150

Selection (*Cont.*):
    test validation, 150-152; and EEOC
        guidelines, 261-269
    and utilization procedures, improvement
        of, 264-266
    and values, 167-169
Selection interview, 120-124
    conducting, 125-128
    preparing for, 124-125
    rating scales, 121-123
    techniques, 128-130
Self-report vs. traditional test scores, 268
Sex differences, on SCII, 160-161
Simulation:
    interview, assessment center, 221-222
    in training and evaluation, 82-83
Situational test, and selection, 17-18, 83
Situational testing, 4
    assessment center, 223-224
16 PF, 185, 187-188, 190-191
Skills and Attributes Inventory (SAI), 34-
        38, 41-46
Socialization, and moral judgment, 200-201
Social type, 159
SPY Scale, 237
SRA Verbal, 185
State-Trait Anxiety Inventory (STAI), 237,
        238, 247, 249
Statistical Package for the Social Sciences
        (SPSS), 103
Stouffer Nonconformist Tolerance Scale,
        169, 170, 171
Stress, and selection, 16
Strong-Campbell Interest Inventory (SCII),
        16, 156, 236, 243, 246, 247, 249,
        250
    Police Officer Occupational Scale, 159-
        160
    race and sex differences in, 160-161
    in selection, 161-164
    technical information about, 157-158
Strong Vocational Interest Blank (SVIB),
        157, 159, 160, 205
Super Market Institute, selection and utili-
        zation procedures study, 264-266
Supervisory ratings:
    and aptitude measures, 185-186
    BAS system data in, 70
    correlation with personality factors,
        190-191
    in performance evaluation, 20
    and personality scales, 185
    (*See also* Behavior Anchored Scales)

Temperament Comparator, 181
Tenure, and performance measures, 97-103,
        107-108
Terminal performance objectives (TPOs),
        81
Termination, and performance evaluation,
        20
Test(s):
    application of, 152-153
    correlations under actual vs. voluntary
        conditions, 186-189
    design of, 146-147
    development procedure, 147-150
    fairness, and differential validity, 271-
        272
    motivation during, 183
    need for, 143-145
    relationship with behavior and ratings in
        ideal vs. actual conditions, 192-
        194
    traditional scores vs. self-report, 268
    validation of, 150-152
Test battery:
    transportability to another organization,
        38-46
    transportability to nonparticipant in
        consortium study, 35-38
Third International Congress on Assessment
        Center Method, 212-213, 229
Time bind, and equal employment oppor-
        tunity, 280-282
Title VII. See Equal Employment Oppor-
        tunity Act; Equal Employment
        Opportunity Commission (EEOC)
Training:
    of assessment center assessors, 217
    evaluation of, 80-84
    and selection, 7
Transportability:
    in job analysis, 34
    of nonparticipant in consortium study,
        35-38
    from one organization to another, 38-
        46

Uniform Guidelines on Employee Selection
        Procedures, 260
Urban Mass Transportation Administration,
        266
Utilization and selection, supermarket per-
        sonnel, 264-266

Validation:
  Cleveland Police project, 183–184
  cooperative vs. local studies, 269–274
  criteria, content, and construct, 270–271
  differential, and internal validity of validation procedures, 189–194
  extension of selection requirements, 257–258
  external validity of procedures, 185–189
  internal validity of procedures, 189–194
  for psychological tests, 258–259
  of selection, 12
  selection tests, and EEOC guidelines, 261–269
  selection test battery for bus drivers, 266–269
  traditional vs. performance related techniques, 271
  validity of studies, 182–183

Validity:
  of police validation studies, 182–183
  of validation procedures, 185–194
Values:
  FPSRP variables, 236
  instruments in study of, 169–170
  results of study, 172
  and selection, 15–16, 167–169
  study procedure, 170–172

War Office Selection Board, 82, 213–214
Women:
  differential validation and systematic bias, 190, 192
  success-failure comparisons, FPSRP, 242–249
Work experience, relevance of, 126